"GO TO THE WORKER"

WITHDRAWN
UTSA LIBRARIES

"GO TO THE WORKER"

America's Labor Apostles

Kimball Baker

MARQUETTE
UNIVERSITY
PRESS

MARQUETTE STUDIES IN THEOLOGY
NO. 70
ANDREW TALLON, SERIES EDITOR

©2010 Marquette University Press
Milwaukee, Wisconsin 53201-3141
All rights reserved.
www.marquette.edu/mupress/

FOUNDED 1916

LIBRARY OF CONGRESS CATALOGUING-IN-PUBLICATION DATA
Baker, Kimball, 1941-
 Go to the worker : America's labor apostles / by Kimball Baker.
   p. cm. — (Marquette studies in theology ; no. 70)
 Includes bibliographical references and index.
 ISBN-13: 978-0-87462-749-7 (pbk. : alk. paper)
 ISBN-10: 0-87462-749-4 (pbk. : alk. paper)
 1. Labor—Religious aspects—Catholic Church 2. Church work with the working class—United States—History. 3. Catholics—United States—Biography. 4. Catholic Worker Movement. I. Title.
 HD6338.2.U5B35 2010
 267'.182092273—dc22

                                                              2010000375

∞ The paper used in this publication meets the minimum requirements of the
American National Standard for Information Sciences—
Permanence of Paper for Printed Library Materials, ANSI Z39.48-1992.

Association of American University Presses

MARQUETTE UNIVERSITY PRESS
MILWAUKEE

The Association of Jesuit University Presses

Library
University of Texas
at San Antonio

CONTENTS

Dedication ∞ 7
Timeline ∞ 8
Abbreviations ∞ 11
Acknowledgements ∞ 13
Introduction ∞ 15
Preface ∞ 19
Foreword ∞ 25

1 John Hayes ∞ 29
2 John Cort ∞ 53
3 Bert Donlin ∞ 79
   Social Action Vignette: Linna Bresette ∞ 100
4 Joseph Buckley ∞ 101
   Social Action Vignette: Boston Labor Guild ∞ 116
5 Ed Marciniak ∞ 117
   Social Action Vignette: Dennis Comey ∞ 142
6 Thomas Darby ∞ 143
7 Karl Hubble ∞ 169
8 Charles Owen Rice ∞ 191
9 Philip Carey ∞ 213
   Social Action Vignette: New Orleans ∞ 238
10 George Higgins ∞ 239

Suggested Reading List ∞ 259
Index ∞ 261

Dedicated to
the members of
the Catholic social-action movement

and to
Terri, my wife, muse, and best friend

"Go to the worker, especially where workers are poor;
and in general, go to the poor."
Pope Leo XIII, *Rerum Novarum*, 1891

"Come writers and critics
Who prophesize with your pen
And keep your eyes wide
The chance won't come again
And don't speak too soon
For the wheel's still in spin
And there's no tellin' who
That it's namin'.
For the loser now
Will be later to win
For the times, they are a-changin.'"
Bob Dylan, *The Times They Are A-Changin'*, 1963

TIMELINE

1886	American bishops persuade Pope Leo XIII not to ban Knights of Labor membership
1891	*Rerum Novarum*, Leo XIII
1906	*A Living Wage*, John A. Ryan
1911-22	Xavier School of Social Sciences, NYC
1913	Kansas governor appoints Linna Bresette factory inspector
1919	*Bishops' Program for Social Reconstruction*
1919	Social Action Department (SAD) established
1919-45	John Ryan's tenure as SAD Director
1923-56	New York Workers School (later Jefferson School of Social Science), flagship school of Communist network
1926	*Oratre Fratres* founded, liturgist Virgil Michel links personal reform and social reform
1929	Stock market crashes
1931	*Quadragesimo Anno*, Pope Pius XI
1932-45	Presidency of Franklin D. Roosevelt
1933	Dorothy Day's Catholic Worker movement starts
1935	Committee of Industrial Organizations (CIO) formed
1935	National Labor Relations Act passes
1935	Jesuits' leader declares worldwide fight for social reform and against Communism
1936	First Catholic labor schools, Philadelphia and NYC
1936-40	U.S. Senate hearings on violations of workers' rights
1936-44	Reynold Hillenbrand's rectorship, St. Mary of the Lake Seminary, Chicago
1937	*Divini Redemptoris*, Pius XI
1937	Association of Catholic Trade Unionists (ACTU) established

1937	Memorial Day massacre of Chicago steelworkers
1938	1st National Catholic Social Action Conference, Milwaukee
1938-41	*The Chicago Catholic Worker*
1939	Nazi-Soviet Pact, end of Popular Front era in U.S.
1939	Pius XII replaces Pius XI as Pope
1939-64	*The Wage Earner*
1940	Father John Delaney establishes Jesuit ISO office, NYC
1940	CIO President Philip Murray unveils Industry Council Plan
1940	Father Charles Coughlin goes off the radio
1940-44	John Hayes' tenure as Catholic labor-school coordinator
1941	Hitler's armies invade Russia
1941-45	U.S. involvement in World War II
1942	U.S. government adopts "Little Steel formula"
1943-61	*Work*
1944	CIO Political Action Committee (CIO-PAC) created
1944-80	George Higgins' tenure at NCWC/USCC
1945-2001	George Higgins' *Yardstick* column
1945-54	John Cort's *Commonweal* column "The Labor Movement"
1946	*The Problem of American Communism in 1945*, Father John Cronin
1946	113-day UAW strike against GM ends
1946	*Catholic, Jewish and Protestant Declaration on Economic Justice*
1947	Taft-Hartley Act passes
1948	TWU's Mike Quill breaks with Communist Party
1948	United Rank & File Educational Committee forms

1948-55	XLS in fight against corruption on NYC waterfront
1949	Francis Cardinal Spellman opposes NYC cemetery workers' strike
1949-50	CIO expels 11 CP-dominated unions
1950-54	McCarthy era
1955	Cleveland conference on Catholic social action's decline
1955	AFL-CIO merger
1957-60	U.S. Senate hearings on labor racketeering
1962-65	Vatican II
1965-76	Farmworkers organize
1968	Walter Reuther takes UAW out of AFL-CIO
1968	Martin Luther King assassinated while in Memphis to support sanitation workers' strike
1970	Reuther dies in plane crash
1980	Boycott of J. P. Stevens textile products
1980	Monsignor George Higgins retires from USCC
1980s–now	Renewed energy for union organizing
1981	UAW reaffiliates with AFL-CIO
1981	President Ronald Reagan fires PATCO strikers
1986	American bishops' letter on economic justice
1987	St. Joseph's Institute of Industrial Relations (Phila.) director Dennis Comey dies, Institute later renamed for him
1988	Xavier Labor School, NYC, closes
2001	Oklahoma 22nd "right to work" state
2009	65th birthday of The Labor Guild, Boston
2010	79th anniversary of *QA*, 119th of *RN*

ABBREVIATIONS

ACA	American Communications Association
ACTU	Association of Catholic Trade Unionists
ACTWU	Amalgamated Clothing and Textile Workers Union
ADA	Americans for Democratic Action
AFL	American Federation of Labor
AT&T	American Telephone and Telegraph
CCIP	Catholic Conference on Industrial Problems
CCW	The Chicago Catholic Worker
CIO	Committee (later Congress) of Industrial Organizations
CIO-PAC	CIO Political Action Committee
CISCA	Chicago Inter-Student Catholic Action
CLA	Catholic Labor Alliance
Comintern	Communist International
CP	Communist Party
CPUSA	Communist Party of the United States of America
CRA	Catholic Radical Alliance
C.S.C.	Congregation of Holy Cross
CUA	The Catholic University of America
CW	Catholic Worker (movement)
CW	*Catholic Worker* (newspaper)
DLI	Diocesan Labor Institute
FBI	Federal Bureau of Investigation
FEWOC	Farm Equipment Workers Organizing Committee
GM	General Motors
IHC	International Harvester Corporation
ILA	International Longshoremen's Association
IMA	Illinois Manufacturers Association
ISO	Institute for Social Order
ISU	International Seamen's Union

IUE	International Union of Electrical, Radio and Machine Workers
JOC	Jeunesse Ouvrière Chrétienne
LL	*The Labor Leader*
NAM	National Association of Manufacturers
NFWA	National Farm Workers Association
NIRA	National Industrial Recovery Act
NLRA	National Labor Relations Act
NLRB	National Labor Relations Board
NMU	National Maritime Union
NRA	National Recovery Act
OPM	Office of Production Management
PATCO	Professional Air Traffic Controllers Association
PWOC	Packing-house Workers Organizing Committee
QA	*Quadragesimo Anno*
SAD	Social Action Department
SIU	Seafarers International Union
SJ	Society of Jesus
SWOC	Steel Workers Organizing Committee
TWU	Transport Workers Union
UAW	United Auto Workers
UE	United Electrical Workers (see UERMWA)
UERMWA	United Electrical, Radio and Machine Workers of America (same as UE)
UFE	United Financial Employees
UFW	United Farm Workers
UFWOC	United Farm Workers Organizing Committee
UMW	United Mine Workers
URWDSEA	United Retail, Wholesale, and Department Store Employees of America
USCC	United States Catholic Conference
USCC	United States Chamber of Commerce
WE	*The Wage Earner*
XLS	Xavier Labor School

ACKNOWLEDGEMENTS

A line I love in "Talkin' Union Blues" reminds us that as much as we've moved on from the folks in previous generations (or think we have), we need to remember that "we're standing on their shoulders." That line certainly applies to the members of the Catholic social-action movement, and my main acknowledgement is to them. I am privileged to have met and talked with John Hayes, John Cort, Bert Donlin, Joe Buckley, Ed Marciniak, Karl Hubble, Charles Owen Rice, and George Higgins, all of whom have since died. Their passion for social justice burned brightly, and still lights our way.

I thank also the other members of the Catholic social-action movement I met and talked with, all key parts of the movement's story: Kay Taft, active in Chicago ACTU with her husband Andrew; Bob Senser, assistant editor of *Work*; Norm McKenna, a *Wage Earner* editor; Fathers John Quinn, John Fahey, and Ed "Maxie" Roche, teachers in the Hillenbrand network of labor schools; Tom Lilly, Sr., a labor lawyer and longtime Xavier Labor School teacher; Owen Dailey, an assistant to Father Phil Carey in that school's final years; Detroit ACTU members Tony Kaiser, Mary Ellen Riordan, Bob Forbes, Judge Joseph Sullivan, and Bill Ryan; Father Ron Heidelberger, teacher in one of the Detroit area's parish ACTU "conferences"; Monsignor Jack Egan, longtime head of Chicago Catholic Action; New York ACTU attorney John Sheehan; Father George A. Kelly, assistant to that chapter's chaplain, Father John Monaghan; George Donahue, a leader of the chapter throughout its existence; Helen Haye Cort, also in New York ACTU and later the wife of John Cort; and John O'Gara, an excellent writer for *The Chicago Catholic Worker* and *Commonweal*. All of these labor apostles recalled experiences of a decade to a half-century earlier lovingly and as if they had happened the day before, and each of them has greatly enriched these pages. Tom Lilly, Sr., was especially steadfast in his support.

Good research depends on good source material. I thank the archivists and their staffers at The Catholic University of America (CUA); Wayne State University (WSU); Chicago Historical Society (CHS); University of Notre Dame (UND); Loyola University of Chicago (LUC); the Archdioceses of Detroit (AD) and Chicago (AC); the Jesuit Province in New York City (PR); and Fordham University (FU).

(The abbreviations correspond to those used in the footnotes for each chapter.) Their guidance has been indispensable.

Next, I express my appreciation to several experts in Church and labor who reviewed drafts of this work; I benefited tremendously from their comments. *Primus inter pares* is Father Edward Boyle, who died in 2007 but who, thank God, lived long enough to contribute to (see Preface) a book he never let me give up on. Deep gratitude is due also to Thomas R. Donahue (see Foreword), who started in the milieu portrayed herein and rose to the top post in organized labor; CUA associate archivist William Shepherd, in at start and finish; renowned Catholic social-action scholar Patrick Sullivan, CSC, PhD; Joseph McCartin, an esteemed professor of American history at Georgetown University; and William Bole, a penetrating writer on Catholic social and labor issues. A better group of reviewers would be hard to find.

This work started life as an unfinished doctoral dissertation at The Catholic University of America. I owe special thanks to my dissertation advisor Dr. Gary Gerstle, now at Vanderbilt University, whose knowledge of U.S. history is profound and who was instrumental in this book's topic finding me; and to Dr. Myron Lounsbury of the University of Maryland, where I received my M.A., for helping to develop in me an American Studies sensibility. I hope I've displayed it in this volume.

Finally, I'm immensely grateful to Marquette University Press director Andrew Tallon and manager Maureen Kondrick for readying and launching this literary vessel so skillfully. And thank you, David Nahan, for a much needed dose of photo clarity.

Photo Credits: **19.** The Labor Guild of Boston. **29.** The Catholic University of America Archives. **53.** Helen Haye Cort. **79.** The Donlin Family. **100.** The Catholic University of America Archives. **101.** Father Kevin O'Donoghue. **116.** The Labor Guild of Boston. **117.** Loyola University of Chicago. **142.** Temple University Archives. **143.** College of New Rochelle. **169.** Archdiocese of Detroit. **191.** The Pittsburgh Press. **213.** Fordham University Archives. **238.** Library of Congress. **239.** The Catholic University of America Archives.

INTRODUCTION

People don't find topics, topics find people. At least that's my viewpoint after writing this book.

Its topic is social justice—worker justice, to be specific. I've come to consider this topic as a natural outgrowth of paired pursuits of mine, spiritual enlightenment and social justice.

After much soul-searching, I long ago arrived at the belief that all human beings are equally children of a higher power and thus equally one another's sisters and brothers. Other searches, of social conscience and scholarship, have led me to the companion belief that wherever people form communities—from the national or even global level to the grassroots—we owe each other just and fair treatment in our economic and social dealings.

When I look around the U.S. economic and social scene, what I find most disturbing is the damage being done to Americans' spirituality, economy, and society by the elevation of unrestrained free enterprise to the pinnacle of America's treasury of values. I respect free enterprise, but only when it's in balance with another treasured human and American value, the one we call "the common good."

Throughout American history, especially from the Gilded Age on, limitations on the free enterprise system have by-and-large been so weak and ineffective that economic individualism, and the runaway materialism which accompanies it, have reigned supreme. America's workers have borne the brunt of such tyranny—and by "workers" I mean nearly all of us, excepting only the owners of economic enterprises and their small circles of top managers. This super-rich and dominant elite has redefined "workers" to exclude as many of us as possible so that any thunder of resistance is stolen before it even begins to rumble.

This book is about a time in America's history when thunder for the common good and against unlimited free enterprise, did rumble, loudly and to the great benefit of the nation's workers, of every variety. Among the "rumblers" then were the members of the Catholic social-action movement, inspired by the need to alleviate Great Depression sufferings, by Pope Pius XI's 1931 call to Catholics to help workers to organize and to bargain collectively, and by U.S. legislation supporting these worker actions.

The story of this movement and of its members, priests and laypeople, is far too little-known, and I am delighted to seek for it a wider audience. I first got involved in it in the mid-1990s, as I gathered material for a doctoral dissertation. The material included interviews with all of this book's subjects alive at the time (eight out of ten), and although I didn't finish the dissertation, the voices of those I interviewed stayed with me and grew into a chorus I had to answer. While I am not a Catholic myself, I feel in such voices a kindred spirit.

This book is my attempt to give voice to some key members of the Catholic social-action movement. As much as possible I let its subjects speak for themselves (through extended quotes which appear in italics), and I've tried to get out of the academic mode in which I started the work and to make it a popular history which can reach the masses of the people as the movement did. The book is primarily a work of advocacy, not academics. I forthrightly promote worker empowerment, in as scholarly a manner as I can and with an effort to clearly delineate between my views and the views of my subjects.

I believe a word must be said at this point about the fact that all ten of these subjects were white males. What this reflects most, I think, is the reality that a movement that started some 75 years ago was unrepresentative and unbalanced in terms of gender and race. Progress since then enables us to make this critical assessment, but it needs to be tempered considerably by the difficulty and incompleteness of such progress and by the fact that our protagonists were among that progress's instigators.

Sizable and significant elements of both the Catholic social-action movement, and the labor movement it closely partnered with, fought hard, by and large, to bring in and empower more women and more people from other groups severely discriminated against, such as non-whites and immigrants (and, in the case of the Church, to bring in and empower more laypeople). *"Go to the Worker"* throws light upon the battles by tracing the huge influence Dorothy Day had on most of the chapter subjects, by detailing the activism and achievements of African-American John Yancey in Chicago, and by highlighting Ed Marciniak's role in widening the scope of Catholic laity, and by citing many other ways in which these movements, and those they reached, became more representative and inclusive.

Introduction

Because of the magnitude and complexity of the challenges the Catholic social-action movement faced and sometimes surmounted, I'm convinced that the movement can be especially helpful and inspiring to Americans today. We live in times that present us with challenges similar to those confronting movement members in the 1930s and 1940s. I think that their challenges resonate with ours for several important reasons.

For one, the movement's labor activists got involved in helping workers because they felt this to be part of a spiritual calling, just as is helping to meet any other human need. Today, when our spiritual pursuits are often divorced from our economic pursuits, this connectedness is refreshing.

For another thing, these activists recognized workers' dignity and true worth. They recognized workers' need to band together in unions for adequate and effective protection of their rights. They recognized workers' having rights *and* responsibilities (e.g. "an honest day's work for an honest day's pay"). Finally, they recognized the tremendous importance of unionists being as active as possible in the creation and maintenance of sound, clean unions.

The ecumenical nature of the Catholic social-action movement is yet another reason why it gives us a useful legacy. Many of the workers it helped were non-Catholics, and its members cooperated with many non-Catholic labor activists. Indeed, the movement's very genius was drawing upon some distinctively Catholic principles and some generally Judeo-Christian ones, then merging all of them with the bedrock principles of industrial and political democracy.

In its heyday from the mid-1930s to the mid-1950s, this "fully Catholic, fully American" movement (the words are those of Catholic social-action giant Edward Cardinal Mooney) presented America with a "third way," a path between capitalist individualism and Communist collectivism. This middle way's travelers were not out to overthrow the American system of free enterprise. Rather, they were out to eliminate the excesses of the system and to radically reshape it, to transform it into an instrument of worker justice and of social justice generally.

Today, many more steps along America's journey, Communist collectivism is largely discredited and capitalist individualism grasps our nation's reins more tightly than ever. The time is ripe for a reawakening of spiritual and societal values which bring people together in justice and inclusiveness.

Everywhere we look today, we see erosion of the worker protections for which many Americans gave their lives on domestic front lines. The labor apostles who people these pages remind us that we need good unions now more than ever. In the mid-1950s, one out of every three American workers belonged to a union. Today, the figure is one out of every ten.

My devout hope for this volume is that it helps workers and all Americans open their minds and hearts to learn and apply the hard lessons which labor activism's long eclipse can teach us. Above all, we must be aware that both employers and workers contributed to this eclipse—employers through too many anti-labor attitudes and workers through not enough full participation in making and keeping strong and honest unions.

Today, by contributing to a resurgence of empowered workers and constructive unions, Americans can revive their spirits and our nation's soul. That prospect will be brought closer by enactment and revision of national legislation, including passage of the Employee Free Choice Act and rollback of the anti-labor Taft-Hartley Act and its offshoots. the main measure of progress, however, will be greater commitment to social justice by the nation and its workers—and that means nearly all of us

The message of this book's labor apostles rings just as true as it did in the early 1930s, when a young priest remarked that "If you look closely into the texts of *Rerum Novarum* and *Quadragesimo Anno*, you will find explosives enough to blow all economic tyranny and social injustice into fragments small enough to be wafted along in the invisible air."

Kimball Baker
Egg Harbor Township, NJ

PREFACE

This is a story that is long overdue! A survey of the work of respected labor historians such as Foster Dulles, James Green, Joseph Rayback and Philip Taft, shows not a single index citation on Catholic labor schools. The evolution of the American labor movement in the 20th century, including its explosive growth in the 1930s and 1940s, is a specific focus of this volume. Yet one notes that those scholarly labor histories are silent on the impact of all faith communities, including such institutions as the Jewish Labor Committee and the Workmen's Circle. It is as if the labor scholars have adopted a schizoid anthropology denying any religious influence in the everyday life of individuals. In defense of this lack of attention, however, one must recognize the sensitivity of public acknowledgement by union activists of any strong faith links in a religiously pluralistic America. Only infrequently, for example, did longtime CIO President Philip Murray publicly acknowledge Pope Pius XI's 1931 encyclical *Quadragesimo Anno* ("Reconstructing the Social Order") as the source of the

Industry Council Plan at the center of Murray's national CIO program, although a comparison of the two reveals startling similarities. Perhaps because of this absence of substantial historical research and supporting data, it is impossible to gauge the actual impact of the Catholic Church on the U.S. labor movement. One can point, however, to the large number of trade unionists who attended Catholic labor schools across the country and ultimately attained leadership positions, including such recent AFL-CIO presidents as George Meany, Tom Donahue, and John Sweeney. As these pages will document, the exchange between these two institutions extended beyond the classroom to involvement in such labor-related matters as Communist infiltration of unions, publication of relatively sophisticated newspapers covering both national and regional labor-management activities, and Church clergy and laity serving on regional and national labor boards. This is all in addition, of course, to the widespread and weekly attention to labor issues from the pulpit.

Thanks to the fast-paced, lucid prose and detailed description of the daily activities of clergy and laity profiled, the reader can make his own assessment as to the importance of these institutional ties. Because of the author's decision to employ extended excerpts from the personal writings of these individuals and from contemporary news articles, the reader gets a visceral sense of this interaction.

Among the signs of the interest in the Church in labor matters is the geographical diversity of the ten individuals highlighted (Chicago—Hayes, Higgins, and Marciniak; Detroit—Donlin and Hubble; New York City—Buckley, Carey, Cort, and Darby; and Pittsburgh—Rice). Another indicator is the remarkably large turnout at the First National Catholic Social Action Conference in 1938, with attendance by 25 bishops, 750 priests, and 1,000 lay and religious activists. But the most telling sign of the Church's involvement is the explosive growth of the labor-school program, moving from 10-15 schools in 1936-37 to well over 150 in the 1940s, with many of them enrolling several hundred adults a year. The unmistakable similarity of the basic school format across scattered geographical locations, and the diversity of the sponsoring Church organizations—diocesan, Jesuit, ACTU, Christian Brothers, etc.—testify to the existence of a national movement. The standard format was one evening a week for a relatively limited time frame (7-9 weeks). Most schools were open to all at little or no

Edward F. Boyle, *Preface*

cost, with a core curriculum of Church social teaching, parliamentary procedure, public speaking, and basic economics and labor law.

These night schools became the main vehicle of the Catholic Church's seeing that its social teaching was disseminated to the ordinary Catholic and to a good cross-section of the non-Catholic populace. That social teaching insisted on the dignity of all workers regardless of job title, bringing a moral claim to the worker's rights to a voice, to respect in the workplace, and to a living wage. The Church's doctrine of the social nature of the person saw collective action, such as unionism, as entirely appropriate. At the same time that doctrine recognized the existence of greed, as well as creativity and initiative, in the capitalist system, thus requiring such countervailing forces as unionism and government regulation.

The roots of the "mission to the worker" ultimately go back to Jewish and Christian scriptures, for example to the life and teachings of Christ as conveyed in passages on His purpose to "feed the hungry, clothe the naked, and preach good news to the poor," or on His task "not to be served but to serve." Among the immediate catalysts of this labor-justice initiative in the 1930s and 1940s were the Depression, with its material and psychological devastation; the emergence of the CIO and its vibrant labor activism; and the promulgation of the papal encyclicals *Quadragesimo Anno* in 1931 and *Divini Redemptoris* ("On Atheistic Communism") in 1937. These documents were quite specific in their call for structural change and for attending to the needs of the working class lest it be lost to Communism or to a capitalist society such as the United States at the time. The emergence of a strong Communist influence in many unions, for instance, generated great anxiety in the nation. Thankfully, more and more children of working-class families strengthened the mission to the worker, as there was rapid growth in vocations to the priesthood, to religious life, and to various lay ministries.

The settings and responses of clergy and lay activists are poignantly captured in the following reflection from Reverend Philip Carey, SJ, subject of one of this volume's profiles: "It was the winter of 1936. The Great Depression ravaged the country. Idle freight cars were parked along the rails for 75 miles to Poughkeepsie. The effects upon the working people of the nation were devastating. It wasn't only that they were cold and hungry and idle. People staggered about in a hopeless daze. Father [Francis] LeBuffe gathered a group of teachers and lawyers and asked 'Can we do anything to give some hope, some meaning to living?' The fruit of this meeting was a simple eight-line letter to the Cardinal Archbishop [Patrick Hayes] requesting to start a worker-education program, and a similarly brief and uncluttered six-line approval—both indicative of the felt need for this ministry."

In 15 short years, such settings were dramatically reversed. The economy was booming and many were living comfortably. Communist inroads to the American labor movement had largely been reversed, and the movement generally had developed resources of its own to undertake extended labor education of an expanding membership. It is not surprising that the changed scene brought in its wake the rapid decline of a popular and highly effective Church-labor liaison.

The decline of Catholic social action was not a disappearance, however. The doctrine on which it is based continues today. It is a theology that finds the official Catholic Church holding the unpopular position of being a strong advocate of unionism in our secular society, even as some Church institutions have a far spottier record in terms of adherence to that position.

Another "take" on the intensity of Catholic social action is to note the variety of forms described in this relatively short volume: the Catholic Worker Movement, the official papal documents on economic and social justice, the sponsorship of summer labor-management institutes in various cities across the nation, the practice of priests offering prayer at regional and national labor conventions, and so on. It is important, however, to recognize that not all Church hierarchs or clergy-lay activists shared this pro-union sympathy. Many saw unionism as identified with Communism or anti-Americanism. Thus as noted here, the "labor apostles" were often burdened by personal attacks.

Some readers might be surprised about this volume's silence on the "spirituality of work." For the most part that issue developed later, especially in the documents of Vatican II and the writings of John Paul II. The issue is the focus of different current initiatives, especially in the various Protestant traditions, under the rubric of "faith-at-work." Rather, the focus of this book is on justice, the empowerment of the disenfranchised through collective action. It is a cause today that still speaks to religious values, as is evident in the dramatic growth of the interfaith organization headquartered in Chicago, Interfaith Worker Justice (www.iwj.org), which in a few short years has grown from 10 to 60 regional affiliations.

🐝 Edward F. Boyle, *Preface* 23

Enough remarks from this writer. Let the reader plunge into the heart of the book. I think you will recognize that the Church-labor engagement in the 1930s and 1940s can legitimately claim to stand alongside establishment of the first Catholic missions across the country, and the development of the nationwide parochial school system, as singular events in the history of the Catholic Church in the United States. We are indebted to the author, Kimball Baker, for all the demanding research and for unearthing this missing chapter in the American labor movement.

Edward F. Boyle, SJ
Chaplain and Executive Director
The Labor Guild
Boston, Mass.

[Author's Note: *Father Boyle died on November 13, 2007, at age 76, not long after penning this Preface. He exemplified the best of Catholic social action, both for 37 years at The Labor Guild (see p. 116) and in every other area of his life. He was a man of many gifts and a gift to many workers. I have dedicated this book to the members of the Catholic social-action movement, but beyond that I dedicate it to Father Boyle in particular. I would have given up on it but for his inspiration and encouragement—and when I told him that, he responded "Don't thank me. It was the Holy Spirit."*]

FOREWORD

As a sophomore at Manhattan College I covered for the college paper a speech on campus by George R. Donahue (no relation), some of whose achievements as a Catholic activist and labor official are detailed in this text. He was then President of the New York chapter of the Association of Catholic Trade Unionists (ACTU), and was also a graduate of Manhattan. It was a life-changing experience.

Donahue was a rugged-looking man in his mid-thirties or early forties who bore the scars of beatings earned trying to give workers on New York's docks a real voice in their union. He spoke of the work of the ACTU and of the need for the involvement in the labor movement of young Catholic social activists. Manhattan faculty member Brother Cornelius Justin Brennan, F.S.C., had, that same year, established the school's Department of Labor-Management Relations, the first full department of its kind in a Catholic college in the United States.

Later that year I changed my major to labor-management, and studied under Brother Justin and another ACTU activist, labor lawyer John Sheehan. Brother Justin insured that *The Catholic Worker*, the journal of Dorothy Day's Catholic Worker House, was widely distributed on campus. I remember vividly that paper's generating lots of lively discussion and healthy controversy.

In my senior year, George Donahue was running an organizing campaign for the Retail Clerks International Association in several New York department stores where the RCIA was trying to oust Communist-dominated locals of the United Retail, Wholesale and Department Store Employees of America. Donahue offered me my first union job as a part-time organizer in those campaigns. And so I began what turned out to be a 47-year career in the trade-union movement, which took me from Local 32B of the Service Employees Union, to the national staff of that union, and then to election as its First Vice-President. That in turn led me to the AFL-CIO as Executive Assistant to then-President George Meany, as Secretary-Treasurer for 16 years, and for a short-time as President.

All of that provided lifetime opportunities to try to assert the principles of the great Catholic social encyclicals Brother Justin had taught and to pursue the cause of social justice for workers. In the course of those years I came to know a majority of the priests and lay social activists profiled in this book. My life was enormously enriched by them and most especially by a long and valued friendship with Monsignor George Higgins, longtime head of the U.S. Catholic Conference's Social Action Department and the subject of the profile in Chapter Ten.

The first major papal encyclical on social conditions—Pope Leo XIII's *Rerum Novarum* (1891), or "On Reconstruction of the Social Order"—laid out a protest against the despotic power of accumulated wealth and called upon owners of industry to recognize not only the rights of their employees to press their just claims for a share of the wealth they produced, but to recognize as well workers' natural right to associate in unions. Forty years later, Pope Pius XI, in *Quadragesimo Anno*, another major encyclical, updated, strengthened, and extended that message.

These papal documents and the U.S. Catholic bishops' formal statement "Social Reconstruction: A General Review of the Problems and Survey of the Remedies" (1919) detailed a program designed to improve the human condition of workers. The program called for minimum wage legislation; insurance against unemployment; a 16-year minimum age for working children; legal enforcement of the right of labor to organize; progressive taxes on inheritance, income, and excess profits; and a variety of other social measures. This program put the Catholic Church squarely on the side of working people and formed the basis for the work of the generation of Catholic social activists detailed in this book.

American unions, unlike some of their European counterparts, had never developed along religious lines and were from their inception secular institutions open to all. The suggestion in *Rerum Novarum* that the "appropriate" associations of workers were those formed along religious lines was simply too far outside the experience of the United States to have validity here.

However, the dedication of a large percentage of the leaders of labor in America derived substantially from their religious inspirations. Jewish, Catholic, and Protestant leaders of the labor movement were greatly inspired by their faiths and by their faiths' respective calls for the advancement of the social condition of workers. In the Catholic realm, the encyclicals and the 1919 bishops' statement provided the practical expression of those concerns and urged Catholic leaders and activists, clergy and laity alike, to work for the fullest implementation of justice for workers in the social order.

Thus was born a generation of Catholic social activists, some of whose stories are detailed here. Individually, they made a mark in their relations with the labor movement. Collectively, they gave birth to a system of trade-union education and to a heightened activism which brought new leadership and new attention to labor-movement struggles before and after World War II and beyond. These activists fought and organized, taught and worked, inspired by their religious principles and heartened by the sure knowledge that their clerical partners brought the weight of the Catholic Church to their side.

The period from the 1930s and into the 1960s was undoubtedly the heyday of Catholic labor social activism, and the individual stories told here make clear the identification of the American church of those years with working people. But that involvement didn't end there. It was carried on during all the lives of these "Apostles to the Worker," and is continued today by many dedicated priests and laypeople.

Newer fields for social activism have somewhat limited the appeal of labor social activism, but its principles are unchanged. Indeed, the encouragement provided by papal encyclicals has continued through *Mater et Magistra* (1961) and *Laborem Exercens* (1981), "On Human Work." I was privileged to be the North American lay commentator at the Rome symposium which marked the issuance of that encyclical, and I was greatly heartened that in it, Pope John Paul II moved beyond earlier encyclical pronouncements that unions were legitimate and necessary and declared them to be "indispensable."

This book tells the stories of 10 outstanding Catholic leaders and educators, but in their tales are interwoven the contributions to worker justice of many, many more activists. It details an era when the Church and all of these activists were "pushing the envelope" to insure workers' rights to organize and to bargain collectively, and to insure the Church's fidelity to those teachings. And when Church leaders as administrators forgot, or put aside, social justice principles in their treatment of the workers in Catholic institutions, these activists were the first to urge those churchmen- and churchwomen-administrators to renew their adherence to those principles and to deal fairly with their workers. In some of today's contestations between the Church and its employees, the voices of such activists are still badly needed and sorely missed.

The sum of it all is that the work described here provided an invaluable assist to a labor movement which has always needed friends and protectors and defenders who share its passion for social justice. The work of these "Apostles to the Worker" constituted some of the finest hours of the American church and helped build some of the finest hours of the American labor movement.

Thomas R. Donahue
Former President, AFL-CIO
Washington, DC

CHAPTER ONE

JOHN HAYES (1906–2002)

"After six weeks as a sixth-grader at St. Carthage Grammar School on Chicago's South Side, I told Father John Hayes, the parish pastor, that I wanted to be a priest. Here I was, a very impressionable 11-year-old kid, newly enrolled in a Catholic school, not from a Catholic background. Father Hayes replied 'Well, it might be helpful for you to be Catholic.'

"Fathers Hayes and Gerald Weber, the parish's other priest, were very impressive. They would come in to religion class, be out on the playground, friendly, warm and loving. I wish every kid had a priest like Hayes or Weber in his or her life."[1]

The speaker of those words was Atlanta Archbishop Wilton Gregory, who from 2001-04 was President of the U.S. Conference of Catholic

---

1 McCloskey, Pat,"Calm Amid the Storm," *St. Anthony Messenger*, Nov. 2002, 1.

Bishops, the first African-American and the first Catholic convert to serve in that position. The holder of the position is elected to it by his fellow bishops.

Father Weber remembered Gregory looking up to Father Hayes (Monsignor Hayes after 1963) as "an excellent model of what a priest should be."[2] Hayes, 95 in the year of Gregory's election, took immense pride at seeing Gregory, whom in 1959 Hayes guided through baptism, First Communion, and confirmation, occupy such a key position in American Catholicism. Hayes died the following year.

Leadership begets leadership, and with Father Hayes, the leadership pattern developed early. Father Reynold Hillenbrand, Rector from 1936-44 of Chicago's major seminary, St. Mary of the Lake, inspired a whole generation of priests to "go to the worker," and wisely chose his friend John Hayes as a key aide. Hillenbrand was ordained from St. Mary's in 1929 and Hayes in 1930. It was a fateful time and a good time to enter a helping vocation. Hayes grew up in Evanston, a well-to-do Chicago suburb.

> Around 1925 I worked through one summer vacation in a steel fabricating mill. The starting (and for some time the finishing) wage was 33 cents an hour. We put in 55 hours a week for $18. Men with families managed to live on it, though not handsomely. They took it and liked it. If they didn't, they could tell the superintendent and be pitched out.
>
> Were we cogs in the production process? With certain qualifications—some jobs required a bit of intelligence or skill—we were.
>
> Of course, we had the benefits of a plant newspaper, a baseball team, and an annual picnic, all humanizing influences. Despite these devices, the men around me didn't seem to be getting any more human. This was no school for the development of one's higher faculties of mind and will. There was too much fear, monotony, and compulsion about the place.
>
> Our work set-up seemed to say that God supplied all the brains and good will to a few men and entitled them to make all the decisions. Such men were good, but not that good. At any rate, they were not invincible; they went down in the depression. Maybe they and other employers made mistakes by keeping out unions and keeping down wages.[3]

---

2 Greear, Priscilla, "Family Shares Roots of Archbishop's Faith," *The Georgia Bulletin*, Aug. 12, 2006, 3.

3 Hayes, John, "Why Workers Should Share in Management Decisions," *Chicago Catholic Worker*, Mar. 1955, 4.

1 ❧ John Hayes

This experience, the stock-market crash, and *Quadragesimo Anno* ("Fortieth Year"), or *QA*, all shaped the outlook of young priest John Hayes. Pope Pius XI issued *QA*, an encyclical, or papal letter, in 1931, saying "We lay down the principle long since clearly established by Leo XIII [the Pope who first addressed workers' concerns, in *Rerum Novarum*, or "New Things," 40 years earlier] that it is Our right and Our duty to deal authoritatively with social and economic problems."[4] In the midst of the Great Depression's catastrophes nationally and internationally, the document offered practical and spiritual encouragement to the millions of people in search of renewal.

Hayes, after graduate study at St. Mary's and in Rome, taught at Quigley Preparatory Seminary (high school) in Chicago from 1934-40 and lived at St. Angela Church. Depression suffering really hit home for him, he recalled, when a well-off family man in that parish lost his job, his house, and his mind. Father Hayes resolved to do all he could to relieve such suffering.

One of the first things he did was become chaplain to the Chicago branch of Dorothy Day's Catholic Worker (CW) movement. This movement began in New York City in 1933, when Day established the first House of Hospitality, or center for feeding and housing poor and needy people. The movement grew rapidly thereafter.

In October 1936, Chicago's CW volunteers met every Sunday in a West Taylor Street house to discuss ideas and make plans according to the "see-judge-act" principle, which came from Young Christian Workers, a group beginning in France as Jeunesse Ouvrière Chrétienne or JOC (the group's followers were called Jocists). The principle was simply to observe your work situation, evaluate it in light of the Catholic faith and its social teachings, and do what you could for positive impact.

This principle strongly influenced Dorothy Day and Catholic Workers everywhere, as did the writings of Virgil Michel, a Benedictine monk and an advocate of reforming the Catholic liturgy—the meanings and practices of worship. For Michel and many CW followers, liturgical reform connected to social reform through a concept known as the Mystical Body of Christ.[5]

---

4 In *Seven Great Encyclicals*, Glen Rock, N.J.: Paulist Press, 1963.

5 Michel, Virgil, *The Mystical Body and Social Justice*, Collegeville, Minn.: St. John's Abbey, 1938.

The concept revolves around the simple belief that all human beings are the children of God and are therefore brothers and sisters of one another. Jesus Christ, both as God's Son and as a human being among other human beings, joins divine and human life into one universal, mystical body.

In this unity, according to the concept, all people are in Christ and He is in them. Thus, when one child of God helps another child of God who is in need, whether of food, drink, clothing, shelter, or worker justice, that helper has ministered to "another Christ"—i.e., to Christ in the other person.

Liturgical reform based on this concept was the driving force of Father Reynold Hillenbrand's social-action efforts, as well as of many of the mid-1930s' activities of Chicago's Catholic Workers. In mid-1936, Fathers Hillenbrand and Hayes visited Dorothy Day at the New York House of Hospitality, and in February 1938 she visited them at St. Mary of the Lake Seminary. These visits greatly encouraged Chicago's CW volunteers, who later in 1938 started *The Chicago Catholic Worker* (*CCW*).

In the movement newspaper *The Catholic Worker* (*CW*), started a couple of years earlier, Day praised *CCW*, saying "As long as you have such friends as Father Hayes you are all right. If you make mistakes they are easily remedied, if the will be right."[6]

In 1936 and 1937, for Hayes and other Catholic social actionists, the CW movement and its national newspaper were a direct route to labor activism. Volunteers went to the steel mills and the stockyards to pass out *CW*, sometimes side-by-side with Communist Party (CP) members passing out *The Daily Worker*. Father Hayes or another priest would address the workers, urging them to join the newly-organizing industrial unions of the Committee (later Congress) of Industrial Organizations, the CIO, or to become active and informed if they had already joined.

Catholic workers were assured (or reassured) that these actions were compatible with Catholic social teachings, and that indeed these teachings say Catholic workers have a duty to join an effective union. Employees gain real power in their workplaces only as members of such unions, the teachings maintain, and unions can be effective only when they present a united front to employers. "[I]t is of the very essence of social justice," Pope Pius XI states in *Divini Redemptoris*

---

6 "Dorothy Day Writes," *CCW*, Aug. 1938, 1.

(1937), "to demand from each individual all that is necessary for the common good."⁷

The Packing-house Workers Organizing Committee (PWOC) began its efforts in 1936. It was a tough task in a tough setting, with working conditions exemplified by the yards' "bloody and dirty" kill and offal departments. Houses in the Back of the Yards neighborhood were "dilapidated, ramshackle affairs."⁸

United Packing-house Workers-CIO President Ben Brown was severely beaten by thugs on the property of the Stockyards Transit Company, allegedly with none of the company's one hundred security guards in sight. This happened during a December 1938 strike for a contract, but with help from Father John Hayes and other Catholic social actionists, the strikers won.

Hayes always seemed to be where he was most needed, and he never backed down in the midst of danger or difficulty. PWOC organizer Frank McCarthy admired him as "a straight-from-the-shoulder encyclicalist," and said "We're all grateful for his talks, and hope to have him out again. I'm Catholic, as are most of our workers, whether Polish, Irish, Bohemian, Lithuanian, Mexican, or Italian. Both as a Catholic and as a union man, I wish there were more Father Hayes's around."⁹

By spring 1938, Catholic social actionists in Chicago, New York City, and elsewhere were making enough headway in strengthening American industrial democracy that the National Catholic Welfare Conference's Social Action Department (SAD) sponsored the First National Catholic Social Action Conference in Milwaukee May 1-4. A thousand students, 750 priests, and 25 bishops attended. Several expanding industries were emphasized, and for each industry there was a speaker from labor, a speaker from management, and a speaker from the Church—usually a priest active in the industry's organizing campaign. John Hayes focused on meat-packing.

> I feel that I can contribute something to the better understanding between the meat-packing industry's management and its wage workers which this meeting proposes to engender.
>
> Let us begin by recalling the Christian and the only rational view of economic society in general—the grand picture painted not only by Pius

---

7   In *Seven Great Encyclicals*, op. cit.
8   Dorney, William, speech, *Proceedings*, Summer School of Social Action, Chicago, Jul. 10-Aug. 12, 1938, Vol. 1, 61-5.
9   "CIO Organizer Pays Us a Visit," *CCW*, July 1938, 1.

XI and Leo XIII but by perpetual Catholic tradition. The meat-packing business or any business is meant to be part of an integrated system, a universe divinely ordained to provide for the material as well as the spiritual needs of every human. Business has tried to secede from that whole; we have tried to subtract part of God's creation—the economic part—from God's dominion....

The ultimate purpose of man's existence is to serve God.... That puts our problems on a high level; but any lower level, such as "business is business," is modified atheism. If some of us can begin to look at economic life that way, to see that each human cog in the machine is tremendously important to his Creator, to believe that every free act, such as paying wages or earning them, merits God's approval or reprobation, it will be much easier to unravel the purely economic knots.

With such an attitude we shall willingly accept other rules of the game besides such mechanical canons as the law of supply and demand. We shall see the need of harmonizing individual enterprise with the necessities of the less enterprising, lest these latter be ruinously handicapped in the struggle to live worthily. We shall temper rigorous economic law with justice, and justice with mercy. If we can't at least get a glimmer of this idea into a few heads, all our scheming will fail; we shall go on fighting, and the casualties on one side or the other will continue to make American economic life as a whole a miserable failure.

I call such an attitude, such a view of society, the fundamental principle. I hope you will pardon me for laboring a truth that is obvious to many of you, a truth proclaimed again and again by the church, but one which has not been generally heard nor heeded.

Other less general principles are derived from this one, for instance the responsibilities of ownership. The use of private property is restricted by the needs of others. In the language of Pius XI the institution called private property, that is, the right of individuals to own, has been given by the Lord of creation that the good He created may serve not the few but the universal family of mankind. This will not be achieved by collectivism; nor, on the other hand, by selfish, sometimes called rugged, individualism. The exercise of ownership is circumscribed by the necessities of people living together in civilized society....

Next is the principle of interdependence. The Pope reminds us that capital could do nothing without labor, nor could labor do anything without capital; both together could do nothing without the natural resources God has provided.

Because this interdependence has been ignored, capital has in the past taken whatever profits it could, usually an exorbitant share. Employers have not usually considered wage earners as co-workers, partners in the enterprise, contributors to its success, worthy of a decent human living because they too are men, deserving some of the profits of business because they help make profits.

Concretely, stock-handlers are infinitely superior to the animals they handle, because they possess immortal souls. Too often management has looked on labor only as a necessary expense, an impersonal element in production costs, an item to be bought at competitive market prices, a somewhat unruly brother to the machine.[10]

For Catholic social action and Father John Hayes, 1938 was a real up-and-down year. A severe economic recession coexisted uneasily with continued energy for worker justice.

Hayes turned his attention immediately from Milwaukee to another national SAD conference, the Summer School of Social Action held in Chicago from July 10 to August 12. It also served as one of nine regional Schools of Social Action SAD conducted to train the priests and laypeople who in turn trained other labor apostles.[11]

At the Chicago conference, Hayes suggested measures for such training—priests' study clubs, series of sermons on the social-action encyclicals and their applications, and labor schools for unionists and potential unionists. All these measures were implemented in Chicago by him and the Hillenbrand-inspired group of seminarians and newly-ordained priests—"Hilly's Boys," they were called.

Instrumental in their commitment and success was the solid backing of their Archbishop, George Cardinal Mundelein. The national press release announcing the Chicago conference quoted from an address he made in March 1938 in a Chicago where recession had put so many people back on the dole that relief funds were drying up: "The trouble with us [the Catholic Church] in the past has been that we were too often allied or drawn into an alliance with the wrong side. Selfish employers of labor have flattered the Church by calling it the great conservative force, and then called upon it to act as a police force while they paid but a pittance of wages to those who worked for them.

"I hope that day is gone by. Our place is beside the poor, behind the worker. They are our people, they build our churches, they occupy our pews, their children crowd our schools, our priests come from their

---

10   Hayes's speech, *Proceedings*, First National Catholic Social Action Conference, Milwaukee, May 1-4, 1938, 250.

11   The other cities were Buffalo, Los Angeles, Milwaukee, New York, Richmond, San Francisco, Toledo, and Washington, DC.

sons. They look to us for leadership, but they look to us too for support. Now when I speak of the Church, I mean not only our clergy, I mean the great body of our Catholic laity, I mean particularly an organized laity."[12]

With the tone thus set, the Chicago conference was a landmark event. It was held at St. Mary of the Lake Seminary, which Mundelein designed in 1920 to reflect an American Catholic Church with Roman roots. In the same sense, Catholic social action's answer to America's economic and social problems as it was presented at the conference was an answer both "fully Catholic and fully American."

The cruelty of economic life was on dramatic display nearby even as the conference proceeded. At O'Donnell's Hotel in the Seminary town of Mundelein (renamed in honor of the seminary's founder), several organizers of the United Shoe Workers of America-CIO were signing up, at that very time, 30 of the 100 employees of an American Maid Shoe Company plant. As the organizers left the hotel, seven men in two cars attacked and severely beat them. Father Hayes and other conference attendees were notified and provided whatever help they could.

Management representatives as well as labor representatives attended this conference and other Catholic social action gatherings, but generally, fewer managers attended than were invited. This didn't stop some managers who didn't show or weren't invited from complaining that Catholic labor activists were biased against management. Responses by these activists that their central message involved labor-management partnership got replies indicating that management's conceptions of partnership were sometimes more one-sided than the conceptions of Catholic social action and of industrial democracy.

Such a clash of conceptions occurred immediately following the Chicago conference, when the International Harvester Corporation (IHC) briefed a group of social-action priests who accepted an invitation by the company to visit its Chicago headquarters. Father John Hayes, part of the delegation, thanked his hosts but took issue with a few of their briefing points.

> With regard to the attitude adopted by the genial officials who spoke to us: I think it is fair to say that there was an effort made to divorce such matters as prices, profits, and dividends from our consideration

---

[12] "Summer Catholic Social Action School for Clergy is Announced in Chicago," NCWC news release, May 16, 1938.

of labor problems. That seems an irrational restriction; it would make all real progress impossible. For it is evident that excessive prices will reduce production and eliminate workers, just as prices set at a level too low will likely reduce wages. Likewise it appears obvious that the share left for wage earners will depend considerably on the amount of dividends... In line with this thought may I make the observation that taxes [IHC representatives had complained about how high they were] will not be reduced by throwing three thousand more families on the public funds, as will likely result from your layoff of that many men at the Tractor Works last Saturday. In the interests of frankness, this layoff might have been mentioned. Has the fact that the C.I.O. lately signed a contract in that plant anything to do with the layoff there?....

With regard to collective bargaining: it is the opinion of Catholic authorities as well as the tenor of federal law that company unions do not provide a medium for generally free bargaining. Whether your various "independent" associations can correctly be dubbed "company unions" is a matter for the National Labor Relations Board to decide.... Still, it is strange that such thoroughly satisfactory organizations should so quickly succumb to the C.I.O. after a brief campaign....

Whatever criticism is contained herein is not directed at the particular officials who were our kind hosts, since they can hardly be held responsible for all the policies of the company, and surely not for the failure of the American economic system as a whole to provide adequately for more than a fraction of the great mass of people depending on it. Rather it has been my purpose to call in question, if not to disprove entirely, the widespread assumption that all is well, that all possible efforts have been made, and that industry has conscientiously and completely fulfilled its responsibility to American society.[13]

IHC's subsequent behavior confirmed the accuracy of Hayes' observations. Over the next several years, it did all it could to oppose Farm Equipment Workers Organizing Committee-CIO (FEWOC) efforts at plants throughout the Midwest. Its supervisors and foremen criticized CIO leaders, threatened a wage cut, made disparaging remarks about CIO buttons, and induced employees not to sign CIO application cards.

On February 8, 1941, following a strike by the union, the National Labor Relations Board disestablished IHC's six company unions, thus clearing the way for recognition of FEWOC locals as the workers' representatives. Father Hayes and other Catholic social actionists stood

---

13   Hayes to International Harvester Company, Aug. 19, 1938. [CUA]

behind the strike every step of the way despite the opposition's considerable Red-baiting—that is, labeling strikers Communists whether they were or not.

Chicago's national Catholic social-action conference, whose hundreds of attendees represented 25 dioceses and 12 religious orders, generated a groundswell of enthusiasm and activity around the country, particularly in the founding and operating of Catholic labor schools. Five of them opened as part of a Chicago-area network established in October 1938, two months after the conference, by Father Hillenbrand's social-action group.

Hayes viewed the labor schools as an important part of a two-pronged response to *Quadragesimo Anno*, the pioneering document which was discussed earlier in this chapter and in which Pope Pius XI affirmed Catholic workers' joining neutral (or secular) unions and called upon these workers to also form associations "side by side" with the unions. The purposes of these associations were spiritual instruction and a better understanding of Catholic social teachings. To Hayes, gatherings along the lines of the Jocist "see-judge-act" principle served the first purpose and Catholic labor schools the second.

The Chicago area's first labor schools, a diverse lot, were located at: Saints Peter and Paul Church, South Chicago, parish of workers at U.S. Steel Corporation's South Works—first Germans and later Croatians, Irish, Italians, and Poles; Holy Name Cathedral; Mother of God Church, Waukegan (north of Chicago), a parish with many Slovenian steelworkers; the CW House of Hospitality on Blue Island Avenue (opened by Dorothy Day during her 1938 visit); and St. Theresa of the Infant Jesus Church, a primarily Irish congregation on the city's South Side.[14]

Father Hayes, as well as the other priests and the lay activists involved, were well aware that in addition to a knowledge of Catholic social teachings, they needed a knowledge of "particular conditions in this country and in one's own community in terms of economic

---

14 Parishes which later hosted schools in the Chicago-area network: St. Anselm; St. Bonaventure; St. Cecilia; Cenacle; Corpus Christi; Epiphany; Five Holy Martyrs; St. Gabriel; St. Ignatius; St. Leonard; St. Mary, Joliet; St. Mel; Our Lady of the Angels; Our Lady of Good Counsel; Our Lady Help of Christians; Our Lady of Sorrows; St. Roman; Sacred Heart; St. Viator, and St. Wenceslas. Also, in 1939-40 there was a labor school for 30 women teachers, nearly all members of the Chicago Teachers Union.

conditions, laws, and unions," and that they then needed to convey all that knowledge in a way which worker-students could understand and which would galvanize them to action. Father Edward Roche, an effective teacher of the Slovenian steelworkers, said "They're tough as nails and they're not philosophers—but if you prove yourself to be a good friend of the workers, they will listen to you and work with you."[15]

Wise labor-school directors made sure to get for their teaching staffs a sizeable number of experienced, articulate, and personable unionists, whether officers or rank-and-filers. One such unionist in Chicago was John Yancey, International Secretary-Treasurer of the United Transport Service Employees-CIO. Yancey was not only one of the most prominent African-American labor leaders in Chicago, but he was a persuasive teacher and speaker who related to fellow unionists on the basis of his experiences in the midst of union struggles.

Other good friends of labor who taught or spoke at these schools constituted a wide cross-section of Chicago's labor scene. They included Arthur Goldberg, a labor lawyer and later a U.S. Supreme Court justice; Frank Delaney, a regional officer of the U.S. Department of Labor's Wage and Hour Division; Isaiah Dorfman, National Labor Relations Board (NLRB); Albert Kuhle, U.S. Social Security Board; Frank Gillespie, Dairy Employees Union, American Federation of Labor (AFL); and Kate O'Connor, Women and Children's Division, Illinois Department of Labor.

Stoking worker interest in Chicago-area Catholic labor schools, and providing their teachers with plenty of real-life examples, was the continued labor ferment in the area in the late thirties and early forties. Two notable examples were the Hearst strike and the organizing drive at Marshall Field's department store, and John Hayes was in the middle of both actions.

In December 1938, the Chicago Newspaper Guild went on strike after unsuccessfully protesting 500 firings over the previous 18 months by the Hearst newspapers *The Chicago American* and *The Chicago Herald-Examiner*, papers which merged during the strike to become *The Chicago Herald-American*. In early 1939, 45 Catholic strikers on the Hearst Guild Strike Committee wrote to the editor of *Novena Notes* that "the strike is just, because the moral right of collective bargaining expressed in the papal encyclicals was denied [the strikers]."[16]

15 Roche, Edward, interview with author, Jul. 7, 1995.
16 Hearst Strike Committee to Ed., *Novena Notes*, Jan. 15, 1939. [LUC]

Novena Notes was a small devotional journal, but since the media at large were suppressing the story, publishing the letter gave the strike committee a chance to outline its grievances. (The Archdiocesan publication *New World* had briefly mentioned the strike two weeks earlier.) In the letter, the committee also thanked Hillenbrand, Hayes, and four other priests "for speaking to us and telling us to persevere in this just strike."[17]

An illustration on a strike-committee brochure showed the pope handing a parchment document ("labor doctrine") to a brawny worker, lunch-box in hand and standing in the forefront of a smoke-belching mill. On the back of the brochure is a selection of encyclical quotes, and inside is a summary of the strike's origins and a note that Hayes and other supporters had visited strike headquarters to provide words of encouragement. All in all, the brochure constituted a rather direct promotion of Catholic social action's "Go to the worker" mandate![18]

In July 1939, American Newspaper Guild President Heywood Broun (like Day a Catholic convert) praised the Catholic labor apostolate's support for the long and difficult strike. Broun, unfortunately, didn't live to see its 1940 settlement, in which labor and management agreed to NLRB representation elections in three to six months—a result the union welcomed.

In 1940, employees at Marshall Field's department store, long a Chicago institution, organized, and at a mid-year meeting voted unanimously to join the United Retail, Wholesale and Department Store Employees of America-CIO. *Telescope*, the employees' newsletter, reported "Speakers at this meeting were Rev. John M. Hayes of Quigley Seminary and Rev. William Boyd of Mundelein and DePaul Colleges. Both gave interesting talks, pointing out the advantages to us as employees and as citizens of a democratic country of becoming a part of the real trade-union movement."[19]

This news was too much for Catholic milliner Joseph Beckmann. He complained to Archdiocesan Chancellor George Casey that Fathers Hayes and Boyd had overstepped their bounds. Casey defended the priests to Beckmann, but then instructed them that in the future, they were not to speak to a labor gathering without Chancery approval. They probably exercised a bit more caution thereafter, but it's

17 Ibid.
18 Brochure, Hearst Strike Committee, Jan. 1939. [LUC]
19 "Speakers at this Meeting," *Telescope*, July 8, 1940. [AC]

doubtful there was much change in local (and national) Catholic social actionists' general policy of "Don't ask and they can't say no."

The clergy and laity of Chicago's labor apostolate knew they faced a tough task, but believing "a little leaven expands the loaf," they pressed forward. Stirred by their commitment and labor's vibrancy, worker-students came in growing numbers to Chicago's labor schools. The school network expanded from five schools in autumn 1938 to twice that many over the next few years.

The network ran until 1943, when it tailed off. Hillenbrand listed several reasons: "The war is one. The lack of labor trouble is another. Return of 'good times' is a third and maybe the most important.... It seems that interest wanes when the effort must be made for the future instead of the immediate present."[20]

Another factor was the death of George Cardinal Mundelein at the end of 1939. Successor Archbishop Samuel Stritch, while generally permissive, was not as active in support of worker justice as Mundelein. In this respect, Mundelein's death echoed the death earlier that year, on March 2, of Pius XI, whose successor as Pius XII was conservative Cardinal Eugenio Pacelli.

The new Pope declared the goal of any society to be "economic prosperity" as measured solely by diffusion of wealth. Also, while his predecessor had distinguished between revolutionary socialism and reform socialism, and acknowledged the latter as an important ingredient of Catholic social action, Pius XII condemned all types of socialism.

Despite the labor-school network's slowdown and a more conservative Church, Catholic social action in Chicago was still very much alive in the middle of World War II, although it was headed in a different direction. (See Chapter Five.)

Father John Hayes was instrumental, as noted, in the achievements of Chicago Catholic social action's early phase. He was a labor advocate, a planner of social-action activities, a teacher in labor schools, and the writer of many of the mimeographed outlines the schools used as texts.

His efforts received wide attention, and in mid-1940, when the National Catholic Welfare Conference (NCWC) sought a full-time labor-school coordinator for SAD, it recruited Hayes for the position, located at NCWC headquarters in downtown Washington, DC. He

---

20 Hillenbrand, Reynold, to Hayes, July 24, 1942. [CUA]

was just what SAD sought—a priest with substantial field experience and a good understanding of the clergy's social-action role.

> *An academic interest in these questions is not enough for the main body of the clergy. It leaves us subject to the accusation of hypocrisy or stupidity or both. I think the Holy Father makes that clear; he does not direct us merely to study the problems of the poor; he says "Go to the worker, go to the poor." There is the rub; it is easy enough to read about these things in the comfort of the rectory, yet even intensive studies are no proof of heroic virtue. But to get out and spend ourselves, as far as we can, in this difficult, non-remunerative, misunderstood, ofttimes novel form of priestly activity, that will take a lot of "push." This sort of thing is still considered eccentric, needless, foolish, even positively harmful, by a few Catholics and some priests.*[21]

Father John Hayes always went out and spent himself, and he did so in his new job. He "picked the brains" of SAD's Linna Bresette, who for several years had coordinated labor-school efforts as one of her many duties (see p. 100), and then he streamlined the process of providing Catholic labor schools with course outlines and bibliographies. Fittingly, a set of his Chicago outlines became one of the most requested items.

In addition, Father Hayes asked the schools' labor apostles to fill him in on their problems and prospects, and incorporated the results into the widely-read monthly he started, *Social Action Notes for Priests*. Also, he took to the road, promoting labor schools and guiding their directors, teachers, and students.

An SAD survey in summer 1939 showed 52 schools in 24 cities. New York, Chicago, Detroit, and Baltimore had school networks. Pittsburgh and Washington, DC, had two schools each. There were single schools in Boston, Buffalo, Indianapolis, Joliet, Kansas City, Kenosha, New Rochelle, Newark, Philadelphia, Richmond, Rochester, St. Paul, San Francisco, Scranton, Sheboygan, Tarrytown, Waukegan, and Wilkes-Barre.[22]

---

21 Hayes, "Work of the Priest," *op. cit.*

22 Most of the 52 schools are identified elsewhere in this volume. Those which are not: the 10 schools of the Baltimore-Washington, DC, Archdiocese (eight in Baltimore, including at St. John Church, St. Martin Church, and Calvert Hall College; and two in Washington, DC, including one for African-Americans); the diocesan schools in Indianapolis, Kenosha, Richmond, St. Paul (at St. Paul Seminary), and Sheboygan; and

1 ❦ John Hayes 43

Over the next few years, the number of schools doubled, thanks to Hayes' firm grasp of the national labor-school helm. From Burlington to Berkeley, Lynn to Troy, Albany to San Diego, Grand Rapids to Jersey City, Peoria to Providence, multiplication of schools meant growth in labor learning.[23]

The coordinator role required Hayes to be part counselor and part chaplain to the priests under his guidance, and this was a calling he fulfilled admirably. He began by taking in, thoroughly and patiently, what they communicated to him.

Sometimes they wrestled with difficulties: "We promise the factory workers in the parish everything but a fan dancer every Mass each Sunday to build up trade for the school," wrote Detroit's Father Clem Kern, "but we mostly get the red-hot unionist and triple-A Catholic, for an average attendance of eight." Father George Vogt, of Rochester, N.Y., wondered "how to hold the men on lines that are not parochial." "[W]e've abandoned the field for too long and now they [worker-students] aren't docile," observed Chicago priest William Dorney. And Father Henry Holleman, of New Orleans, complained about some local pastors thinking of assistant pastors "that these 'young' men with their highfalutin ideas are rebels, almost Communists, idealists, but above all and at any rate not too well mentally balanced. If our hierarchy, *salve reverentia* [with all due deference], would set the pace, and our 'big' pastors would favor capital a little less, we might get some place."[24]

At other times, the labor schools reported triumphs. New Orleans Fathers William Reintjes and Jerome Drolet (p. 238) noted that as a result of labor-school lessons, worker-students sent a release to local newspapers supporting a strike at the Alden Hosiery Mills and stating "We wish to play our humble part in applying the social directives of the Holy Father in our own city and state"; the release was

---

the Wilkes-Barre School of Social Action, jointly sponsored by College Miseracordia and the University of Scranton (with Christian Brothers involvement). St. John's University in New York City made labor courses part of its extensive program to train future civil servants.

23 For an incisive, in-depth look at the interplay of Catholic social action and labor activism in Providence and Woonsocket, RI, see *Working-Class Americanism: The Politics of Labor in a Textile City, 1914-1960*, Gary Gerstle, Cambridge: Cambridge University Press, 1989.

24 Responses to "Survey of Labor Schools," SAD, July 1941.

published and much discussed throughout the community, and the strike was settled the next day. Buffalo Labor College Secretary Frances Engel spotlighted Albert Maggioli, a worker-student who, after hearing about the encyclicals' sometimes-convoluted style, "was surprised to find that each word counted in his work experience." And Father Philip Carey, Director of Xavier Labor School in New York City (see Chapter Nine), commended Philip Troy, the President of Marble Helpers Union Local 10 and a student with two years' perfect attendance; Troy said the school "broadened my philosophy of the worker's problems in a way that helped me direct union affairs fairly."[25]

Hayes absorbed the many tribulations and triumphs and processed them into recommendations and reflections, primarily in *Social Action Notes for Priests*. Drawing upon his experience as a teacher in Catholic labor schools, he helped scores of labor-school educators to focus their classes and students on real-life labor principles, problems, and practices. And since many of the school's teachers were parish priests, he emphasized Pius XI's counsel that they "dedicate the better part of their endeavors and their zeal to winning back the laboring masses to Christ and to His Church."

National labor-school coordinator Hayes recognized that the major purpose of workers' education generally—a growing phenomenon in that period—and of Catholic labor schools in particular, was to develop in their students a sense of responsibility for solving current economic and social problems. Hayes was well aware, he wrote in the March 1941 issue of *Social Action Notes for Priests*, that students were faced with "too many colorful and exciting and dramatic diversions" (his examples of movies and radio would now be items in a much longer list), but he did all he could to "implant a gnawing desire of self-sacrifice for the common good, a deep sense of solidarity and social responsibility."[26] And he took some definite stands in his newsletter on legislation and industry proposals.

In the February 1941 issue, for example, Hayes encouraged priests to support new State Labor Relations Acts and Minimum Wage Acts where they didn't exist or were restrictive. Also, he cautioned readers that a National Association of Manufacturers (NAM) proposal for meetings between priests and businessmen in every industrial town

---

25 Ibid.
26 Hayes, "Creating Interest," *Social Action Notes*, Mar. 1941

was highly suspect, in light of the NAM's "40-year record of anti-unionism."²⁷

Perhaps he had heard from his Chicago friends about the debate scheduled for that month at St. Ann Church in Chicago Heights between two representatives of Catholic social action (Father Boyd, Hayes' companion at Marshall Field's, and newspaperman Harry Read) and two representatives of management—a railroad executive and a representative of the Illinois Manufacturers Association (IMA), the state branch of the NAM. The pairs exchanged viewpoints vigorously, with the social actionists gaining such an edge that the railroad executive ran from the room and Father Joseph Petro, a priest at St. Ann's, declared that "for the first time in history, the workers in this town have their shoulders back and their chins out."²⁸

The incident left a bitter aftertaste, however. Throughout subsequent months, the IMA complained to St. Ann's pastor, Father Joseph Anderson, and to Archbishop Stritch, that management wasn't sufficiently represented at Catholic social-action conferences.

By November, Father Hillenbrand's patience was wearing thin. He responded to a Stritch request that he attend an upcoming conference of the IMA by citing its "anti-labor" stance and its opposition to 16 labor bills pending in the state legislature. Stritch in turn blistered Hillenbrand for having "no hope of planting right principles in the managers and owners of property."²⁹ Hillenbrand attended the event, but the Chicago Church was obviously moving towards a far-different era.

In August 1944, Archbishop Stritch put an exclamation point on the end of the early era by reassigning Father Hillenbrand to an affluent parish in Hubbard Woods, on Chicago's North Shore, an area with many IMA members. There had long been friction at St. Mary of the Lake Seminary between the administration, largely Archdiocesan, and the faculty, largely Jesuit. Several conservative Jesuit faculty members worked for months to undermine Hillenbrand's position, and Stritch was only too happy to replace him with a more conservative rector. "From now on," Father Hayes wrote Father Daniel Cantwell, "the seminary might appear to be safe for the Republicans."³⁰

---

27   Hayes, "NAM Proposal," *Social Action Notes*, Feb. 1941.
28   Read, Harry, to Hillenbrand, Feb. 14, 1941. [UND]
29   Hillenbrand to Stritch, Nov. 16, 1941; reply Nov. 17. [UND]
30   Hayes to Cantwell, Daniel, Aug. 23, 1944. [CHS]

Hillenbrand was made a domestic prelate, or monsignor, in 1946 and went on to years of devoted service in Catholic Action efforts before he died in 1978. At Hillenbrand's funeral, Father Cantwell, by then a leader in Chicago social action, called the 1944 reassignment "the most monumental error ever made in the history of the Archdiocese."[31]

During Father John Hayes' Washington years, he kept in touch with his Chicago friends. He was delighted, for instance, to hear of success for the Back of the Yards Council. Catholic churches and labor schools near the stockyards supported it after its July 1939 formation by Jewish community organizer Saul Alinsky and Catholic activist Joe Meegan, Davis Square Park Community Center director. The group brought together packing-house workers of all faiths to organize and bargain, and thus minimized employer exploitation of workers' ethnic and religious differences.

Hayes also reconnected with his CW origins by forming a "see-judge-act" group of government and education professionals in the Washington, DC, area. Members found many ways to apply their spirituality and their social-action principles in the hectic pre-war and wartime atmosphere of the nation's capitol.

It was an exciting time for John Hayes. He was thrilled to work for, and get to know, SAD director John Ryan, a Catholic University of America economist, and a major inspiration for pre-1930s Catholic social action. Ryan's 1906 book *A Living Wage*, based upon his doctoral dissertation at St. Paul Seminary in Minnesota, was one of the first studies in economic ethics by an American Catholic scholar.[32]

Ryan's spiritual and economic ideas were akin to the Social Gospel movement and the teachings of Richard Ely (author of the introduction to *A Living Wage*), John Commons, and others in the "ethical school of economists" at the University of Wisconsin, with whom Ryan drafted and promoted the earliest U.S. minimum-wage laws. In 1919, Ryan wrote *The Bishops' Program for Social Reconstruction*, a plan for U.S. recovery from World War I.[33] *Quadragesimo Anno* was heavily

---

31 Higgins, George, interview with author, Sept. 15, 1995.
32 Ryan, John, *A Living Wage: Its Ethical and Economic Aspects*, New York: P.J. Kenedy and Sons, 1906.
33 Appendix to Ryan, *Social Reconstruction*, New York: Macmillan, 1920. McShane, Joseph, "*Sufficiently Radical*," Washington: Catholic University of America Press, 1986.

influenced by Ryan and by the democratic and socialistic ideas of German Jesuit Father Oswald von Nell-Breuning, *QA*'s primary drafter.

Hayes was familiar with Ryan's social teachings, but now he could explore the background in which many of these teachings were adopted. The call of *The Bishops' Program* that labor participate in industrial management set the tone for Catholic social action for years to come. For Ryan, such industrial democracy meant workers sharing profits, having a voice in every aspect of their enterprises, and owning enough of these enterprises to play significant roles in management and operational control.

The Bishops' Program resulted from the more active role American Catholics played in U.S. social and economic development in World War I. Among the document's other recommendations were a public employment service; social insurance for the sick, jobless, and elderly; vocational training; abolition of child labor; and paying women and men equal pay for equal work. All the document's recommendations became part of New Deal legislation except for the one on labor participation in industrial management, the heart of *The Bishops' Program*.

In the year of this document's appearance, the Catholic Church in the United States reorganized the National Catholic War Council as the National Catholic Welfare Council. In 1922, as the result of a tug of war between liberals and conservatives within the American Church's hierarchy, the Vatican suddenly abolished the Council and then just as suddenly reinstated it. It became the National Catholic Welfare Conference and kept the SAD, which was formed in 1919 with Ryan as its director.

His assistant director was Father Raymond McGowan, whose sociable, casual style contrasted sharply with Ryan's professorial demeanor. They made a good team, however, and for years McGowan and Linna Bresette ran the Catholic Conference on Industrial Problems (CCIP), whereby representatives of labor, management, and the Church met in industrial cities to resolve problems cooperatively.[34] Indeed, it was Father John Hayes' work with CCIP in Chicago that brought him to SAD's attention.

By the time the Depression hit, John Ryan had a solid national reputation as an economics expert, so it's no surprise that when 1932 Presidential candidate Franklin Roosevelt sought help in that area, he

---

34   Greene, Thomas, "The CCIP in Normalcy and Depression," *The Catholic Historical Review*, July 1991, 437-69.

turned to Ryan. "The Right Reverend New Dealer," radio priest Father Charles Coughlin (see p. 84-85) later called him—sarcastically, although Ryan and his friends proudly appropriated the nickname.

Robert Jackson, head of the New Deal Justice Department's Anti-Trust Division and later a U.S. Supreme Court justice, said Catholic social action inspired New Deal measures for remedying the ills of America's economy and society. Indeed, the labor-industry-government arrangements represented by the National Recovery Act (NRA) and the National Industrial Recovery Act (NIRA) relate directly to QA.

The U.S. Supreme Court declared the NIRA unconstitutional in 1935, but its labor-organizing and collective-bargaining provision survived as Section 7(a) of the National Labor Relations Act (NLRA) passed that same year. Ryan called the NLRA "probably the most just, beneficent, and far-reaching piece of labor legislation ever enacted in the United States."[35]

Hayes' SAD office in Washington was a short drive away from The Catholic University of America (CUA), where many of his Chicago friends came to study during this period, and where he often visited with them. They included Father George Higgins (see Chapter Ten), who would succeed him in the coordinator role at SAD, and Father Daniel Cantwell, mentioned earlier.

Monsignor (from 1936 on) Ryan taught economics at CUA until mid-1939, when conservative Churchmen who had long opposed his ideas were instrumental in a ruling by CUA's Board of Trustees that no faculty member could teach past age 70. The ruling was adopted six weeks before Ryan reached that age, and he was the only one to whom it immediately applied.

Also at CUA was Francis Haas, who in 1937 became a monsignor and the first dean of CUA's short-lived School of Social Sciences (1937-43)—he had directed the university's School of Social Service from 1931-5. Haas, a renowned labor activist and author [see pp. 70-71, 82), was a member of NRA's Labor Advisory Board, chaired the Fair Employment Practices Committee, and was a skilled federal labor mediator.

Haas was from Milwaukee, and Hayes knew him from their participation there in the First National Catholic Social Action Conference,

---

35   Broderick, Francis, *Right Reverend New Dealer John A. Ryan*, New York: The Macmillan Company, 1963, 220.

in May 1938. When they chatted in Washington, they agreed that prospects were excellent for furthering connections between labor and Catholic social action.

Haas, a student of Ryan, applied his ideas and took them a step further. Haas agreed with Ryan that the NRA was a good example of QA's ideal economic organization, but, unlike his mentor, also believed that the ideal would never be approached without years of strengthening unions until they were on a par with management. Labor-management harmony and industry pride, Haas affirmed, must be developed from the plant level up.

John Hayes thoroughly enjoyed his Washington contacts and his association with Ryan, although Ryan was too busy with his researches to spend much time with a junior employee. Hayes spent more time with McGowan, who often recounted the struggles of him and Ryan for worker justice.

On numerous occasions, McGowan said, he and Ryan were called "Bolsheviks," "Communists," "radicals," or worse, but neither of them was ever cowed. They were among the earliest proponents of opposing Communism yet giving priority to championing economic and social justice, thus removing the ills which bred Communism.[36] The charge of being "radical" they unashamedly accepted, as did Hayes, in the sense expressed by liturgist Virgil Michel: "the sense of a person plumbing down to the roots of our system with a new and critical and vigorous constructive activity."[37]

Sometimes their foes were close to home. Michael J. Curley, Archbishop for Maryland and the District of Columbia, was so incensed at Ryan and McGowan fighting for a Constitutional amendment to end child labor that he called McGowan an "omadhaun" ["fool"], accused Ryan of acting in a "cowardly" and "blackguardly" manner, and declared "I shall have nothing whatsoever to do with any School of Social Science, so far as sending men to it, with which John Ryan and McGowan are connected."[38] Further, in 1937 he reassigned McGowan to a remote Maryland parish until Ryan, with help from a couple of Curley's fellow archbishops, got him back.

---

36   In 1920, for example, SAD published McGowan's *Bolshevism in Russia and America*, which included a chapter called "Bolshevism as an Epithet."
37   Marx, Paul, *Virgil Michel and the Liturgical Movement*, Collegeville, Minn.: The Liturgical Press, 1957, 306, 329.
38   Curley, Michael, to Edwin O'Hara, Apr. 12, 1937. [AD]

From his chats with McGowan, Hayes learned that, as he put it, "McGowan and Ryan faced blank walls on many occasions, and their method, which has worked out better than open warfare, was to sit quietly and eventually dig under the wall or see it collapse."[39] Hayes wrote that in a letter to his friend Father Cantwell, and followed the McGowan-Ryan approach in his own contacts and travels as SAD's national labor-school coordinator.

Several times in 1941-43, Hayes visited the Diocesan Labor Institute (DLI) in Connecticut, sponsor of labor schools in 12 of the state's cities and towns.[40] DLI worker-students often struggled to apply their lessons in Communist-dominated or -influenced unions. This was a difficult task, because these worker-students had to balance union democracy with their fight against fellow unionists for whom union control was a steppingstone towards the CP's expressed goal of overthrowing the United States.

The task was tough, but DLI members tackled it valiantly, and Hayes helped them stay balanced. DLI Director Father Joseph Donnelly said "We credit Father Hayes with much of the success that we have been able to attain. He guided our beginnings and he has been not only a help but an inspiration."[41]

Father Hayes was always strong, always unassuming, and always there. Undoubtedly, he would have gone on adding to his record of SAD achievements, but in 1944 he came down with tuberculosis. Doctors advised him to move to a dry climate, so he got reassigned to a teaching position at Incarnate Word College, San Antonio, Texas.

John Hayes didn't let his labor activism die out, however. He spoke at strikes and organizing meetings for garment workers, bakers, and meat-packers, and contributed articles on labor topics to the Catholic weekly *Alamo Register* and to Chicago's monthly *Work*, which started in 1943. (*The Chicago Catholic Worker* didn't survive the onset of war.)

Hayes' pace did slow down, however, giving him time to reflect, particularly about the final months of World War II and about the shape of the postwar world. Even before American entry into the war, he ob-

---

39 Hayes to Cantwell, Aug. 23, 1944. [CHS]
40 Bridgeport, Bristol, Hartford, Meriden, Middletown, Naugatuck Valley, New Britain, New Haven, New London, Norwalk, Stamford, Waterbury, and Willimantic.
41 "Report to Bishop," Diocesan Labor Institute, Hartford, Conn., June 30, 1944.

served in *CCW* that the United States possessed "physical resources, to be sure; we can unite our resources for such an ignoble purpose as war." But he then wondered "Have we the intellectual and moral health to join forces to give the jobless a share in economic life as well as permission to vote at regular intervals? Our experience in this country over the past 10 years would seem to suggest that quite possibly we have not." By shortly after the war's end, Hayes and many others expressed a frustration that "a share in economic life" meant little more to the average worker then than it did when he made that observation.⁴²

Over the next decade, Hayes continued doing whatever he could for Catholic social action. He moved back to Chicago in 1953, where he was Mercy High School chaplain and later pastored at St. Carthage's (where this chapter opened) and at Epiphany Church. In 1954, he formed the St. Thomas More Service Club, a see-judge-act group for writers.

Hayes was always hopeful, but he was also increasingly disappointed in the results of the Catholic social-action movement and its labor schools, and in the movement's future prospects. Many of the schools trooped on into the mid-1950s, but dwindled away rapidly thereafter.

"There is almost as great a dearth of social justice in the average man," he said around that time, "as there was a generation ago. He is a rather unusual individual who is willing to make sacrifices for the common good, or even thinks of it."⁴³

> *Today things are somewhat different in that plant I worked at 30 years ago. Not only are wages higher but the workers have something to say about their jobs. They don't have very much to say. They don't say it directly but through their elected and hired representatives. That's all right. Most of them are neither imaginative nor glib. Their spokesmen argue for them about wages, vacations, lay-offs, and a few other things. A suggestion box is located in each department.*
>
> *Back in 1931 Pope Pius XI said it would be a good idea, although not his main idea, for the work contract to give some share in management to the workers in a plant.... A new study manual on "Workers' Participation in Industry," published by the International Confederation of Free Trade Unions in Brussels, Belgium, resembles at times the approach of Pius XI in "Quadragesimo Anno": "Workers [the manual says] will seldom get interested in joint efforts to increase production un-*

---

42 Hayes, "An American Tragedy" Part 1, *CCW*, Oct. 1939, 4.
43 Hayes, speech, Social Action Conference, New Orleans, Labor Day 1956. [WSU]

til and unless they are strongly enough organized to make sure that they will benefit equitably by the increased production. But there are other reasons than the desire for more pie. The demand for workers' participation is part of the movement toward more democracy."

Is there any hope of further participation? Times are pretty good, and personnel policies are more refined than formerly. My guess, however, is that most American workers would warm up to the proposal of further "participation in industry" only if their leaders will do most of the production, spadework, and planning.[44]

We live in times that are obviously very different from when Father John Hayes ventured that guess. But in any times, and especially now, his guess is a challenge to all America's workers, non-union and union, rank-and-file and officer, to speak up, to exercise their power, to link up with other workers, and to claim their rightful shares in America's enterprises. They can say "thanks" to Father Hayes while they're at it.

---

44 Hayes, "Why Workers Need More of a Share," *op. cit.*

CHAPTER TWO
JOHN CORT(1913–2006)

In the winter of 1936-37, in the converted storefront of a New York City tenement house, recent Harvard graduate John Cort walked among a small group of workers as they studied copies of *Quadragesimo Anno* (*QA*). Using a popular commentary on it, Cort patiently guided the workers as they struggled their way to an understanding of phrases from the document:

> When on the one hand we see thousands of needy victims of real misery for reasons beyond their control, and on the other so many round about them who spend huge sums of money on useless things and frivolous amusements, we cannot fail to remark with sorrow that justice is poorly observed.
>
> Immense power and despotic economic domination is concentrated in the hands of a few.... [A]ccumulation of power, a characteristic note of the modern economic order, is a natural result of

unrestrained free competition which permits the survival of those only who are the strongest. This often means those who fight most relentlessly, who pay least heed to the dictates of conscience."

[T]he whole economic life has become hard, cruel, and relentless in a ghastly measure.

Even more severely must be condemned the foolhardiness of those who neglect to remove or modify such conditions as exasperate the minds of the people, and so pave the way for the overthrow and ruin of the social order.

Every effort must be made that at least in the future, only a fair share of the fruits of production be permitted to accumulate in the hands of the wealthy, and that an ample sufficiency be supplied to the workers.

[N]ot only is man free to institute associations [connected with their occupations], legally and functionally of private character, but he also has the right of "freely adopting such organization and such rules as are judged best for the end in view."

[T]he wage contract should, when possible, be modified somewhat by a contract of partnership. ... For thus the workers and executives become sharers in the ownership or management, or also participate in some way in the profits.

It is rightly contended that certain forms of property must be reserved to the state, since they carry with them an opportunity of domination too great to be left to private individuals without injury to the community at large.

[I]f we examine matters diligently and thoroughly we shall perceive that this longed-for social reconstruction [*On Reconstruction of the Social Order* was QA's subtitle] must be preceded by a profound renewal of the Christian spirit from which so many of those engaged in economic activity have in many places unhappily departed. Otherwise, all our endeavors will be futile, and our social edifice will be built not upon a rock, but upon shifting sand.

Undoubtedly, the first and immediate apostles of the workers must themselves be workers, while the apostles of the industrial and commercial world should themselves be employers and merchants.[1]

John Cort's worker-students brought to their study of QA the essential ingredient for its understanding: the students had all felt the sting of social injustice in their workplaces. Some of them, in fact, were feeling this sting even as they studied. They were seamen on strike, and had come to the classroom from the roiled-up New York City wa-

---

1   In *Seven Great Encyclicals*, Glen Rock, NJ: Paulist Press, 1963.

terfront seeking help in their fight to cast off the yoke of the corrupt International Seamen's Union and to get better representation.

John Cort brought to his students a deep knowledge of Catholic social teachings, knowledge he had gained since his conversion to Catholicism a year and a-half earlier. After his conversion, he enlisted in the Catholic Worker (CW) movement founded by Dorothy Day and her followers in New York City, and moved into the CW House of Hospitality there, the first of many such centers. It was at 115 Mott Street in Manhattan's Lower East Side, and housed the storefront classroom used by Cort and his students.

The CW movement was based on the concept that social reform goes hand-in-hand with personal reform, and involves performing acts of charity and justice—including worker justice. In this view, helping workers claim their rights is as vital a part of the gospel of Christ as feeding the hungry, clothing the naked, or sheltering the homeless.

A favorite CW quote is the Bible passage (Matthew 25:31-46) where Jesus tells his listeners that whenever they've helped any of the needy, "ye have done it unto me." Thus when Dorothy Day looked at the seamen in Cort's class and at other strikers, she could say, as she did in summer 1936 in the movement's influential publication *The Catholic Worker* (*CW*), "When workers are striking they are following an impulse, often blind, often uninformed, but a good impulse—one could even say an inspiration of the Holy Spirit. They are trying to uphold their right to be treated not as slaves but as human beings. They are fighting for a share in the management, for their right to be considered partners in the enterprise in which they are engaged."

An earlier issue of *CW* is what got John Cort interested in Dorothy Day and her movement in the first place. It was the issue of December 1935, and Day's observation "We choose to spend the salaries we might be making if we were business-like on feeding and sharing our home with the homeless and hungry" stirred Cort's mind and imagination.

To this new Catholic, lonesome for fellowship and moved by the human suffering in the midst of the Depression, *The Catholic Worker* meant challenge and connection, and after visiting CW's Boston center he sold the paper, a penny a copy, in front of churches around the city.

> *In April 1936 Dorothy Day came to Boston to give a talk in the dingy room of our headquarters in the South End. I was late for the*

meeting, and by the time I got there, she was speaking already. Suddenly, bang, without ever to that moment having given the proposition any serious thought at all, I decided to chuck my $15-a-week reporter's job, go down to New York City, and work for room and board.

What was it about Dorothy Day that had such an effect? Certainly not physical attraction, although she was by no means an unattractive woman. In fact, the face was striking, the cheekbones high, and the eyes large and strangely slanted. She was tall and imposing in figure, but round-shouldered and a bit stooped as though she were already feeling the weight of the burdens she had assumed. She was then thirty-eight years old—young, as I look back now from a snow-capped eighty-nine, but to me then, a mere boy of twenty-two, she was old.

She was not a forceful speaker in the usual sense. She spoke in a low, conversational tone, and the content of her talk was much like the articles I had read in the paper, personal and anecdotal, full of people, places, and events, with occasional quotes from the Gospel or a favorite writer. She probably included one of her favorite quotes, from The Brothers Karamazov: "Love in action is a harsh and dreadful thing, compared with love in dreams."

What moved me was something else, something that shone through the harsh and dreadful life she was living on behalf of the homeless and the hungry. I remember sitting in that dingy room and thinking, "This woman seems to be getting a lot of fun out of life, and I would like to get some of that for myself."

As much as anything, what attracted me was a quality of humor and laughter, but with a base deeper than the humor and laughter you might get from a good comedian. In one word it was a quality of *joy*. Not perfect joy, perhaps, but close enough. Leon Bloy wrote once that "joy is an almost certain sign of the presence of the Holy Spirit." Whatever she had—fun, joy, Holy Spirit—it moved me.[2]

John Cort volunteered for Dorothy Day's New York City venture that very evening, and she was delighted to gain such a thoughtful and eager helper. Cort lived among her compassionate cadre for the next two years, sleeping in a dormitory with nine other men and countless bedbugs; serving to the homeless (and eating) cornflakes for breakfast, soup and bread for lunch, and thin stew for supper; and working for worker justice the rest of the time.

No task was more essential at the time, or more exciting. In 1935 the U.S. Congress passed the National Labor Relations Act—also known

---

2   Cort, John, *Dreadful Conversions: The Making of a Catholic Socialist*, New York: Fordham University Press, 2003, 2-3.

as the Wagner Act—which gave workers the right to organize freely and bargain collectively. In 1936 and 1937, workers across the nation responded with fervor and determination, forming unions wherever they could and in many cases gaining effective representation for the first time.

In 1935, a half-dozen large industrial unions—unions organized by the mass of workers in an industry—formed themselves into the Committee for Industrial Organizations. In October 1937, this group broke away from the American Federation of Labor (AFL), whose unions were composed of widely-scattered groups of skilled craftsworkers. This action by the Committee (in 1938 renamed the Congress of Industrial Organizations, or CIO) threw the doors wide open for unionism in meat-packing; maritime industries; coal-mining; and the manufacturing of steel, autos, rubber products, textiles, and a host of other commodities.

Dorothy Day, John Cort, and many other American Catholics fought vigorously and valiantly in the fierce 1930s struggles for worker justice because they felt that in the papal encyclicals *QA*, *Rerum Novarum*, and *Divini Redemptoris* (also known as "On Atheistic Communism"), they had potent medicine to apply to the nation's severe social and economic ills.

These encyclicals encouraged Catholic workers to join neutral (or secular) unions. *QA* called upon clergy and laity to find and train "apostles of the workers" and thus become labor apostles themselves. The combination of a fervent labor apostolate and an awakening labor movement packed a powerful punch.

The challenges involved in answering Pius XI's call were manifold and daunting. The social-action encyclicals called for an end to class struggle (they were, after all, responses to Communism and revolutionary socialism, which were active in Europe in the late 19th century and in places around the globe in the early 20th century) and for its replacement by cooperation among labor, industry, and government. Industry owners, as good stewards of their properties, would provide for an industry's managers and workers to share justly in proceeds and production decisions, and the government would pass laws to facilitate such industrial democracy, stepping in only to help make certain this objective was reached.

In the real world of the United States in the 1930s, however, "rugged individualism"—Catholic social action's name for unrestrained capitalism—ran as rampant as it could, little chastened by the Great Depression. Nearly every agreement industrial owners/managers (including many Catholics) made with organized labor was made grudgingly and after bitter, long-drawn-out opposition, and was unmade if possible as soon as it could be. Communists in the labor movement, therefore, continued to find fertile soil for their class-struggle arguments. Catholic social actionists had to fight on two fronts.

At the same time, they had to assure Catholics that they could join a union and still be good Catholics. The social actionists excelled at this task, which got easier as time went on and many more Catholics understood their message.

In addition, they had to inculcate enough Catholic workers and enough other workers with the teachings of the social-action encyclicals to significantly impact the labor movement. Results here were mixed. The labor apostles' impact was substantial but not nearly as substantial as it might have been, for reasons this volume will explore.

Dorothy Day and John Cort were right in the middle of the earliest labor-organizing struggles. Two months into the seamen's strike mentioned earlier, the strikers voted to go back to work, but they'd made their point. A month later, they formed themselves into the National Maritime Union (NMU) and affiliated it with the CIO. In the National Labor Relations Board election to determine whether seamen wished to be represented by the corrupt International Seamen's Union-AFL or the newly-formed NMU, the NMU won on 52 shipping lines and the ISU on only six.

The New York City waterfront was not a place for the faint-hearted. During the 1936-37 strike, CW volunteers established a waterfront outpost where strikers could eat and gather. Cort got his waterfront baptism of fire there when he joined the strike's picket lines just as police were clearing a path through them for strikebreakers, or scabs. All of a sudden, he felt himself being shoved along a sidewalk by the backside of a policeman's horse.

The boss of the waterfront and a leader of the strikebreakers was International Longshoremen's Association-AFL head Joe Ryan, a Catholic who regularly attended Mass and never used profanity, but who also piled up ill-gotten gains and used goon squads to keep honest workers and their friends in line. He didn't intimidate Dorothy Day, however.

Ryan accused all the leaders of the seamen's strike of being Communists, another example of Red-baiting. (Some of the strike leaders <u>were</u> Communist, but Ryan painted all the leaders with the same Red brush.) Dorothy Day responded on the front page of *CW* with a letter addressed to "AFL Union Leaders, Especially Joseph P. Ryan." The letter called them and him "Bolsheviks themselves," alleging that since "they are not trying to deproletarianize the worker, as the Holy Father advises, helping him to become an owner, to have a share in the management of the calling to which he is engaged, they are denying the right to private property."[3]

Dorothy Day covered the top labor stories and wrote perceptively on them for the CW paper. To get the scoop on the ultimately victorious sit-down strike at the General Motors plant in Flint, Michigan, from the waning days of 1936 into February 1937, Dorothy Day actually climbed through the windows of the plant to obtain the viewpoints of the sit-downers. They contended that they were just preserving the plant for its owner until their injustices were redressed.

In May 1937, Day was in Chicago covering a strike against Republic Steel Company, the last hold-out against the organizing drive of the Steel Workers Organizing Committee. She interviewed steel-workers at Sam's Place tavern, strike headquarters. A few days later, 10 strikers were killed by police in what is now known as the Memorial Day Massacre. Most of the victims were shot in the back.

As for John Cort, teaching workers *QA* gave him insight into Pius XI's call on Catholic unionists to form "side by side" associations. The Pope's concern was that in countries with no Catholic unions (e.g. the United States), Catholic unionists would get work-related instruction but no spiritual guidance, especially in relating their faith to encyclical principles. Cort conveyed this insight to *CW* readers and mulled over what to do about it.

Meanwhile, he plunged further into labor activism, and in the process distanced himself somewhat from Dorothy Day. She increasingly came under the influence of Peter Maurin, a sort of philosopher-in-residence at New York's House of Hospitality. Peter had distilled his five-plus decades of roustabout life into an assortment of aphorisms, including "Strikes don't strike me" and "When the organizers

---

3   Cort, *Dreadful Conversions*, op. cit., 28-9.

try to organize the unorganized, then the organizers don't organize themselves."[4]

Day, though remaining empathetic to struggles for worker justice, joined Maurin in focusing almost wholly on spiritual discipline rather than temporal discipline. As Cort moved more deeply into workers' struggles, his interests and Day's continued to diverge. She later called him "my wayward son"[5], but always regarded and treated him with affection and respect.

Cort's comments in CW on "side by side" workers' associations caught the eye of Catholic unionists. Marty Wersing, President of the Edison Electrical Workers Union, responded to Cort that Catholic employees of the Edison Company, while they made up the majority of its 40,000 workers, were too often indifferent to union organization. He added that Communists were apt to be his union's most active members because, despite their widely-advertised aim of revolutionary overthrow of the U.S. government in favor of a worker state, they "made a religion of their devotion to the trade union movement."[6]

On February 27, 1937, Cort met with Wersing and nine other Catholic unionists and formed the Association of Catholic Trade Unionists (ACTU). The founders saw it as the "side by side" association called for by Pius XI. This was unlike Father John Hayes' conception, but Catholic social action had room for many variations in approach.

The group assigned Cort and Wersing, its only union official, to draw up a constitution. They immersed themselves in the social-action encyclicals and other landmark documents of Catholic social action, including the writings of John Ryan.

Ryan's teachings, as outlined earlier, blended the encyclicals; Midwestern progressivism; and the ideas of social, economic, and political democracy. These teachings spread widely during Ryan's 1919-45 directorship of the Social Action Department of the National Catholic Welfare Conference.

Surrounded by their awesome array of resources, with Cort at a typewriter and Wersing dictating, the two men went to work.

> *Whose idea it was to shape the program in the form of rights and duties I do not remember. This approach was off the beaten track of U.S.*

---

4   Ibid., 13-4.
5   Ibid., 18.
6   Ibid., 81.

labor history, which has been strong on rights but weaker on duties. The program went like this: "The worker has a right to—1) Job security. 2) An income sufficient to support himself and family in reasonable comfort. 3) Collective bargaining through union representatives freely chosen. 4) A share in the profits after a just wage and a return to capital have been paid. 5) Going on strike and picketing peacefully for just cause. 6) A just price for goods bought. 7) Decent working hours. 8) Decent working conditions.

"And the worker has a duty to—1) Perform an honest day's work for an honest day's pay. 2) Join a bona fide union. 3) Strike only for just cause and after all other legitimate means have been exhausted. 4) Refrain from violence. 5) Respect property rights. 6) Abide by just agreements freely made. 7) Enforce strict honesty and a square deal for everybody inside the union. 8) Cooperate with decent employers who respect workers' rights, thus bringing about a peaceful solution of industrial war by setting up guilds for the self-regulation of industry, and by establishing producer cooperatives in which the worker shares as a partner in the ownership, management or profits of the business in which he works."

Several things are noteworthy about this list, other than the weak grammar and the sexist language. The word "guilds" was a synonym for what Pius XI had in mind in Quadragesimo Anno and was identified more accurately as vocational groups or industry councils. The idea was to make it possible for workers to share, through their unions, in control and decision-making, both at the level of plant and industry as well as at the level of the national economy.[7]

In April 1937, this program was approved by ACTU's founding members. Among the New York chapter's earliest steps: starting a weekly publication, *The Labor Leader* (*LL*), with labor news from a Catholic perspective; applying social-action principles, such as by supporting strikes which the members determined to be "for just cause"; and setting up the Catholic Labor Defense League, through which lawyers in ACTU's ranks offered pro bono representation to workers having problems with organizing, rank-and-file activism, and workplace issues such as pay, benefits, and discrimination.

In 1941, ACTU added 11 chapters—Pittsburgh, Detroit, Chicago, San Francisco, Cleveland, South Bend, Saginaw, Milwaukee, Newark, Seattle, and Trinidad (Colorado). ACTU labor schools, where unionists learned their rights and responsibilities, were established in New

---

7 Ibid., 84-5.

York City and Tarrytown, New York; Detroit and Bay City, Michigan; Pittsburgh; Chicago; San Francisco; Newark; Cleveland; and Gary.

ACTU chapters and labor schools varied in terms of the openness of their enrollment or membership policies. More often than not they welcomed non-Catholics, non-unionists, and women, although some were restrictive in one way or another. Generally, openness increased as time went on.

On August 11, 1939, representatives from chapters of ACTU convened in Cleveland for the group's first national convention. Measures adopted emphasized the laity-based nature of the organization, and called for each chapter to have a priest as chaplain and for each diocese with an ACTU presence to have a priest-director. National oversight was minimal, but a second convention was held in Pittsburgh August 31-September 1, 1941.[8]

By and large, ACTU did not provide Catholic workers with the sizeable amount of spiritual instruction Pope Pius XI hoped for from a "side by side" association, a fact which disappointed John Cort although it never diminished his commitment to the organization. It's also true, however, that ACTU labor schools always had a class on the ethics of Catholic social action, and that this class was almost always taught by a priest.

Most ACTU chapters had corporate Communions, nocturnal adoration societies, worker retreats, encyclical anniversaries, holy hours, and days of recollection; and some ACTU chaplains conducted more of these events than others. Generally, however, ACTU activities were more practical than devotional.

The New York chapter's chaplain was Father John "Doc" Monaghan, a Fordham University professor who never forgot his days as an involved parish priest, according to Father George Kelly, an ACTU associate chaplain. Monaghan, according to Kelly, "wanted a worker's mind and muscle recognized as being no less important to economic prosperity than the money of investors or the moxie of entrepreneurs. What concerned him most, however, was the fact that the minds of workers were seldom molded with the ideas of Christ."[9]

---

8   Oberle, Joseph, *The Association of Catholic Trade Unionists*, New York: Paulist Press, 1941. This pamphlet is an excellent source on ACTU's beginnings.
9   Kelly, George, *Inside My Father's House*, New York: Doubleday, 1989, 51.

The strikes New York ACTU initially supported shaped its development and enabled its members and labor-school students to effectively apply their lessons. The five questions ACTU members and students used to determine whether a strike was just were: Are the demands reasonable? Have all other means been exhausted? Are there good chances for success? Do the possible good effects outweigh the possible adverse affects? Will just means be used in pursuing the strike?

The first ACTU-supported strike, in 1937, involved Woolworth stores, whose saleswomen were on strike. In response to the unwelcome publicity this gave Woolworth heiress and society figure Barbara "Babs" Hutton, a gossip column noted that Babs gave $11 million to charity. The column appeared at a time when a Woolworth's saleswoman was getting less than $10 a week for 60 hours on her feet.

Cort and fellow Actists (the common term for ACTU members) went uptown to the big Woolworth's on 14th Street and marched on the picket line with posters like the one proclaiming "'BABS' GAVE $11,000,000 TO CHARITY, BUT 'THE WORKER IS NOT TO RECEIVE AS ALMS WHAT IS HIS DUE IN JUSTICE'—POPE PIUS XI."[10] This was undoubtedly one of the first papal pronouncements on a picket-line sign.

The strike was lost, but the young saleswomen made many friends for their cause, and inspired salesgirls at Grant's 5&10 not far down the street to go on a sit-down strike—all the rage that year. The Grant's strikers won, gaining a contract and a 10-percent raise. Cort's contribution was sneaking the salesgirls out on Sunday morning and taking them to Mass, then sneaking them back in!

Here are some other strikes with ACTU involvement:

- Editorial employees at the *Long Island Daily Press* figured that maybe the reason the paper's printers were making more money than its reporters was that the printers had a union and the reporters didn't, so they joined the Newspaper Guild and decided to strike. After a "good show" by several hundred ACTU-supported picketers, the strikers won a decent settlement.
- At the Gem Razor strike in Brooklyn, involving 800 workers, a small CIO union asked New York ACTU for help. The chapter's members voted to support the strike, and arranged for Father William Brennan, a local pastor, to speak to the strikers, who were

---

10   Cort, *Dreadful Conversions*, op. cit., 87.

mostly Catholic. His rousing talk, Actists' picketing with the strikers and distributing copies of *The Labor Leader* (often next to Communist Party distributors of *The Daily Worker*), and Cort's and Brennan's persuasiveness with a rigid and skeptical management, contributed to a good contract and no wage cuts. In addition, violence was averted through opposition to it from Cort and Joe Flynn, a veteran organizer lent to the strike by John L. Lewis' United Mine Workers. Flynn was so impressed by ACTU that he joined it, bringing several other organizers with him.

◆ Up the Hudson River in Stottsville, New York, some 500 CIO Textile Workers Union members at Atlantic Mills walked out because management refused to arbitrate a 12.5 percent wage cut or to sign a union contract. Shortly after the strike began, the local priest had spoken against the union from his pulpit at Sunday Mass, and the union members appealed to ACTU for help.

In his remarks the priest had said, "Strikes and unions are a detriment to the country. The CIO is imbued with Communistic tendencies. If a union is necessary, why can't we have a local union formed and controlled by our own men and women?" In other words, a company union. It turned out that the superintendent of the mill was a parishioner. So too were most of the workers, but their influence was not as weighty, it seemed, as a single superintendent's.

That night I spoke to a crowded meeting of the strikers and told them what men like Detroit Archbishop Edward Mooney, San Antonio Bishop Robert Lucey, and Monsignor Francis Haas had said in defense of the CIO. Bishop Lucey, for example, had said "[N]ow, in the providence of God, a better day has dawned for the teeming masses of the people. By enormous effort the CIO is lifting labor from its lethargy. Literally millions of semiskilled and unskilled wage earners are enrolling under the banner of organized labor."

I quoted the popes in support of the worker's right and need to join a trade union to win a wage that would be enough to support a family "in reasonable comfort." I stressed the advantage of a strong national union as against a weak local organization whose leaders would be dependent on the boss for their livelihood.

The response was good. As I spoke, looking down at those anxious faces, I could sense a kind of lightening of the atmosphere as the Catholics present began to realize that they could stop worrying about any conflict of loyalty between their union and their church.

The strike wound up with an agreement to submit the wage cut to an impartial arbitrator. Under the circumstances, that result had to be considered a victory for the strikers.[11]

Another location of intense ACTU activity was the New York waterfront. As discussed earlier in this chapter, that area was an early site of labor activism for both Dorothy Day and John Cort. Joe Ryan was a formidable foe of such activists, as he and his International Longshoremen's Association-AFL were hooked up with organized crime, shipowners fearful of labor strife, and cops and politicians on the take. "If the problem of the CIO was Communist influence," Cort noted, "the problem of the AFL was racketeer influence."[12]

George Donahue, a Manhattan College graduate who took a job on the docks because it was the only work he could find amidst Depression doldrums, had a waterfront baptism of fire a lot worse than Cort's. Donahue was a checker, the worker responsible for receiving freight for shipment.

A mob-controlled checker could sign a receipt with a fake name, an act which would not be discovered until months later. In the meantime, the freight "delivered" to the checker would have been shanghaied and sold.

Donahue refused to sign a fake name, was badly beaten, and was left unconscious on his pier. After he came to, he went to the meeting of his union local scheduled for that evening, told his story to the 150 workers assembled, and won a unanimous vote of support for his action. The mob got him fired, however, and he was labeled an "outsider" when he came back as part of ACTU's efforts to clean up the corruption.

Despite these efforts and *The Waterfront Labor Problem*, a 1938 exposé of that corruption by labor activist Father Edward Swanstrom,[13] it would be about 15 years before the reformers made significant headway against the racketeers. When that happened, however, Catholic social action would again be right at the heart of the struggle. (See Chapter Nine.)

---

11   Ibid., 92-4.
12   Ibid., 105.
13   Swanstrom, Edward, *The Waterfront Labor Problem*, New York: Fordham University Press, 1938.

Donahue's education and experience both came in handy for ACTU as he edited its newspaper (*The Labor Leader* quickly evolved from a mimeographed newsletter into an influential printed tabloid with circulation in many ACTU cities), helped in union struggles, and taught in labor schools. Cort, Donahue, several of Donahue's Manhattan College friends well-schooled in Catholic social action by Brother Justin Brennan of the Christian Brothers—these and other ACTU pioneers were examples of the kind of lay labor apostles envisioned by Pope Pius XI and needed by their country.

ACTU's labor-school network started in fall 1937, and by its second year had four schools. One was at Fordham University's downtown branch in the Woolworth Building, 233 Broadway; the others were at St. Mark the Evangelist Church in Harlem, St. Joseph's School Hall in the Bronx, and the College of New Rochelle just north of New York City. (See Chapter Six.) Each school met one night a week for 10 weeks in fall and again in spring, a common arrangement for Catholic labor schools.

With Catholics and Communists squaring off in labor-union elections and meetings, and Catholic unionists squaring off against employers in organizing drives and negotiating sessions, public speaking and parliamentary procedure were required courses in most Catholic labor schools. Other frequently-required courses were ethics, labor history, and current labor problems.

The labor-history course was invaluable. Too few American workers had a really good idea of what their forerunners paid—in life, limb, and otherwise—for social justice in the workplace (and such a lack is still widespread in the U.S. workforce and throughout American society). Labor schools brought such sacrifices to their students' attention through study of a variety of sources, including labor histories and articles.

John Cort himself authored many of the articles selected. In the fall of 1938, Cort, still living at the NYC House of Hospitality, was stricken (as John Hayes was two years later) with tuberculosis. In that era before anti-TB drugs, Cort had to spend most of the next several years in sanatoriums in the Bronx or Long Island. This enforced rest enabled him to reflect deeply upon labor developments and to share his reflections with readers, which he did in *Commonweal*, *The Catholic Worker*, *The Labor Leader*, and other widely-read periodicals. Here's an example, from the article "Labor and Violence," in the November 10, 1939 issue of *Commonweal*:

> A common practice in many "open shop" towns—a practice still frequent, but especially so before the days of the Wagner Act—is the jolly custom of "taking the Reds for a ride." The definition of a Red is, of course, any outside union organizer and, in many cases, any worker who stands out as a leader in urging his fellows to join an outside union or to strike for higher wages, shorter hours, etc. To "take for a ride" usually means to beat into unconsciousness, and frequently involved murder, tar and feathers, forcible ejection from the community, and other niceties of social ostracism.
>
> Those who "take for a ride" are plant foremen, promotion-seeking employees (usually called "loyal workers"), company police or service men, professional union-busters from detective agencies ("finks"), deputy sheriffs, regular police, vigilante committees, American Legionnaires, and so on. Different as these groups may seem, they all have one important thing in common. They all represent the employer, and if the employer did not want them to act, and in most cases pay them for acting, they would never dream of acting. For all the vile deeds they have committed over the course of the years, American employers must, at any rate, take almost complete responsibility.
>
> Famous cases of this sort in recent years are: the brutal beating of Dick Frankensteen, CIO organizer, by Ford "service men" in May, 1937, while Dearborn [Michigan] police stood by and watched; the near-murder of organizer Blaine Owen in 1935 by agents of the Tennessee Coal and Iron Company (a subsidiary of U.S. Steel); and the beating of Sherman Dalrymple, president of the CIO's Rubber Workers union, in Gadsden, Alabama, by agents of the Goodyear Tire and Rubber Company. (Note that these are all prominent companies, established leaders of American industry, the type that like to say "Of course we believe in collective bargaining.")
>
> Another type of labor violence attributable to employers is the organized raid or attack on strikers with intent to demoralize, thereby breaking up the strike. In many cases picket violence supplies a partial excuse for such raids. Notable examples of this tactic are the Homestead Strike of 1892, in which Henry Frick hired several hundred Pinkertons to mow down the striking employees of Carnegie Steel; the Ludlow Massacre of 1914, by which the Rockefeller interests broke the strike of their Colorado miners; and the Toledo strikes of 1934, wherein agents of the Auto-Lite Company clubbed, shot and tear-gassed striking members of the Auto Workers Union.

> Our American employers have probably grown less crude over the years, but it is surprising how few of them have changed underneath that surface polish.[14]

Government documents were another valuable labor-history resource. The 1936-40 proceedings of the U.S. Senate's LaFollette Committee, for example, recount in detail industries' use of espionage and vigilante squads, mistreatment of union organizers, delayed negotiations, discrimination against union workers, inflated prices at company stores and houses, and refusal to implement or improve pensions and other benefits. Some of this still sounds distressingly familiar.

In summer 1943, John Cort was able to leave his sanatorium at the time, the Nassau County Sanatorium, for a few months of full-time work for *Commonweal*, but not so full-time as to keep Cupid away. Cort met and dated ACTU volunteer Helen Haye during this period, and in the next year, despite the fact that his TB resurfaced and he had to go back into the Bronx sanitorium where he was first treated, a springtime engagement to Helen softened the blow. He faced two more years of bed rest, but at least he now had a constant companion to help him through them.

The articles Cort wrote from his sanatoriums constitute a clear window into the course of organized labor and Catholic social action from the 1930s into the 1950s. His insights are particularly helpful in understanding these two movements as they faced their common foes, Communism and unrestrained capitalism.

The path of the Communists in these years was circuitous and contradictory. In the 1935-39 period, commonly known as the Popular Front era, members of the Communist Party of the United States of America (CPUSA) had instructions from the Moscow-based Comintern (Communist International) to cooperate with American reformers and reform groups when possible, as in the labor movement. In so doing, CPUSA's theory went, Party members would become so entrenched in unions that when the Comintern gave American Communists the signal to overthrow the U.S. government, the American labor movement would be in the vanguard of the revolution.

Things worked well for the Communist Party (CP), up to a point. In the mid-1930s, when forceful, craggy-browed John L. Lewis hired organizers for his United Mine Workers Association and the CIO in-

---

14 Cort, "Labor and Violence," *Commonweal*, Nov. 10, 1939, 68-9.

dustrial unions he led out of the AFL, he included quite a few Communists because they had experience and skill in organizing, a shortage occupation.

The downside—a big one—was that Lewis and many other union leaders (though not all) neglected to release the Communists when their organizing was done. He later admitted he made a mistake in the matter. Regardless, by summer 1939 the CPUSA effectively controlled eight large CIO unions; shared control, as part of a Left coalition, of four others; and had members in key positions at CIO headquarters.[15]

On August 23, 1939, Russian dictator Josef Stalin, seeking to protect both his country and his plans for empire-building, made a nonaggression pact with Hitler and Nazi Germany. In a few pen strokes, the American CP became a fifth column within the United States, which was preparing to join Hitler's enemies. During the pact's 22 months, labor-movement Communists manipulated strikes to hamper defense preparedness, thus going against the common good of their unions.

Complicating the situation further, on June 22, 1941, Hitler changed his war plan and invaded Russia. All of a sudden, American Communists were "allies" again.

From that point and throughout World War II, Communist unionists ludicrously became cheerleaders for speed-ups (companies speeding up production to get more output from workers without increasing their wages) and for piecework or incentive-pay schemes. Since maximum American production was needed to help Russia eject Hitler's armies, the CP'ers favored any production boosts, even unjust measures which were opposed by other unionists—and which, at one

---

15   Howe, Irving, and Lewis Coser, *The American Communist Party: A Critical History*, New York: Da Capo Press, 1974, 385. The eight unions: American Communications Association; International Fur and Leather Workers Union; International Longshoremen's and Warehousemen's Union; Maritime Federation of the Pacific; International Union of Mine, Mill and Smelter Workers; State, County and Municipal Workers of America; United Cannery, Agricultural Packing and Allied Workers of America; and United Electrical, Radio, and Machine Workers of America. CPUSA also controlled strong sections of the United Automobile Workers and the United Shoe Workers of America. At CIO Headquarters were Lee Pressman, chief counsel and advisor to CIO Presidents John L. Lewis and Philip Murray; and Len De Caux, editor of *CIO News*.

time, these CP'ers themselves had vehemently opposed. This whole unfortunate series of events dealt a body blow to the cause of reform, including labor activism and Catholic social action.

The rugged, or selfish, individualists in capitalism's ranks greeted the gyrations of labor's CP'ers with great glee—and used these gyrations to Red-bait Catholic and other non-Communist unionists and to question their patriotism. During the war, these boosters even pointed to CP unionists as examples of how non-CP unionists should act, then Red-baited the latter some more. Red-baiting played well in the realm of public opinion, thus further pushing labor down as it struggled for worker justice.

Pushing labor down was unrestrained capitalism's pursuit since labor's huge gains in 1936-37. (Actually the pursuit can be said to have started with Gilded Age greed and to be just resuming after a brief lull.) In 1938, conservatives in industry, politics, and even segments of the AFL engineered a backlash against President Roosevelt and his New Deal, and by mid-1939 much labor legislation was being rolled back. John Cort bore faithful witness against this rollback in his perceptive and far-reaching writings.

Pre-World War II defense mobilization boosted employment, but also featured intensification of labor-rights violations, union busting, profiteering, employment turnovers, and general uncertainty. As the United States prepared for and entered the war, labor's expectations and management's expectations diverged widely.

Management wanted to preserve the status quo throughout the war. Although CIO unions had won recognition and contracts from many companies, most of these companies refused to accept the union shop or to grant one or another union the sole and exclusive bargaining rights for all of a firm's workers.

The union shop was essential to any fair, effective system of labor-management relations. Under a union shop, an employer's hires may be members of a union or not, but if they are not, these hires must join a union within a certain period of time (unlike with the open shop).

Most Catholic social actionists affirmed the duty of Catholic workers to join a union, and linked this duty to the union-shop arrangement. Workers in a union shop, asserted eminent economist Monsignor Francis Haas, risked jobs and even lives to gain recognition for their union, and paid monthly dues to support it. They also set wages, hours, and other standards that non-union employers approximated in order to keep unions out, thus creating better conditions for non-union workers as a result of what union workers did.

Given such a situation, Haas continued, simple justice requires non-union workers to join a union so that they enjoy the benefits not of others' sacrifices and contributions, but of their own. Joining also answers the dictates of charity, since union members, as workers who are stronger—better paid and treated as a result of union efforts—help non-union, or weaker, workers by encouraging them to join a union.[16]

The centrality of the union shop for the Catholic social-action movement and the labor movement explains why these movements were natural partners, and why social actionists supported labor's position regarding labor-industry-government roles in wartime. This position was that labor would fully cooperate with the government's war effort, while the government, for its part, would accommodate union security and growth by requiring corporations to accept union-shop arrangements. Labor also wanted government to ensure labor leaders an equal policy-making share with business leaders.

Business, unsurprisingly, envisioned a different quid pro quo. Corporate leaders wanted to coordinate military-industrial policy and wanted the government to discipline labor through no-strike pledges and binding contracts.

Management fared far better than labor. President Roosevelt, who was politically timid at this juncture and preoccupied with diplomacy and war preparations, neglected labor's advocates. Government agencies awarded many lucrative contracts to anti-union firms, and recruited wartime administrators who came primarily from the corporate world and allied professions and who "treated labor leaders and workers as clients, not equals," in the words of labor historian Melvyn Dubofsky.[17]

An example of this imbalance is what happened in late 1940, when CIO President Philip Murray proposed his Industry Council Plan. Murray, a devout Catholic of Irish and Scottish heritage, centered his plan on the kind of cooperation among labor, industry, and government called for by *QA*. Murray attributed the general design of his proposal to the social-action encyclicals.

---

16 Blantz, Thomas, *A Priest in Public Service*, Notre Dame: University of Notre Dame Press, 1982, 59-60.

17 Dubofsky, Melvyn, *The State & Labor in Modern America*, Chapel Hill: University of North Carolina Press, 1994, 171.

Murray knew whereof he spoke, having learned labor from the bottom up. He mined in western Pennsylvania coalfields at 16, became president of his United Mine Workers local at 18 and vice president of the entire union at 33, and headed the United Steel Workers in 1937 after leading its whirlwind organizing drive. He unveiled his plan just after taking CIO's helm in 1940.

The plan called for each major industry to have a council with equal representation by labor and management and with a government chairperson. Each council would know the government's defense-production requirements for its industry, and thus could both expand industry production and coordinate with other industries. In addition, each council would employ and train the jobless, prevent orders going to facilities unable to handle them, utilize idle facilities, and maintain bargaining and consumer-price levels. A national defense board chaired by the President would oversee the industry councils.

In the Murray plan, organized labor's direct participation in industrial administration would extend down to the plant level, a provision representing a significant advance over the labor-industry-government partnership of the early New Deal's National Recovery Administration, on whose Labor and Industrial Board Murray had served. The CIO felt that the plan would serve as the model for a postwar reconversion capable of strengthening the nation's industrial democracy.

The Murray plan was sensible and shrewd. Half or more of the workers in many industrial areas in the United States were Catholics, and the Catholic social-action movement and its encyclical teachings were widely known and influential in these areas. The plan, however, encountered strong opposition.

Office of Production Management (OPM) Director William Knudsen, previously chief executive officer of the General Motors Corporation (not a union-shop company at that time), opposed any labor-industry-government administration of production, as did many other business leaders. Also in opposition were the AFL and John L. Lewis, Murray's predecessor as CIO President. Lewis had just resigned from that office, carrying out his vow to do so if Wendell Willkie failed to keep FDR from a third term.

Knudsen deputy Sidney Hillman, organized labor's most prominent representative in government, contrasted the plan unfavorably with what he felt he could arrange as head of OPM's labor division. Hillman, it turned out, seriously overestimated his clout—but before he discovered that he'd done so, the Murray plan fell to the powerful combination of interests just outlined. Again bearing witness was John Cort, on this occasion in the August 4, 1942 issue of *Commonweal*:

> Since American employers have been running industry pretty much as they pleased, it is only natural that they should look upon the Murray Plan with a cold and clammy eye. Their general reaction is: "Haven't we given up enough power to government and 'that man' [FDR] without having to give up the rest to labor leaders and our own employees?"
>
> This employer attitude was put in a neat nutshell by C. E. Wilson, General Motors president, at a Detroit conference in March 1942 called by the War Production Board to promote the [Donald] Nelson plan of management-labor committees in that city's war plants. Curt Murdock, president of the Packard local of the United Auto Workers, CIO, asked Mr. Wilson "whether GM planned to set up joint management-labor committees" with "an equal voice" in war production.
>
> "The question sounded all right," Mr. Wilson replied, "until the questioner said 'with an equal voice.' Any committee" of this type can only be a suggestion-and-advisory committee to the management." (From The New York Times, March 25, 1942)
>
> One can't dismiss Mr. Wilson's attitude as arrogant reaction and try to forget about it.... Wouldn't he rather share the control of plant and industry with labor than lose control of both to federal bureaucrats? That is the really important and basic question.... Perhaps if Mr. Wilson were to take a good look at Washington, and then, steeling himself, another good look at the implications of that bottleneck for the whole business of industrial management, and then finally, one last good look at the <u>greatly increased</u> efficiency of companies that have given labor an "effective voice" in production policies—well, perhaps he could then begin to understand why such statements as his own bother some people, personally and impersonally, very much indeed.
>
> In short, I am afraid that both employers and labor leaders have a lot to learn in this country about such things as efficiency, justice, charity, and humility before we can hope to see any real harmony between capital and labor, either during or after the war.[18]

Well before America entered the war, it was clear that labor was going to be subordinate in war administration, not equal—thus the huge strike wave of 1941. Some unions succeeded in gaining security in the form of "maintenance of membership," meaning that with the award of a defense contract, all current members of a union remained on its

---

18 Cort, "Are We Missing a Bus?," *Commonweal*, Aug. 14, 1942, 394.

books for the contract's duration. The government regularized this arrangement early in the war as its provision for union organizing and collective bargaining.

Government portrayed wartime collective bargaining as voluntary labor-management cooperation, but unions knew that if they couldn't control the rank and file, they could lose union security and face military interference. And companies knew that if they refused to reach agreements with labor, the National War Labor Board would mandate and enforce settlements.

The major war aims, understandably, were ensuring maximum production and restraining inflation. Government aimed to control wage inflation by the "Little Steel" formula"—so named because it was part of the July 1942 settlement of a labor dispute between United Steel Workers of America and the "Little Steel companies—Republic, Youngstown, Bethlehem, and Inland. According to this formula, wartime wage increases could not exceed 15 percent of what wages were in January 1941.

The other side of the inflation coin, of course, was price inflation. Wartime prices rose 45 percent by the end of 1943—three times the percentage of the wage-increase formula. "When the mine workers' children cry for bread," John L. Lewis unforgettably declared, "they cannot be satisfied with a "Little Steel" formula.[19]

Compounding this situation, and increasing the lop-sidedness of labor-management relationships at that point, was the fact that from 1940 to 1943, corporate pretax profits tripled to $27 billion while the average annual earnings of employees grew only half as rapidly. Unions had earnestly subscribed to no-strike pledges when the war started, but workers' patience was wearing thin and their working conditions were deteriorating.

Labor's cause wasn't helped when John L. Lewis took the United Mine Workers into a long 1943 strike, directly challenging the President. Lewis and the UMW got what they wanted, but, as Melvyn Dubofsky states, "they fed rising public antagonism against trade unions and fueled the influential anti-labor members of Congress and their many allies who came to honeycomb the federal administrative bureaucracies during the war years."[20]

---

19   Dubofsky, *op. cit.*, 189.
20   *Ibid.*, 191.

The anti-labor forces had industrial unions down and aimed to keep them down, such as by 1943's Smith-Connally Act, which, among other repugnant things, outlawed union contributions to political campaigns. The unions' response was CIO-PAC, a political-action committee formed to protect a decade's worth of labor advances and to help gain for industrial workers the equal voice and participation which they were being denied.

In an article in the October 20, 1944 *Commonweal*, John Cort pointed out that CIO-PAC did help labor's cause in that year's fall elections, generating considerable financial support for the President and for Democratic candidates who backed labor. Help from the Committee provided the margin of victory for many of the candidates it endorsed.

Organized labor was nearing representation of 35 percent of the civilian labor force, a very healthy figure. Union membership had grown from 3 million in 1933 to 8.5 million in 1940, 10.5 million in 1941, and 14 million in 1945.

Despite these achievements, labor was in a weak position late in the war and in postwar. It was on the defensive, and the "powerful, unscrupulous forces" arrayed against it had painted it into a corner.

Many labor activists and Catholic social actionists still wanted to emphasize giving workers a stronger voice and equal partnership in their enterprises, whether through joint labor-management committees, proactive contract drafting, or other means. There were not enough such advocates, however. Management took advantage of its wartime role to become the dominant force in governmental and judicial oversight and in regulation of labor-management relations. It remains so yet.

Much of the public, for its part, was fed up with management, labor, and government. Faced with domestic chaos and tremendous uncertainty about the future, most Americans just wanted to get as much prosperity, leisure, and uncomplicated day-to-day living as possible.

Consequently, labor was reduced to including its specific solutions in such over-arching, widely-accepted goals as full employment, social and economic security, and consumerist abundance. Worker frustrations exploded in a wave of strikes in late 1945 and throughout 1946, even as strikers knew that greater unrest added to labor's unpopularity. One of the biggest of these strikes—the 113-day UAW strike against GM in 1945-46 (see Chapter Three)—almost achieved, against tremendous odds, a landmark victory for the cause of true industrial democracy, but the strike was defeated and frustration mounted even higher.

Management's intransigence was coupled with a concerted and expensive effort by the National Association of Manufacturers (NAM) and other big-business organizations to stir up public opinion against labor and to lobby for anti-labor legislation. During this period, for example, state NAM branches urged Congress to repeal the Wagner Act, prompting Catholic social actionist Father Karl Hubble (see Chapter Seven) to remark "It is as if they were asking Government to take a walk and inviting Labor out behind the barn to fight the whole thing out again."[21]

In strike after strike throughout the following months—and there were more strikes in the first two months of 1946 than all during the war—big-business interests ratcheted up their anti-labor campaign. Many strikes were lock-outs disguised as strikes, enabling employers to claim lessened war profits and thus reduce income taxes and excess-profit taxes. Many other strikes were the result of 1946 expiration of wartime wage-price contracts. But whatever the case, labor was cast in the role of trouble-maker.

Workers kept a wary eye on Congress and prayed that Harry Truman, the haberdasher-turned-President who succeeded Roosevelt upon his death in April 1945, might give labor a fair deal. They hoped for the best but feared the worst—and pretty much got it.

Capital's anti-labor crusade heavily impacted public opinion. A January 1947 Gallup poll asked people to identify the most important national problem and 40 percent said "strikes and labor problems." Only 9 percent said that in a poll five months earlier.

In May 1947, a month before the Taft-Hartley Act passed, a Gallup poll asked people whether the President should approve a law "that cuts down labor's power a good deal" (46 percent said "Yes") or veto it (38 percent said "Yes"). An August poll, however, showed that only three fifths of respondents were familiar with Taft-Hartley, with 33 percent of them for it and 38 percent against. (The Act is discussed in Chapters Four and Five.)

The first three of the May poll's four work categories (Business-Professional, White Collar, Farm, Manual Labor) showed similar majorities in favor of restricting labor. Capital successfully marginalized labor by defining as "management" multitudes of employees who were

---

21 Hubble, Karl, note, "NAM Seeks Wagner Act Repeal," nd. [WSU]

thus left essentially unrepresented, or by restricting the definition of "labor" to the most manual or menial of occupations. Such marginalization cast a long shadow into the future.[22]

As for John Cort, spring 1946 found him still in that Bronx hospital, dashing off pages of support for labor's struggles. On a personal note, he had cause for great joy, as doctors "sent me out into the world again with approval to work."[23] He returned to ACTU as managing editor of *The Labor Leader* at $40 a week, continued writing for *Commonweal* (where he was starting what would become nine years of the column "The Labor Movement"), and exchanged long-awaited wedding vows with Helen Haye. By this time, Helen had graduated from the College of New Rochelle (see Chapter Six for the story of the labor school there, which she attended) and gone to work for Local 32A of the Hotel Service Employees Union. She and John were a dynamic marital and labor duo.

Life's mysterious ways over the following decades took Cort through many twists and turns. He was a Boston Newspaper Guild organizer and helped breathe new life into the Catholic Labor Guild of Boston, which, as The Labor Guild, still operates—the last of the old-time Catholic labor schools (see p. 116).[24]

Later, Cort ran for the Massachusetts state assembly and barely lost, supervised a Peace Corps region in the Philippines, and administered Massachusetts' anti-poverty agency and later the Model Cities program in Lynn. Also, he wrote *Christian Socialism* in 1988 and *Dreadful Conversions: The Making of a Catholic Socialist* in 2003.[25]

Christian Socialism compares and contrasts ideas of capitalism, industrial democracy, Communism, and socialism, then relates these ideas to spiritual beliefs and moral and ethical foundations. *Dreadful Conversions* is Cort's autobiography.

Both books testify powerfully to the blend of spiritual and social justice driving Catholic social action's labor apostolate. They are also effective antidotes to defenders of American Communists' role in the

---

22 Gallup Poll, *Public Opinion 1935-71*, Vol. 1, New York: Random House, 1973.
23 Cort, *Dreadful Conversions*, op. cit., 142.
24 Throughout its history, the Guild has conducted classes in a number of Boston-area communities, including Norwood, Haverhill, Lowell, Lynn, North Andover, and Salem.
25 Cort, *Christian Socialism*, Maryknoll, NY: Orbis, 1988.

U.S. labor movement prior to the CIO's ejection of 11 Communist-dominated unions by late 1950. Such defenders often either omit or soft-pedal Communism's revolutionary aims and how these were pushed in the 1930s and 1940s, openly or surreptitiously, to the detriment of the common good of U.S. workers. In addition, these defenders (often, ironically, in company with religious or political conservatives) consistently downplay what John Ryan called the "genuinely radical" nature of Catholic social teachings and their blending with reform socialism.[26]

Americans have a long way to go in understanding that the "socialism" in reform socialism is not a dirty word, and that we have allowed the Communists and revolutionary socialists—the fiercest enemies of reform socialism and of reform in general—too big a part in controlling our definition of what socialism means. We're making progress in this regard, however, and John Cort is among those we can thank for that progress.

John Cort made it to 94, survived after his death in 2006 by Helen and their 10 children.[27] Until just a couple of weeks before he died, he was in the choir at St. Thomas Aquinas church, Nahant, Massachusetts, his resonant bass voice singing the old hymns loudly and clearly. So rings out to us his message of spiritual vigor and worker justice.

---

26   Broderick, *Right Reverend New Dealer John A. Ryan*, New York: The Macmillan Company, 1963, 272.

27   Barbara, Nick, Paul, Mary Liz, Becky, Lydia, Susan, Alice, David, and Julia.

CHAPTER THREE
BERT DONLIN (1910–1999)

I was in Chicago in the fall of '30, and I was working on West 14th Street, in a restaurant, and the banks closed, down the street from the restaurant. And when I came out at one o'clock—I was working a split shift, I looked to go to my room until five and come back then—the street was just loaded with people. And if you ever saw desolation—people just whipped, they couldn't speak, their breath was gone. I heard one woman say "We had two thousand three hundred dollars, our settlement with the railroad company, in that bank."[1]

Sixty-five years after that episode, Bert Donlin was still able to convey the shock and sadness he felt at witnessing the human fall-out of the Great Depression. A few years before the episode, Donlin, a teen-ager in Miller, South Dakota, had to drop out of high school to help support his family. He was raised a Catholic, although he recalled the disconnect he felt whenever he passed his parish priest's house and saw

---

1 Donlin, interview with author, Jul. 12, 1995.

a photo of President Herbert Hoover in the front window. In 1929, he was in Minneapolis when the stock market crashed. When lay-offs began, he figured it was time to ride the rails and see the country.

> I traveled in about 20 states. First I went to Omaha, then Sioux City, Chicago, Cleveland, Buffalo, Baltimore, DC for a little while. I had learned enough in restaurants that I could pretty well walk into any joint in town and get work. My shoes were so worn out that I had to wear cardboard in them. I'd cut about that much [holds hands up] out of a cardboard box. It was about that thick [indicates with fingers]. We'd cut cardboard in the mornings and put it in our shoes.
>
> We found out in Cleveland that if you could get to Buffalo—where Father Baker ran a mission in Lackawanna, New York, the Polish sector of Buffalo and a steel-mill area—and work in a wood-yard for three hours, you could get new soles and heels in your shoes. So we took the freight train and ran into Conneaut, Ohio, where there was a rotten s.o.b. of a railroad bull we called "Conneaut Clem." He just loved to shoot at bums trying to hook a ride. So we had to catch the train outside of town, going at a good clip. I kept a suitcase with me, kind of a thick one, oh, a little bit of an upper class thing. I had a good suit in the suitcase, but kept my few valuables in a rubberized raincoat that I wore all through the Depression.
>
> In any case, we got to Buffalo eventually, and with concentration I threw my suitcase down. Well, then I'm committed, I gotta move in the dark, and I have to grab that side ladder. My feet came out from under me, so I got back straight, and finally I climbed up on top and watched and saw an overhead coming—you had to get down—and by gosh we slowed down and we got in. I traveled as far back as to where I thought I threw my suitcase out, and found it. When I got those shoes, I felt like a new man.
>
> At the time I left for my travels, they were burning corn in South Dakota, great big yellow ears of corn. Ultimately I ended up in P.A., and saw the poor miners sitting out there in big mountains of coal, every plant in Wilkes-Barre and coal fire left, nobody mining. Farmers in the West were burning corn because they couldn't afford the price on the coal from P.A.
>
> Then I traveled through grape country. On Lake Erie shores, I saw big Concord grapes—honest to God, they were an inch thick, very big, never saw them in my life that big out in South Dakota—and I said to a farmer, "Isn't it getting kind of late in the year for those to be out there and not being picked?" And he said "What are we going to do? Two of our biggest shippers"—they shipped carloads of grapes to Chicago—"are being sued for freight." So there they were at a standstill, grapes falling

3 🐝 Bert Donlin 81

> on the ground, apples falling on the ground in New York state, and out West they had to shoot cattle because they were starving to death for lack of hay. The crops hadn't been good and you certainly couldn't buy hay. So the whole country just ground to a halt. People starvin' for lack of fruit out there, and in the East they were starvin' for lack of starch products from corn and the things that corn makes. I saw that kind of a lesson, I saw that all happen at once.[2]

History in the making galvanized Bert Donlin into action. When he got settled for a while, working in New York City later in the Depression, he became active in the Democratic Party and took parliamentary procedure classes at City College of New York to sharpen his political skills. The preparation paid off.

Upon his return to South Dakota in the mid-1930s, he became chairman of the Democratic club in his home county. And when he relocated to Detroit for an auto-industry job, he remained active politically and became an influential participant in the affairs of his union, Chrysler Local 7 of the United Auto Workers (UAW) union.

The UAW in Detroit at that time—the defense-mobilization period before World War II—was a good arena in which to fight for social and economic justice while sharpening political skills. The union had grown from 30,000 members in 1935 to 400,000 in 1938, after being a founding union of the Congress of Industrial Organizations (CIO) and conducting vigorous organizing drives.

In terms of UAW politics, in Detroit the union was a battleground between the Communist Party and its allies on one side and, on the other, a democratic-socialistic coalition led by Walter Reuther and including the local chapter of the Association of Catholic Trade Unionists, or ACTU.

The auto industry was central to labor-management relations in Detroit. It was also central to Catholic labor activism in that era.

Father Frederic Siedenburg, SJ, Executive Dean of the University of Detroit and a member of the committee which created the Social Action Department of the National Catholic Welfare Conference, was an expert on the automotive industry. He and other social actionists, local and national, played a vital role in UAW organizing drives and sit-down strikes of late 1936 and early 1937, which after massive struggles resulted in the union's acceptance by General Motors (GM) and Chrysler.

---

2 Ibid.

Monsignors John Ryan and Francis Haas, as well as Fathers Raymond Miller (an author of widely-used encyclical commentaries) and Jerome Hannan of Pittsburgh, made the case that the sit-down strikes were morally justified. Miller, for example, contended that they were self defense, used only because civil authorities failed to prevent unjust employers from violating the workers' rights to a living wage and to decent working conditions. A sit-down strike might be more physical than other strikes, Haas noted, but he contended that it was more effective in that it withheld property from (or preserved it for) an owner until injustices were redressed.[3]

The centrality of the auto industry in Detroit's labor and Catholic social-action scenes was also reflected in the Detroit ACTU chapter's preferred organizational form—the "conference," or cell (akin to a Communist Party cell in a union). The national headquarters of ACTU suggested that where a significant number of ACTU members came from one union, workplace, or industry, these workers form a conference to meet separately and strategize regarding particular problems or prospects and how to deal with them. Also recommended was that such workers be prepared for their chapter responsibilities by Catholic labor schools; in the case of Detroit, the schools were first run by the Archdiocesan Labor Institute and later by the chapter itself.

Bert Donlin was already well-trained in activism when he joined Detroit's ACTU chapter, which recruited him because, in his words, "they thought I was a radical." As a second-shift chief steward, he couldn't attend many meetings of his ACTU "conference" because most of them were in the evening. He was aware of them, however, and recalled that "a phone call or two kept me abreast of what was discussed."[4]

The conference method worked well in Detroit, largely a one-industry, one-union city with huge, behind-the-scenes struggles in the dominant union. Also, the leadership of Catholic social action in Detroit was excellent, with Edward Mooney as Archbishop and Paul Weber as President of the ACTU chapter.

Weber was a brilliant, dynamic journalist and the President of the Detroit Newspaper Guild. As an active Catholic layman and a skilled

---

3 "Morality of the Sit-down Strike," *American Ecclesiastical Review*, Apr. (Ryan) and July (Hannan) 1937. Miller, speech, *Proceedings*, Summer School of Social Action, Chicago, Jul. 10-Aug. 12, 1938.

4 Donlin, interview, *op. cit.*

union leader, Weber led the chapter's labor activities with a hard-nosed style which, had it been employed by a priest in that role, would likely have drawn charges of clericalism, that is, inappropriate involvement by priests in political or secular matters.

In May 1937, when Edward Mooney arrived in Detroit to take over as Archbishop (he had been Bishop of Rochester), he was already a foremost leader of Catholic social action. In 1936, he became the Church hierarch responsible for the National Catholic Welfare Conference, a position he held with distinction for a decade. With the Conference's Social Action Department in his purview, he and the Department's John Ryan and Ray McGowan spearheaded American Catholics' forceful, impassioned response to the papal injunction "Go to the worker."

Mooney, Weber, and other Catholic social actionists in Detroit spent late 1937 and much of 1938 helping labor consolidate its period of rapid, sweeping advance. The two major sides in UAW's internal struggles split their time in that period between fighting each other and fighting UAW President Homer Martin, a onetime preacher who mistook workers' liking his labor advocacy for workers' wanting him to be UAW's absolute ruler. Not until March 1939 was a truce declared, when the union presidency went to R. J. Thomas, a "bread and butter" unionist belonging to neither side but acceptable to both.

The major fight in Detroit, however, was still the conflict between unrestrained capitalism and worker justice, and Archbishop Mooney made clear to the city's business community exactly where he stood. In May 1938, as a speaker at the Economic Club, foremost gathering place for Detroit's corporate executives, he told his lunch-time listeners that runaway capitalists had developed "iron necessities in a world apart from Christian obligation and sentiment." They concentrated wealth in the hands of a minority, he added, and thus had created "an increasingly large class of propertyless wage-earners—an American proletariat.

"You may think what I'm saying is 'Communist', or 'socialist', or 'radical', or 'un-American,'" the Archbishop went on. "But the most effective way to spike the guns of agitators and revolutionaries is to treat with the workers whose grievances they are ready to exploit for their explosive and subversive ends."[5]

---

5   Mooney, Edward, speech, Detroit Economic Club, May 9, 1938. [AD]

Archbishop Mooney was candid, but also appealed to listeners who differed with his viewpoints to get together with him in an attempt to resolve their differences. Mooney's blend of firmness and conciliation, the hallmark of his successful leadership style (he became Edward Cardinal Mooney in 1946), ran up against one seemingly immoveable obstacle, however—Father Charles Coughlin.

In the late 1920s, Father Coughlin aired a show on radio—then still quite a novelty—to attract parishioners to his new church, the Shrine of the Little Flower [St. Theresa], in the Detroit suburb of Royal Oak. The approach worked, the church grew phenomenally, and the young priest's mellifluous voice and populist message became a winning combination in Depression doldrums. By 1935, Coughlin's *Golden Hour of the Little Flower* was a national program with 40 million listeners and a passionately loyal following, especially among Catholics.

Father Coughlin's ego, however, was as huge as his popularity, and soon he began to see enemies around every corner. He replaced populism with blatant appeals to prejudice, including anti-Semitism, and, in the late thirties, with growing praise of Hitler and Mussolini. Catholic authorities from Pope Pius XI down demanded that Coughlin be reined in, but Bishop Michael Gallagher, Mooney's predecessor, refused to act.

Mooney took over the Detroit Archdiocese with the understanding that he would silence Father Coughlin. He was moving slowly and deliberately to do so, with Coughlin resisting every move, when the radio priest made the Archbishop's task much easier.

Coughlin had already turned on labor, at one point attacking the CIO as "Red in its conception, in its method, in its objective, and in its effective personnel."[6] But on November 11, 1939, in the midst of a UAW strike of Chrysler, he went too far. He devoted his radio talk that Sunday afternoon to an all-out effort to break the strike.

Three days later, UAW responded with a rally in Cadillac Square, in the heart of Detroit. Forty thousand auto workers, about half of them Catholic, filled and overflowed the square and cheered on speaker after speaker as they rebutted Coughlin's confused musings and championed the workers' cause.

Foremost among the speakers was Monsignor John Mies, Pastor of Holy Rosary Church, who had loaned the church's parish hall to Detroit's recently-formed ACTU chapter to use as its temporary head-

---

6   Coughlin, Charles, editorial, *Social Justice*, Feb. 8, 1937.

3 ❦ Bert Donlin

quarters. Bert Donlin, as both a Chrysler worker and a chapter member, was among the many listeners for whom November 14 became a day of celebration on the 1939 calendar.

Before that day was out, Father Ray Clancy, head of Detroit's Archdiocesan Labor Institute, a network of several dozen Catholic labor schools, appeared on the radio on behalf of Archbishop Mooney and refuted Father Coughlin point by point. Clancy asserted that Coughlin is "in error in his knowledge of the facts" on the Chrysler strike, and concluded "Father Coughlin has misused the papal encyclicals."[7] In less than a year, the radio priest was off the air.

As winter 1939-40 turned to spring, Detroit workers had another cause for celebration: Ford Motor Company's long-time resistance to the UAW was finally broken. Henry Ford's legend as automotive genius hid his record of seriously mistreating workers, most notoriously by using Ford's "Service Department"—henchman Harry Bennett and his army of several thousand thugs and spies—to keep workers in line. But not even the globally-distributed photo of these thugs' May 26, 1937 beating of UAW officers Walter Reuther and Richard Frankensteen ended Ford's unfair labor practices.

In February 1941, however, the U.S. Supreme Court backed the two-year-old National Labor Relations Board (NLRB) action against these practices, and Ford's long-withheld recognition of the UAW seemed imminent. Instead, the company dragged its feet, and on April 1, Ford workers, spontaneously and unanimously, just stopped working.

What followed—an all-night gathering around the union hall at the "Rouge," Ford's huge River Rouge plant—was, recalled gathering leader Emil Mazey, "among the most exciting events in my whole experience in the labor movement. It was like seeing men who had been half-dead suddenly come to life. And did they come to life! It was hard to keep things going, hard to organize, so eager were they just to mill around and talk and let some steam go. That night you really understood what the union could mean to men."[8]

The strike was far from over. A fierce week-long struggle ensued, with Chrysler and GM workers rallying to the cause. It prevailed when, in an NLRB election in late May, Ford workers overwhelm-

---
7   Clancy, Raymond, broadcast, WMBC radio, Nov. 15, 1939. [WSU]
8   Cook, Fred, *Building the House of Labor*, Chicago: Encyclopedia Brittanica Press, 1963, 126.

ingly chose UAW to represent them over an AFL union jerry-built by Harry Bennett himself. What was Bennett's response? "The election was a great victory for the Communist Party ... and the National Labor Relations Board."[9]

Given the fact that since the Nazi-Soviet pact of 1939 the U.S. labor movement's Communists were doing all they could to disrupt the nation's defense preparedness, Bennett's attribution was ludicrous. So were the manipulations and gyrations of labor's Communist Party (CP) members, antics never clearer to Bert Donlin and his UAW and ACTU mates than in June 1941.

> Charlie Williams was a member of our local. The executive board met on Sunday morning at 10:30 and Williams got up and offered a motion that we go on record condemning the situation in Europe as "an imperial bloodbath." That same day, somebody got ahold of him and gave him the new Party line. Hitler had opened a front on "brother" Stalin. So from the executive board meeting in the morning, that "imperial bloodbath" became "a progressive struggle against Fascism." That's how fast things changed. So that got us off to a rough start. You could be right in either case, or you could be wrong in either, but if you use the labor union first, and use it for your purpose and not for the labor movement, you're using it for international purposes.
>
> Later the Comrades went on record in favor of the no-strike pledge. We had the no-strike pledge shoved down our throat, and R. J. Thomas, our then-President of the UAW, went along with it, for lack of enough on the ball to take 'em on. And it was probably an ideal thing, but not to make it a part of our real existence. I said "I'm for the no-strike pledge if they're for taking down the reasons for creating strikes. If they want to get in the picture and get mad with us, I'll play their games and we'll all hold hands and get along." Charlie Williams and the Stalinists, they took it right to heart—all the labor movement existed for was the no-strike pledge, and they wanted to open the Second Front <u>now</u>, or yesterday. We weren't ready for it. We had to ship barges, and motors, and little boats, and tanks, and pontoons, to Russia to get them well-armed before we dared even think about a Second Front. But no, they wanted it now, period. Every meeting we had to beat them down on that.[10]

The main reason many rank-and-file UAW unionists, and many of their shop-floor leaders like Donlin, became increasingly frustrated

---

9   Howe, Irving and B.J. Widick, *The UAW and Walter Reuther*, New York: Random House, 1949, 105.

10 Donlin, interview, *op. cit.*

over the no-strike pledge was the inequality of wartime sacrifice between labor and management, a point expanded upon in Chapter Two. By mid-war, management got the military-industrial complex it wanted (and has had for decades since). It began planning ways of keeping labor subordinate to it after the war, and of getting back as much as it could of the open-shop environment prevailing before the Depression and labor's awakening.

Unionists, for their part, saw more and more as World War II went on that the workers' rights part of what Americans fought for was in such grave danger that instead of an equal place with management at the workplace table, they'd be lucky not to be shoved *under* the table. This kind of frustration impelled John McGill, of UAW's Buick Local 599 in Flint, to say "We gave up the right to strike. Our brothers and sons are dying in the trenches. Can anyone show any sign that the men who sign checks have made any sacrifices?"[11]

UAW unionists needed look no farther than what happened to their hard-charging leader Walter Reuther to find an example of wartime labor being given short shrift. Around the time CIO President Phil Murray proposed his Industry Council Plan, Reuther unveiled an innovative, detailed proposal to convert idle automobile plants to airplane production. Under the plan, companies would pool their resources and place them under a labor-management-government board of aviation production.

This key feature of the plan—labor-management equality, with joint participation in production matters and decisions—marked Reuther as a labor up-and-comer, indeed as a whole new breed of labor leader, one who took care of both "bread and butter" issues and the deeper level of worker empowerment. That feature, of course, also marked him as a danger to management's supremacy, thus dooming his plan to extinction—ironically, at the hands of former GM chief executive officer William Knudsen. So much for equality!

Industry's cost-plus profits from wartime contracts, prices for food and other necessities rising at a much higher rate than wages—these factors were unjust and upsetting enough. The thing that really stirred workers up, though, was companies pushing production to inhumane and unrealistic extremes.

Piecework, speed-up, incentive pay, whatever name it bore, it meant pitting workers against each other to get pay raises which were equally

---

11   Howe and Widick, *op. cit.*, 112.

divided with the company and which endangered worker health and safety. UAW's rank-and-file came out strongly against such behavior, as did Reuther. Also, he resigned from the War Manpower Commission in 1943 because of his displeasure with government's wage and manpower freezes.

Incentive pay was just one of many issues Bert Donlin had to deal with as a chief steward of UAW's Chrysler 7. The chief steward was the workers' main representative on the shop floor and, as collective bargaining matured, the position took on increasingly greater responsibilities. The chief steward, for example, often had to oppose company actions which threatened employee protections.

> *I was chief steward for a department of 450 or 475 people. It was 1943, a Friday afternoon shift in the daytime. You know, when a guy's got a paycheck in his pocket, and the bars are open, it doesn't take much to get some excuse to walk out. So they fired 10 black women, sweepers. There had been a man scooping the floor after it was swept. So the bosses took him off of it and told the girls "You are going to now do your own scooping." Well, they said "We're women and we aren't supposed to." And the bosses go "Where in the world is that said?" In other words, they said "When a woman sweeps her house, she doesn't pick up the kid to handle the dustpan, huh?" So they said "You either do that or you're fired." That's what the women wanted, and they said "Well, we're goin' out." So they fired 'em.*
>
> *I wasn't representing janitorial people but I did have a sizeable majority of black members, the black constituency of my department—a big bay half a mile long. So the women said "We're going out, they're no good," and I said "Now just a minute. You're not going out unless you want to go out on your own and have fun or something." And I said "I'll tell you once and let's just get things straight. If you're going to walk out, don't walk once. Run out." I said "And when you come to the union hall, run right by it, because we're not recognizing you one iota." So I gave that pitch and they accused me of being a company stooge. They were all fired up. They were thinking of that check and maybe of getting drinks down at the bar—bars cashed checks in those days. So I kept them in." Instinct told me that there's more than meets the eye here, when they'll fire 10 black girls over that one guy, on a Friday night with our paychecks in our pockets.*
>
> *Oh, my God, was the company hot. They got hold of my foreman, they said "Does he do any work at all down there?" He said "No, he tries to, but they always come and get him, they're always on his back about something, and he was tonight busy tryin' to keep them in, and he did*

3 ❦ Bert Donlin

keep them in." They said "That's the problem, that's what we're talkin' about." And do you know what they wanted? They wanted a strike. Some cords in Cleveland had blown up and we were going to be short three or four production days in materials. So the workers were going to be laid off or strike. I kept 'em in, therefore the company had to lay employees off at a cost of eighteen thousand dollars in unemployment-insurance funds.[12]

Donlin's example illustrates how hard it was for union locals and their leaders to play their rightful roles "in a war for which they were called upon to make sacrifices but from the control and direction of which they were rigorously excluded," as Irving Howe and B. J. Widick observe in *The UAW and Walter Reuther*.[13] The fight was doubly difficult when, as with Chrysler 7 and other locals, they went through periods of Communist control.

In the case of the speed-up, labor's Communists had become its most ardent proponents, whereas back in the Nazi-Soviet pact era they were among its most ardent foes. Reuther "has only two things to offer you," the Lucas County (Toledo) Communist Party alleged in May 1941, "war and speed-up." In mid-war, it was U.S. Communist Party head Earl Browder who offered war and speed-up, even claiming that "incentive pay would force better profits on unwilling employers."[14]

The relationship in UAW between its Communist-controlled side and its Reuther-controlled side was a "survival of the fittest" struggle from start to finish. Whichever side won would direct a huge and influential organization and likely would largely determine the direction of CIO, which at that time was divided fairly evenly between Communist-controlled unions and unions not in Communist control. A change in CIO's direction would in turn have a sizeable affect upon national affairs generally.

Most Americans have no idea how close CIO was to being taken over by the Communist Party. As it was, the Communists did CIO incalculable damage at a time when capitalism's rugged (selfish) individualists were waiting to steal labor's bacon.

---

12   Donlin, interview, *op. cit.*
13   Howe and Widick, *op. cit.*, 124.
14   Moody, Blair, "A Communist?: Reuther Gives His Side of the Story," *Detroit News*, May 19, 1941. *Daily Worker*, Feb. 5, 1943.

The major lesson unionists can learn from that damage is also the major prescription for union revival: organize endlessly, participate fully in your local's governance, and be the best unionist you can be. In too many locals in the 1930s and 1940s, only a small percentage of the membership played an active part in meetings and other activities.

According to Bert Donlin, Chrysler 7 meetings sometimes fell five or ten members short of the 16,000-member local's quorum of 170. In Bohn Local 208, Paul Weber noted that Actists and their rank-and-file followers succeeded in ending, in two elections, Communist control. Lacking experience and training, however, most of the group stopped attending meetings and thus lost both control of policy and the confidence of its members. The Communists regained control and kept it.

The internecine warfare in UAW, fierce and fateful as it was, had its comic dimensions—comedy *noir*, perhaps, but comedy just the same. With so many groups of activists, whether Communists, Actists, Trotskyists, Socialists, or what have you—how could it have been any different?

> *The main divisions of Trotskyists were the Cannonites, the Shachtmanites, and the Lovestoneites. They hated each other, the three of them did. To get even with the Shachtmanites, the Cannonites said Dr. Shachtman's followers were actually the left wing of ACTU. That was caused somewhat by us in Local 7. See, we had mostly Shachtmanites, and a few of the Cannonites, and very few Lovestoneites. So they all hated each other, but they didn't hate each other as much as they really hated ACTU. ACTU was a real devil to get mad at, for them.*
>
> *So one day we had a judge out to speak, and the first thing the president of the local did, opening the meeting on Sunday, was to announce that one of our previous presidents, William Marshall, expired, and he said "Let's all bow our heads for a moment of quiet reverence." So we all bowed our heads. And the judge came on and said "My, what a wonderful feeling it was today to watch this body of dedicated people and to see you all together and bowing your heads for your departed brother. This shows real fellowship."*
>
> *That Sunday, we were voting for elections commissioners, and that's where elections could be stolen or held up. So we had a hell of a crowd and we all hated each other, we had "our guns parked under our seats." And the poor judge coming out with that line.*[15]

---

15 Donlin, interview, *op. cit.*

3 🐝 Bert Donlin

In July 1944, a group of presidents and shop committeemen from UAW locals formed a "Rank-and-File Caucus" and called for rescinding the no-strike pledge, pressing for independent political action by labor, and electing UAW leaders pledged to those measures. This move directly challenged both of UAW's main sides, which opposed rescission, and the Reuther side barely managed to arrange for a pledge reaffirmation to be followed by a later referendum.

The rank-and-file caucus attracted a third of the referendum's votes. The approach of war's end, however, made the issue moot, and most of the rank-and-filers returned to the Reuther side.

As for independent political action by labor, it was already underway with the CIO Political Action Committee (CIO-PAC) and its support for labor's friends running for office, including President Roosevelt. Bert Donlin was right in the middle of the action.

> Next came '44. Here's Dewey, a home-state boy, from Owasso up here. He's a big-shot district attorney in New York City—oh man, you don't get any bigger than that, do you? And he's running, and oh, he's going to carry it like Grant took Richmond. So around and around we went, and not much excitement. I was Secretary of the Legislative Committee of Local 7 at that point. We had to get something off the ground and show some activity, and the name of the game was voters—[in 1940] we lost by 30,000 votes, is all—so we pulled one out of the hat and got the registered voters campaign going, in which we gave five $100 war bonds, free chances, if they would show their chief steward their registration. Then we had a registration drive.
>
> Oh my God, the auditorium of the local was full and members were in line around it. Other locals got in the act too—they weren't going to let us run away with it. I put releases out, and my local went on record with it as our policy. I put out one release for each of the news services and one for each of the daily papers. It was a low Sunday, and by God the papers took the release and just changed a couple of words and shoved it in—and there was copy all over the country. R. J. Thomas was in DC and he said "That's my local union." We got things stirred up on the West Coast, and stirred up in the rest of Michigan here—a lot of the locals turned out with it.
>
> We had a hell of a drive going—we called it the Neighborhood Registration Drive Committee—and I went to this old Irish priest's house on the East Side, Father McConaughey, and I said "Father, would you mind just announcing ... we have a non-partisan group put together in which we're getting people registered"—and I couldn't keep from smiling when I said "nonpartisan"—"and we're attempting to register people

regardless of which party, we don't care which party, just so they take part in their citizenship." And he said "Oh, sure, sure you are. Not much you're not interested in which party." And he was a life-long Republican, so he threw me off the porch.

So another guy went up to him, guy who'd been in a lot of fights and knew the score, he went up to the door and said "Are you the head guy around here?" Father McConaughey said "Why, is there anything I can do for you?" Father liked this approach by the other guy, so after he asked for help, McConaughey said "Well, yeah, you can use our hall here for the drive, and we'll announce it at Sunday Masses." We got a lot of people registered there. I couldn't get it done but the other guy could.[16]

What drew Bert Donlin into the Reuther-controlled caucus was Donlin's Democratic activism. For others, the primary motivator was ACTU's Catholic social action (a secondary motivator for Donlin), or Shachtmanite Trotskyism, or a wide variety of socialisms. Walter Reuther was shaped by the German Social Democratic ideas of his immigrant father Valentine, who in the United States championed Eugene Debs. The younger Reuther was a member of the Socialist Party before 1938, when he became active in the Democratic Party. His overriding loyalty was to industrial democracy through unionism.

In June 1945, Reuther displayed the same boldness and initiative in helping prepare American society for reconversion from wartime to peacetime that he had displayed in helping prepare the nation for conversion to defense production. In a brief filed with all war-production agencies, Reuther recommended that in postwar, "Increased production must be supported by increased consumption, and increased consumption will be possible only through increased wages." Industry would pay these "out of the high profits it is making. It will not have to charge higher prices."[17]

Little attention was paid to Reuther's input. In August, President Harry Truman, to combat inflationary pressures at war's end, issued Executive Order 9599, announcing a national policy of permitting wage increases only if they did not result in price increases; Reuther saw in this announcement an opportunity to put his reconversion ideas into play, and he seized the opportunity quickly. Two days later, he opened UAW's current round of negotiations with GM by propos-

---

16   Ibid.
17   Reuther, brief, "Postwar Reconversion," June 30, 1945.

ing that workers be given a 30-percent wage increase and that it not be accompanied by an increase in the price of GM cars.

He assured GM that if it proved these proposals could not be realized in a way which would make the company a nice profit, he would settle for a wage-rate increase of less than 30 percent. When company negotiator Harry Coen said he didn't think the average worker on the picket line cared much about wage theories, Reuther replied that if the company told a worker it couldn't grant him or her a wage increase, the worker would say "Let me look at your books to see why you can't."[18]

This "show us your books" challenge and its underlying premises became a national sensation. Their key effect would have been to make labor a full partner in a national reconversion venture grounded in social justice and economic democracy. Reuther's proposals brought America to a crucial cross-roads in its history.

The outcome was fairly predictable, although the strength and boldness of these proposals gave them considerable impact. GM refused them and UAW, in its turn, went on strike in late November.

President Truman appointed a fact-finding board, asserting on December 28 that GM's "ability to pay" was a legitimate matter for the board's consideration. GM immediately withdrew from the board's hearings, and on January 10 the board recommended that GM pay a 19½-cent hourly-wage increase (somewhat lower than 30 percent) and that it not raise the price of its cars. Unsurprisingly, UAW accepted these recommendations and GM refused them.

Truman was by-and-large a labor supporter, but he was new in his job and rather indecisive throughout this strike. Not only did he allow GM to directly challenge his authority with no tough response, but in a concurrent negotiation, between the steel industry and the United Steel Workers (CIO head Philip Murray's union), Truman caved in to that industry's pressure on the administration to permit wage and price increases together. The administration approved a lower hourly-wage increase (18½ cents) with nothing said about prices; and other unions made similar agreements.

The proposals Walter Reuther hoped would be pace-setters for the postwar era of labor-management relations were thus dealt a body blow, although it's a wonder they got as far as they did. Top corporate interests, who formed the nation's most powerful economic sector, were dead-set on keeping power, not sharing it; government was their

---

18 Transcript, GM-UAW negotiations, Oct.-Nov. 1945.

enabler; other labor leaders put worker empowerment on the back burner; and labor's Communists gave the coup de grâce to Reuther's proposals, thus clearly exposing the hypocrisy of their claims of priority for worker justice.

American CP'ers had just embarked on their latest about-face—this time in the direction of independent political action to support the Soviet Union's postwar empire-building—so they felt freer to let their rough edges show. While UAW was negotiating with GM, James Matles, President of the Communist-controlled United Electrical Workers-CIO (UE), was secretly negotiating with GM on behalf of the 30,000 company workers UE represented. UE and GM made an agreement on the basis of the steel formula outlined just above, and UAW eventually had to settle for the same outcome.

As largely predetermined as many of these outcomes appear to be, the road not taken still draws us like a magnet, especially now that unions represent only 12 percent of America's industrial workers—down from 35 percent at the end of World War II. Fortunately, workers and other Americans are increasingly discovering why unions were and are sorely needed. Hopefully, they will also discover why there was a close bond between Catholic social action and democracy.

Take in one hand Reuther's proposals, with their strong sense of economic interrelatedness. Take in the other hand the central message of Monsignor John Ryan, the progenitor of much of Catholic social action: "The encyclicals reassert and restate the traditional doctrine, that economic as well as other human actions are subject to the moral law, that buying and selling, borrowing and lending, employing and serving, wage-paying and rent-paying, are either right or wrong, good or bad, just or unjust. None of these practices, or any other industrial practice, can claim immunity from the moral law or asylum in an immoral vacuum."[19]

Catholic social action and reform socialism were natural partners except for the spiritual dimension, as important as that exception is. There were few more devout Catholics than John Cort, Father John Hayes, and, in Detroit, Paul Weber, yet they all worked well with socialists (as did most Catholic labor apostles).

Earlier in this volume we explored how and why such cooperation took place in the cases of Father Hayes and John Cort. Weber's case

---

19 Ryan, "Commentary on Encyclicals," SAD, 1936.

was similar in many ways, although he had a distinct and somewhat different perspective.

Paul Weber brought to his role as president of Detroit ACTU the sharp skills in union infighting he had learned in local Newspaper Guild battles. And he brought to his role as editor of the ACTU chapter's newspaper *The Wage Earner* (*WE*), formerly *The Michigan Labor Leader*, a wealth of professional expertise. Yet he was a fighter who looked for ways to form alliances and a devout religionist who made his newspaper widely known and respected for its hard-news coverage of the secular sphere of labor.

Weber's core principle was in Catholics establishing a permanent minority in unions. "Unionism," he maintained, "is part of their religion and through the unions they seek a Christian democracy."

Weber saw Catholics and Communists as presenters of the two fundamental philosophies of unionism, with the Catholic philosophy being social reconstruction according to encyclical principles and the Communist philosophy being "class hatred and despair of human decency." He maintained that if the permanent minority he envisioned "stays on the job day in and day out, whether there are any Communist issues or not, it is capable not only of dealing with a momentary threat, but also of giving the type of sustained leadership which bars the opposition permanently from recouping its foundations."

To Weber, socialists were "the largest and most powerful of the ideological groups in labor. These people started out from Marx and are working to the right. At present, they have abandoned the class struggle, the liquidation of private property.... They are anti-Communist and anti-totalitarian.... In unions, we find it wise and necessary to cooperate with them."

Weber, hoped ACTU would "attract to the Christian program of social reconstruction a vast array of non-Catholic 'fellow-travelers' who will again find in the ancient faith the solution to their human problems. Indeed, we confidently hope that among these will be many of our misguided but often sincere Marxist brethren, who are thrice dear because they are the sheep which are lost."[20]

Weber's combination of uprightness, straight talk, and direct action galvanized Bert Donlin and many other Actists, and channeled their

---

20 Carey, Philip, editorial, *Xavier X-Ray*, Jan. 19, 1944, 2.

efforts constructively. Donlin, who in postwar years continued to be a labor and political activist, crossed paths with Weber frequently.[21]

> Paul Weber was a sharp dude. I remember one day we were at his office downtown. It was on Adams Street at that point, 46 West Adams. And three or four guys from Ford Motor Company came down with a leaflet—it looked like a dictionary, with all this tired-looking copy, you know. Paul took a look at it and said "Yeah, I can just see the average Ford worker taking that home for the weekend, and getting out his bottle of Stroh's, and drinking it and reading the hell out of that. Let's get real. Just a minute." Suddenly, he grabbed a pencil and scribbled "Joe Schmo for President! This is the kind of a guy we need." And he scratched out everything else. "With this kind of a guy we'll know that we've got a voice in the operation of this union, on behalf of the membership and not for treason." Bang! He cut some more, nothing left of it. They took it home and thought they had some really good stuff. And they won.[22]

Wage Earner editor Weber cut right to the heart of every important labor story. On October 26, 1945, just as the portentous GM strike started, he commented in *WE* on its possible consequences: "If Reuther succeeds in forcing GM, one of the country's largest industrial empires, to redivide the fruits of its production, the day of gigantic profits in American business will be done. Every union will then insist that the profit and price structure be examined in collective bargaining and wage increases be absorbed out of profits if possible. The result may not be the end of capitalism but it will certainly be the beginning of a new kind of capitalism."[23]

One satisfied reader of *WE*, Archbishop Mooney, when asked by his friend Syracuse Bishop Walter Foery about the GM strike, not only recommended that newspaper to him but gave him a gift subscription. Mooney expressed support for UAW's position, with its linkage of wage/price increases, adding "Underneath this evident and soluble question, there are ideological issues which were kept under cover during the war effort. The unions are pressing for an advance in employer-employee relations which the industrialists term 'socialistic'

---

21 Upon his death just over a decade ago, Donlin left behind wife Marilyn and daughter Marilyn Greiner, both of Warren, Mich. The author appreciates their providing Bert's photo and agrees with them that "it's characteristic of his style."
22 Donlin, interview., *op. cit.*
23 Weber, "Economic Democracy," *Wage Earner*, Oct. 26, 1945.

but which, in fact, falls far short of what the social encyclicals would call for.

"General Motors has been particularly backward in its outlook in this regard as even during the war it set itself definitely against having management-labor committees to promote better relations in the interest of the war effort, while many other large concerns set them up and found them very useful. In confidence I can say that friends of mine in high circles in General Motors who are excellent Catholics in a sacramental sense are utterly allergic to Catholic social doctrine."[24]

Reuther, too, liked and valued *The Wage Earner*. He told its staff "Your defense of the principles of democratic trade unionism has earned you the gratitude of democratic forces."[25]

Reuther's historic proposals for worker justice boosted his already-strong standing among UAW's rank and file, and delegates to the union's convention in October 1946 elected him President by 104 votes. Apparently hedging their bets, however, they reelected George Addes as secretary-treasurer and put in R. J. Thomas and Richard Leonard as vice-presidents. All three were allies of the Communist-controlled caucus.

A year of vigorous—and sometimes vicious—politicking ensued, but Reuther's foes overplayed their hand and Reuther swept the 1947 convention. The huge Ford Local 600, long a Communist stronghold, went for Reuther, whose candidates won a majority of the executive board, secretary-treasurer (Emil Mazey), and two vice-presidencies (John Livingston and Richard Gosser). A highlight of the sweep was R. J. Thomas' defeat in his own local, Chrysler 7, with Bert Donlin leading the charge.

Walter Reuther had an obvious genius for uniting often-disparate elements of the workforce, a deep commitment to social justice and industrial democracy, and a position of great power. He was hamstrung, however, by labor's need, described in Chapter Two, for including specific solutions in over-arching, widely-accepted goals. (See page 75.)

This need grew out of the U.S. labor movement's history, the story of a fight from below against power above. Workers and their organizations had to conquer insecurity and a sense of inferiority, resulting in concentration on meeting immediate needs and in a strategy of "no ultimate aims." Another result was "circling the wagons" for protection

---

24 Mooney to Walter Foery, Dec. 19, 1945. [AD]
25 Gahagan, Marguerite to "Dear Friend," Mar. 8, 1951. [AD]

when better protection would have come from explaining the immediate and longer-range needs of workers to the public, press, and politicians, thus enlisting stronger support.

In this context, the NAM and other anti-labor propagandists had a field day in the postwar run-up to the Taft-Hartley Act (see next chapter). They created fears of a "labor colossus" without labor leaders generating an effective response. Ironically, these leaders, pressed to conform to a business-dominated society, sometimes reflected its worst traits. In the words of labor historian Herbert Harris, "pursuit of the highest possible profit was transposed into pursuit of the highest possible wage, while control over a resource, a process, a patent was translated into control over a work territory."[26]

During much of this run-up, Walter Reuther was simply surviving and cementing his leadership. The defeat of his power-sharing strategy meant a forced march, against his better judgment, back to a strategy of not straying too far from bread-and-butter issues, at least until times became more propitious for a deeper, longer-term agenda.

Herbert Harris compared the typical postwar labor leader to "the man who, to keep his own house from burning, not only has to put out fires next door and across the street, but also has to adopt drastic measures of fire prevention. He therefore is turning attention to methods and proposals that can generate jobs for all, without boom-and-bust cycles, as the only economic environment in which unionism can prosper, or even survive." He fights for a future "linked with steps toward democratic national planning to keep the wheels turning and to ensure full employment and full production."[27]

Criticism of such a labor leader, or of Reuther specifically, for being trapped in the rhetoric and reality of consumerist abundance, and for thus displaying a materialism contradictory to social justice underpinnings, has some validity. A strong case can be made, however, for Reuther's stance being protective camouflage, especially given his postwar emphasis on such issues as economic empowerment and racial justice.

For example, in September 1945, in *The New York Times* article "Our Fear of Abundance," Reuther called for maximum effort "to wipe out the slums and substandard housing, both rural and urban, which

---

26   Harris, Herbert, "What Taft Taught Labor," *New Republic*. Aug. 8, 1947, 22.

27   *Ibid.*, 24.

sap the health and dignity of millions of American families. We have spent millions to destroy cities. Let us be lavish in the equal challenge and more creative assignment of building homes and rebuilding cities in the United States."[28]

In addition, Reuther wasted no opportunity to promote racial justice and equality in the workforce and in society generally. He hadn't forgotten the searing experience of Detroit's race riots in June 1943, when he and other UAW members had worked with local African-Americans to calm the situation and to address the riots' causes, including injustices in the hiring, promotion, and treatment of workers. It was a time, recalled Walter White, head of the Detroit branch of the National Association for the Advancement of Colored People, when "white union members fought against white mobbists to protect Negroes, and Negro unionists fought Negroes in protection of white fellow workers."[29]

The saddest fact about postwar workers, whether in Detroit, Chicago, New York, or other cities around the nation, was their lowered sights in comparison to prewar workers. Young Chicago priest Daniel Cantwell had the boldness and insight to observe to President Roosevelt, in a November 1941 letter, that "our laboring people are looking for and deserve more than a share in the 'cash' produced by industry; they are looking for a share in the control, the planning, and the prestige of the jobs in which they work.... Genuine cooperation in industry, it seems to me, is the only frontier to which our people look today in the clouded future. They are nervous; they will not stop at revolution if they think it [this frontier] is being closed against them, even though they know they will lose all anyway."[30] Postwar workers were nervous too, as the 1946 strikes show, but they were willing to settle for a lot less than the workers described in Cantwell's letter.

What these workers deserved was also deserved by postwar workers and is deserved by today's workers. Donlin, Reuther, Cantwell, and the many other friends of justice described in this volume remind us that the worker-justice frontier has yet to be fully opened.

---

28   Reuther, Walter, "Our Fear of Abundance," The *New York Times*, Sept. 16, 1945.
29   Cook, *op. cit.*
30   Cantwell to Franklin Roosevelt, Nov. 20, 1941. [CHS]

Social Action Vignette
LINNA BRESETTE: SOCIAL ACTION TRAILBLAZER

In 1921, prominent Catholic social-action priests John Ryan and Ray McGowan faced a tough challenge. The national Social Action Department had just been formed, and a priority task was finding a field secretary—someone who could organize labor-management-government conferences promoting worker justice, and who could then crisscross the United States to publicize and attend the conferences.

The resume of one applicant, Linna Bresette, kept surfacing. They liked the fact that for 11 years she was a teacher and school principal in Topeka, Kansas. They were impressed that she then became a Kansas factory inspector—indeed, the first one in that state to focus on women workers. But they were puzzled to see that she had just been forced to resign her state job—until they dug deeper and discovered why.

In 1913, Kansas Governor George Hodges hired Bresette for the factory-inspector job and charged her to explore how the state could best protect the welfare of working women. For two years, as she went through factories and other workplaces investigating and improving women employees' wages, hours, and working conditions, she gathered the material she needed to complete her mission.

The answer, she concluded, was establishment of a state industrial commission, and she drafted a bill to accomplish that purpose. Opposition was fierce—she was, after all, blazing a trail through terrain where men predominated—but she carried the day with a forceful, impassioned speech to the legislature which had supporters lining up, said a local paper, "like a harvest crew at a free-lunch counter."

Bresette became commission secretary, and until 1921 her blend of friendliness and firmness gained the respect and cooperation of most employers. Resistant employers, however, got her ousted.

Ryan and McGowan, no strangers to employer intransigence and reprisal, quickly hired her. She gave to SAD 30 years of distinguished service and to today's workers a legacy of pioneering activism.

CHAPTER FOUR
JOSEPH BUCKLEY (1919–2001)

I became interested in Catholic social action because of the encyclicals. I went to the seminary prep school in Brooklyn, and when I was in school, Pius XI wrote Quadragesimo Anno, *in 1931. I had just started high school, and it was introduced into our religion courses and somewhat into our social studies courses. I became quite interested.*

We had the Roosevelt revolution at that time, so there were stories about social action every day in the papers—the beginning of the organization of the CIO and so forth. The AFL had been around since the 19th century and the CIO was coming to the fore, and legislation being passed helped the CIO to grow almost as a rival union in relation to the AFL—not really, but they took quite different approaches. One was industrial and one was craft. Then my family was involved in these things—I had a couple of uncles who were union members.

> *I went to college in 1936. At that time, there was a group of priests who were interested in social action, including a young priest of the Brooklyn Diocese named Edward Swanstrom, whose doctoral dissertation became the classic 1938 study* The Waterfront Labor Problem. *In 1933 Swanstrom began to hold discussion groups at the Knights of Columbus on* Quadragesimo Anno *and* Rerum Novarum, *and that was the informal beginning of Brooklyn labor schools, Brooklyn social action.*
>
> *Out of those discussions came a group of parish priests who, on a volunteer basis and if their pastors approved, formed themselves into the Priests' Social Action Committee. Swanstrom became a bishop and the director of Catholic charities, and had a very modern view of what charity should do: look at the causes of corruption, the causes of unemployment. That's why he turned to the encyclicals to see what he could learn from them. Both have three major points: organization—the economic and social picture from a Catholic perspective; legislation, the laws to help workers organize; and moral reform.*
>
> *When I was in college from 1936-38, I was coming home and there was a labor school in my home parish—St. Sylvester's, in Ozone Park— and on vacations I would drop by there. The teacher, Father Richard Lavelle, was fascinating in the way he handled discussion on the four ills of society—maldistribution of wealth, concentration of ownership and control, a lack of organization, and false notions of the government's role.*
>
> *The Priests' Social Action Committee in Brooklyn was unofficial, but Diocesan Bishop Thomas Molloy—a brilliant man and a patrician New Englander, from Nashua, New Hampshire—was very interested in social doctrine and supported us. The Committee decided that what people needed was to know what the social-action encyclicals had to say. It was not to be just discovery, because the people the priests wanted to attract were people who would influence the social order in some way or another, however small. The original labor schools which developed out of all that had three basic courses: Catholic social doctrine; a combination of public speaking and parliamentary procedure, both of great importance then and now; and the history of American labor organization.*[1]

The Brooklyn Priests' Social Action Committee (PSAC) was part of the great flowering of Catholic labor schools and other labor-outreach activities across America. But while there were more similarities than differences among these activities, each activity, each labor school or

---

1 Buckley, Joseph, interview with author, June 12, 1995.

school network, had its own strategies, student and curricular policies, sources of support, relationships with diocesan and other Church authorities, and leaders; and these leaders had differing styles and personalities.

Cooperation among the various ventures was usually attempted, but its degree of success depended upon how compatible one venture was with another. Consider, for example, the relationship among the PSAC and the two Jesuit labor schools in New York City, Xavier Labor School (XLS) in Manhattan and the Crown Heights Labor School in Brooklyn.

The Crown Heights school's director, Father William Smith, also an English teacher at Brooklyn Prep High School, was a good publicist for the labor school, but had a rather specialized and exclusivist concept of it. He viewed the school as a way station along the road to developing "a selected group of leaders who are ready and willing to make real sacrifices in a spiritual way." His aim was to produce "conservative Christian workers," and he even created a society called the Crusaders of Christ the Worker.[2]

This group ran side-by-side with the labor school and took on as members only those who demonstrated in the labor school that they were worthy of such status. For Father Smith, meaningful interaction with labor did not start until that point.

As World War II neared, and Catholic labor apostles wondered about the impact of their labor schools up to that point and about how that impact would be affected by a war and a postwar period, a round-table discussion on those topics was held at the American Sociological Society's 1940 convention in Chicago and Father Smith was a participant. His presentation revolved around an article he wrote around the same time for the Jesuit magazine *America*.

The article quoted from a letter to Smith from a former student at his labor school: "I have attended all the schools and study groups in New York City, including your own Crown Heights School, and I ask you a straight question: What concrete plan of action has evolved from any or all of these study groups?

"Unemployment has been our most acute problem for 12 years," the letter writer went on. "What cure is offered by your study groups? You

---

2 Smith, William, response, "Survey of Labor Schools," SAD, July 1941. "An Open Door to Opportunity!," Crown Heights Labor School, nd [FU].

may tell me that the School is intended to train Catholics to carry Catholic ideals into their trade unions. But ideals must be reduced to practical solutions before they can become effective. The only present solution offered through trade unions is the Marxian solution of state slavery. The working man can get a picture of what the Communists offer. What do Catholics offer? The reason I no longer attend your school is because I am looking for action. Study that starts and ends with study looks to me like Catholic talk taking the place of Catholic action."[3]

Father Smith didn't name the student quoted, but the letter expresses sentiments almost exactly like those expressed in long conversations which Xavier Labor School director Father Philip Carey (see Chapter Nine) had in August 1940 with Ernest Sleeper, a student coming into the XLS fall term, director Carey's first term.[4] There's an instructive contrast in the differing response to these sentiments by Fathers Smith and Carey and in how their varying concepts of a Catholic labor school's role affected their schools' relationships with the Brooklyn PSAC schools.

Despite a "not guilty" response by Father Smith to the letter writer quoted in *America*, the writer was on the mark regarding the lack of concrete, practical, union-based action inherent in Father Smith's approach. Smith did a lot of good—he was one of the best excoriators of the excesses of "rugged individualism"—but he had such high expectations that he seemed perpetually disappointed with the results he got. In contrast, Father Carey took Sleeper's criticisms as constructive, welcomed him, a non-Catholic, into his first group of students, and saw him blossom into a respected student-body and union leader.

So disappointed with his results was Father Smith that after only two years of his labor school, he concluded "Brooklyn is not a good labor-school town and we do not think it will be."[5] The Brooklyn Priests' Social Action Committee, with a different approach, reached a different conclusion—one philosophically and practically more attuned to XLS, with which it would work closely in the future. But first, World War II intervened. Father Buckley:

---

3   Smith, "There Is a Need and Future for Labor Schools," *America*, Feb. 1, 1941.
4   Carey, Philip, "Notes on Ernest Sleeper," Aug. 7, 1940. [FU]
5   Smith, "Report on Crown Heights Labor School," Oct. 1945. [FU]

We were avidly following events, and we saw in the labor movement great hope, we saw the support of organization in the papal documents. Any way you look at Catholic ethics, it is inherent that if you organize for the common good, it makes sense, because existence is coexistence—we are social by nature. We felt that the major problem with the unions in those days was non-participation on the part of the members, because they were either indifferent or unequipped. The Communists were a problem, but in Brooklyn we never saw battle with them as our goal. We saw our goal as positive development of people who knew our Catholic social teachings.

However, when the war started, many of the priests who were leaders in social action went into the service as chaplains. Their reasoning was that a lot of those whom they were going to have to deal with pastorally were going to be in the service, therefore they should go in so they could understand these folks and their experiences. Lavelle, Joseph Hammond—the real soul and spirit of Brooklyn social action—so many of them went into the service. And the rest of us, some still seminarians, just tried to hold things together until they got home.

I was ordained in 1943, and I began to teach in the labor schools of the Brooklyn Priests' Social Action Committee in 1944. My first labor-school teaching assignment was at the Colon Council Knights of Columbus Hall on Long Island. The reason I taught there was that Father Hammond had been running the program and then went into the service, so they needed someone to replace him.[6]

The Brooklyn PSAC actually raised its level of labor-school activity in mid-War, despite considerable obstacles, and continued increased activism in postwar—especially after 1947, when the diocese gave the committee official status by forming it into a social-action department with office space, a budget, and a charge to focus on labor relations. It grew into the 1950s until it had 23 labor schools, including, in Brooklyn, schools at St. Cecilia's, St. Boniface's in Borough Hall, St. Brigid's in Ridgewood, St. Michael's and Thomas Dongan Knights of Columbus in Bay Ridge, St. Therese in Flatbush, and Baron de Kalb K. of C. in Sheepshead Bay; and, in Queens, St. Michael's in Flushing, St. Sebastian's in Woodside, and Dominican Commercial High School in Jamaica.

As the network expanded, it established three schools with advanced courses and called them institutes. They enabled students who completed the first year—Catholic social doctrine, public speak-

---

6 Buckley, interview, op. cit.

ing, and American labor history—to then select from a wide range of other courses.

Buckley and other Brooklyn social-action priests met with XLS director Father Carey and his staffers regularly; indeed, Buckley remembered Carey addressing the opening session of St. Sebastian's labor school in Woodside. Many students went to a Brooklyn PSAC school for some courses and to XLS for other courses, and the brochures of the Brooklyn network and XLS frequently listed course information for both efforts. Also, there was a considerable interchange of teachers, such as Walter Maggiolo of the U.S. Conciliation Service and Joseph Schuyler and several other professors from Fordham University.

Father Buckley saw Carey as "a very true, thoughtful, quiet, cautious guy." Buckley had some reservations about XLS priests playing what he saw as too active a role in certain labor situations. Carey, for his part, feared sectarianism—adherence to dogmatic union factions—and felt that labor schools run by the diocese or by the Association of Catholic Trade Unionists (ACTU) sometimes concentrated too much on "organizational and tactical movements" in unions and not enough on the "spiritual and moral formation" of union members. (PSAC priests became, over the years, honorary chaplains of ACTU.) Agreement between XLS and the PSAC, however, outweighed disagreement by a wide margin.[7]

Father Smith, on the other hand, Buckley saw as "difficult, assertive, and protective of his own turf. I think he felt kind of overwhelmed, and rightly so, since we built up a network of schools and institutes all over the Diocese and he had only the Crown Heights school."[8] After World War II, Smith discontinued the Crown Heights school and became director of St. Peter's Institute of Industrial Relations in Jersey City, New Jersey. The Brooklyn network remained fairly active into the late 1950s, despite the diocesan Social Action Department's postwar acquisition of such new responsibilities as helping displaced refugees with resettlement and employment, and Father Buckley was right in the thick of things.

> I taught at St. Cecilia's when I was appointed to social action and also had to find a place to live here. This was a pretty interesting place to run a school because we had dockworkers, truck drivers, cemetery workers, and some management people—although St. Cecilia's doesn't produce a

---

7 Ibid. Carey to Richard McKeon, Oct. 2, 1948 [FU].
8 Buckley, interview, *op. cit.*

lot of them. I also taught at the labor schools at St. Joseph's High School and at Dominican Commercial High School. I taught many different subjects, and made up most of the outlines for our labor schools.

The kind of people who came to the schools would obviously depend on the place. We soon stopped calling them labor schools and began to call them labor relations schools, then labor-management schools. As we went along, we began to offer, very early on, programs for Catholics who were in management. And we'd have such programs as "How to Be a Shop Steward," "Negotiating a Contract," and "Supervision Skills."

Hammond was the guy who got the teachers. They were all unpaid, by the way. They were people who were teaching in the colleges and graduate schools, or were active in the unions—presidents, shop stewards—or were in government, such as the U.S. Conciliation Service and the New York State Labor Relations Board. The Board produced a lot of teachers whom we used in Brooklyn—they lived somewhere around the Diocese—and in those days, Brooklyn was Brooklyn, Queens, Nassau, and Suffolk. Father John Boland, the Board's Chairman, was a good friend of ours and an excellent and competent teacher, as was Board attorney Louis Crisano.

The students were all adults who were there voluntarily and who chose from among our offerings those things which they thought would best help them with their jobs or situations. I found discussion very easy. Students weren't reluctant to express their opinions or to say "We really don't know about this, that, or the other so we've got to do some research, we've got to get someone here to help us." Many of them went on to become rather important in their unions. I still meet people today who talk about their times in labor schools as among the great learning experiences of their lives.[9]

Whether Catholic social action was Brooklyn Diocese, ACTU, or Jesuit, it took good leaders to produce good leaders. Father Buckley remembered that as a seminarian, he sat in on many ACTU meetings on particular strikes and was always impressed when ACTU chaplain Father John Monaghan not only displayed vast knowledge of the specifics of a strike, but zeroed in on its meaning by asking questions such as "What is the morality of this strike?" and "What is justice here?" Many priests, including Buckley and George Kelly—an assistant to Monaghan whose high regard for him was noted in Chapter Two—considered Monaghan their role model for leadership.

---

9 Ibid.

In Kelly's case, Monaghan counseled him to apply practical morality through "A Look at Labor," the weekly column which Kelly, with Monaghan's encouragement, wrote for *Catholic News* under the pen name A.C. Tuohy—a thinly-disguised variation of ACTU—and through Kelly's other writings on labor. In the immediate post-World War II era, Kelly's writings contributed significantly to an understanding of labor happenings.

The major national event affecting the labor movement in that era was the 1947 passage by the U.S. Congress, over President Truman's veto, of the Taft-Hartley Act, which crippled the union-shop approach and thereby emasculated American unionism. From the standpoint of Catholic social-action principles, the finest writing about this assault on labor—an assault which was mounted by America's rugged (selfish) individualists and their political allies soon after labor flexed its muscles in the mid-thirties, and which had picked up a full head of postwar steam—was Kelly's *Primer on the Taft-Hartley Law: A Moral Analysis*, published in 1948.[10] Kelly noted that Catholic social action is based on the moral imperative that economic activity—a piece of legislation, in this case—must advance the welfare of people affected and help them be virtuous in their conduct. His position is on common ground with other worker-justice advocates regarding their specific objections to Taft-Hartley, such as that the Act masquerades as amendments to the Wagner Act but in reality undercuts it.

The major objection of Kelly and other critics is that Taft-Hartley creates a huge loophole in the Wagner Act's union-shop provisions, which had been the major legislative protection of workers and the cornerstone of Catholic labor activism, as we saw in Chapter Two. There, we outlined economist Monsignor Francis Haas's position on the need for, and the centrality of, the union-shop approach. Kelly, in writing about Taft-Hartley, effectively summarized union shops' advantages, such as maintaining membership, preventing employer discrimination, disciplining recalcitrant workers, and enforcing quality standards.

The Taft-Hartley Act's huge loophole is Section 14(b), which allows states to pass legislation outlawing union shops. In 1948, the states which had done this (the so-called "right to work" states, a colossal misnomer since these states have denied millions of workers effec-

---

10 Kelly, George, *Primer on the Taft-Hartley Law*, Rochester: Christopher Press, Inc., 1948.

tive union representation) were Arizona, Arkansas, Florida, Georgia, Iowa, Nebraska, North Carolina, North Dakota, South Dakota, Tennessee, and Virginia. To these 11 have since been added Alabama, Idaho, Kansas, Louisiana, Mississippi, Nevada, Oklahoma, South Carolina, Texas, Utah, and Wyoming, although the pace of addition has slowed considerably, Oklahoma being the only state added within the past decade.

Many "right to work" states have experienced decreases in wages, benefits, living standards, safety, health, working conditions, unemployment insurance, and worker compensation. There have been increases, on the other hand, in poverty and bankruptcy. In addition, when wages fall in a state, its income-tax and sales-tax revenues fall, meaning that it has less funding to finance education, transportation, and other programs attractive to new industries and businesses, and that productivity and expendable consumer income become sluggish.

Of all U.S. laws ripe for repeal or for a massive overhaul, Taft-Hartley leads the list. There were repeal attempts in 1965 and 1966, but they were filibustered to death; the Landrum-Griffin Act made a few revisions in 1959; and overhaul attempts nearly succeeded in both the Carter and Clinton Administrations. President Truman, in vetoing the Act nearly 60 years ago, called it a "slave-labor bill" because of how it exalts employer mistreatment of the American workforce, and his critique rings just as true since that time as it did then.

What does the Taft-Hartley Act overlook? Consider this excerpt from the U.S. Supreme Court case *Abood v. Detroit Board of Education*, 1977: "A union-shop arrangement has been thought to distribute fairly the cost of union representatives' activities among those who benefit, and it counteracts the incentive that employees might otherwise have to become 'free riders'—to refuse to contribute to the union while obtaining benefits of union representation that necessarily accrue to all employees."[11] There are strong echoes here of the ideas of Monsignor Haas and other Catholic social actionists.

Renewal of union health and strength, a development to be ardently desired and worked for, will require repeal of the Taft-Hartley Act or its top-to-bottom revision. Recent study of Taft-Hartley's effects by such researchers as Steven Abraham of SUNY-Oswego's Business School; Paula Voos of the Rutgers University Labor Program; and

---

11 *Abood vs. Detroit Board of Education*, U.S. Supreme Court, 431 U.S. 209 (1977).

Deborah Ballam of Ohio State University's Business Law Program, demonstrates that the Act has severely hampered the American labor movement's effectiveness.[12]

Father Kelly's prescient critique of Taft-Hartley focused on other flawed provisions, including outlawing of the secondary boycott. This is a union acting against a business because of its association with another business the union is trying to organize. Kelly contended such a boycott is moral if the good to be gained outweighs adverse consequences.

In addition, the Act excluded supervisors, preventing them from organizing (the Foremen's Association of America was quite active at the time of enactment, especially among first-level supervisors in the auto industry) and enabling them to act in an anti-union manner. The Act also adjusted the timing of worker elections to favor employers, and permitted courts to enjoin labor so as to unduly interfere with collective bargaining. Generally, the Act equates the unfair practices of labor with the unfair practices of business, as if labor and business were on a par. The reality is that in American society and in Taft-Hartley, business is pushing labor down and aims to keep it there.

Another labor development in which Kelly, Buckley, and other Catholic labor activists fought vigorously and effectively for worker justice was the 1949 strike by 240 employees—mostly grave-diggers—of the New York Archdiocese's Calvary Cemetery. This was a classic case of "physician, heal thyself" in the arena of Catholic labor-management relations. It seemed as though every major diocese in which there were substantial efforts to apply Catholic social teachings was tested by a labor action against the diocese as employer.

What made this particular strike so widely-publicized and even scandalous was the extreme anti-labor stance adopted by Archbishop Francis Cardinal Spellman, arguably the most prominent Churchman in the United States at that time. This stance was most graphically displayed in newsreels and news photos of seminarians as strike-breaking

---

12 Ballam, Deborah, "The Impact of the National Labor Relations Act on the U.S. Labor Movement," *American Business Law journal*, Vol. 32, 1995. Abraham, Steven, "The Impact of the Taft-Hartley Act on the Balance of Power in Industrial Relations," *American Business Law Journal*, Vol. 33, 1996. Voos, Paula, "Expanding Voice for Professional and Managerial Employees," Labor and Employment Relations Association, Dec. 2005.

grave-diggers. Spellman, who ordered them—often to their great consternation—to perform that task, stood by watching them work.

In addition, Spellman improperly intervened in strike negotiations, showing up to sway the workers and their wives by appealing to their religious loyalties. The Cardinal was shocked when the strikers courageously stood up to him and voted down the Archdiocese's woefully inadequate initial offer 183-0.

Many Catholic social actionists, in the New York area and throughout the nation, braved Spellman's wrath and retaliation and rallied to the cemetery workers' cause. New York ACTU strongly supported the workers, marching on their picket lines and providing them with legal representation by attorneys John Sheehan and John Harold. Father Kelly, in one of his A.C. Tuohy columns, outlined the Catholic teaching that workers have a natural right to organize in trade unions and their employers have a corresponding duty to recognize and deal with these unions.

Approximately 25 percent of the workers attended the St. Cecilia's labor school Father Buckley was running at the time.

> When the strike happened, everybody was choosing up sides, and I got a call from the cemeteries director of Brooklyn, a Monsignor Mullaney, saying "What are you doing, and with whom? You're on the wrong side now, with that Committee." I denied that I was taking sides, and said "How about I come over and talk with you about this?" That never happened, because I was a young priest and he was a big monsignor. Maybe Cardinal Spellman called him and said "Get that guy off this thing." Turns out it wasn't even a Brooklyn issue. Calvary Cemetery, while it's in Brooklyn Heights, was owned by the New York Archdiocese.
>
> Actually, the Brooklyn Priests' Social Action Committee was taking, in terms of that strike, a very objective kind of look. We were trying to get at the facts, which is difficult to do in any strike: "What do they actually make?" "What do they really want?" And so on. All of us involved, in the sense of working with the workers themselves, were trying to get them to think through two things. One was the main economic issue. They were asking for a five-day week with the same salary as they were being paid for five and a-half days. Obviously this amounted to a raise, but they argued their position for a lot of reasons—difficulty of the work, time off, and so forth. Also, aside from their salary, undertakers gave the workers tips, money they didn't have to report. So I was talking with them about the living wage, the family wage, and their wages compared

with those of other people. I worked with them on those things, with some degree of success.

The other issue Cardinal Spellman raised was that cemetery workers were organized by the United Cemetery Workers. It was affiliated with the Food, Tobacco, Agricultural and Allied Workers-CIO, a union with Communist leadership. It happened that the local here, Local 293, had no Communists in it at all, and was under that union only because no other union was organizing cemeteries. So I thought that was a false issue.

It was a memorable experience. I tried to hold those people together, in hopes that they wouldn't be unfairly treated. The results were mixed. After several months of struggle, the workers were granted an eight-percent wage increase, their demand for a five-day work week was sent to arbitration, and they shifted representation to the Building Service Employees-AFL, a union which Spellman regularly dealt with regarding the many building projects of the New York Archdiocese. As for retaliation, the Cardinal immediately cut off the Archdiocese's sizeable contribution to New York ACTU, and later upbraided priests who he felt had been disloyal to him during the strike.[13]

Buckley's participation in that strike and in other major strikes of that era, such as the telephone workers' strike in 1947 and the Wall Street workers' strike in 1948, enabled him to gain penetrating insights into what workers face. The telephone workers' strike, which was pretty much forced on the National Federation of Telephone Workers by AT&T's refusal to negotiate on an industry-wide basis, dragged on for a few months and then collapsed, but it had a good result in that it was eventually followed by formation of the Communications Workers of America, a union representing all telephone-industry workers as opposed to a federation. The Wall Street strike was called by the United Financial Employees Union (UFE), whose workers were primarily clerks, tellers, and other white-collar employees; and while UFE failed to organize these financial workers, Buckley was struck by the fact that when he identified workers capable of recruiting for the union and tried to approach them, they would come up for promotion into management. "If I get active with the union," they told him, "I'll never get a management position."[14]

Employers' increasing classification of white-collar workers (and other types of workers) as managers when they were really workers

---

13   Buckley, interview, *op. cit.*
14   Buckley, interview, *op. cit.*

in need of union representation became a major roadblock to labor organization and a clear symptom of the slowdown of labor activism and Catholic social action. In the middle or late 1950s, according to Buckley, the Brooklyn school network saw its registration and attendance figures shrink. It went from 23 schools and three institutes, with a total enrollment of probably two thousand, to two schools by 1960. The refrain running through everyone's mind was "What happened?"

> For one thing, the priests who came into Catholic social action in this later period were not as enthusiastic about the schools as Hammond and I and the other earlier priests were. They had other fish to fry and more interest in other things. You had to be very patient and be ready for disappointment and few results when you used the approach Brooklyn used: inviting laypeople to come, forming a faculty, giving students what you thought would be good training, and hoping they would then go out and form others using that same training.
>
> We had some notable successes, however. One fellow, Joseph Collins, became President of the Civil Service Employees union. He started in this very parish, just going to labor school because he had little else to do. Tom Donahue, longtime Secretary-Treasurer of AFL-CIO and for a brief period in 1995 its Acting President, is also a product of these labor schools. [Note too that AFL-CIO President John Sweeney attended Xavier Labor School in 1955, in his senior year at Iona College. He worked as a grave-digger and building porter to help pay his tuition, and had already become a union member.[15]]
>
> When we talk about why the labor schools no longer functioned, was it because there was no longer a need? It's true that the right to organize became more accepted and that people became more affluent, so perhaps there was less of a *felt* need. People now are very reluctant to get into unions because of again-rampant individualism. "I don't need unions. I can deal with my workplace on my own. My boss likes me, so what's the big deal?" That's a bad attitude. It's very difficult to buck up against American individualism, very difficult.
>
> In the 1930s, we worked with Temporary National Economic Committee reports, the start of a comprehensive, overall look at the economic situation. Using specific percentages, they revealed the great maldistribution of wealth in this country. Those percentages are worse today! Worse! There's more wealth, so the groups that are way down at least have something to eat, but the concentration of ownership and control is much, much greater. So we haven't added a lot of influence.

---

15 Ibid. Fahey, Joseph, "The Making of a Catholic Labor Leader," *America*, Aug. 28, 2006, 16-18.

One thing we lack today, I think, is a sense of crisis. For some reason, encyclicals after Quadragesimo Anno didn't seem to move people as much. Some of this could be attributable to Pope Pius XII's economic conservatism and constant emphasis on private ownership's priority.

Whatever the case, for some reason Brooklyn social-action priests in the later period were not as convinced of the value of lay education. This, combined with growing affluence and with the labor movement losing a lot of its steam in the 1940s, explains much of what has happened. Just think—in 1950, there were roughly 20 million people in unions out of a workforce of some 60 million. Now, 45 years later, there are roughly 11 million people in unions out of a workforce of some 100 million.

Something else, and this is a criticism I make to union people today, is that they've lost their organizing zeal. There are plenty of places in New York and elsewhere which could be organized with their help, but not enough organizing is going on. We had great organizers come out of our labor schools, folks like Joe and Angie Conlon, retail clerks in the Candy Workers Union. But with affluence and the unions' loss of steam, of moral propulsion, too many unions act like the old business unions. They don't go out and say "Is there an issue of injustice here? If so, let's organize." Instead, they say "How much in dues will we get if we organize this place, and how much will it cost us to do so?"

The bottom line is, we need Catholic social action as much as, if not more than, we ever did. When we lost its strong impulse, we lost something very, very good in the Church and in our country.

After the social action impulse waned in Brooklyn, I was plunged into something entirely different. The Bishop decided he was going to build high schools, and he needed principals for them. He looked at people who had teaching experience, and my name came up because of the labor-school teaching. So they sent me back to school to get a Master's degree in education, which I did, from Fordham University in 1961. From that year until 1969, I was Principal of the 2,700-student Bishop Reilly High School [now St. Francis Prep]. I later served as assistant to the superintendent of education for several years. I also continued helping out however I could in the ministry of St. Cecilia's. [Father Kevin O'Donoghue, who served as pastor of that church and provided the photo opening this chapter, credited Buckley with helping him get settled into the pastorate, and with being "an influence for good on everyone whose life he touched."[16]]

I still feel, as an unreformed democratic socialist, that if we don't get people in this country organized around their work, we're never going to achieve a good social system in the sense that Pope Leo XIII, perhaps

---

16 O'Donoghue, interview with author, Feb. 7, 2007.

rather naively, and later Pius XI, envisioned: people organizing around their work for the good of the workers in body, mind, and spirit, and for the common good. This is the only answer I know to American individualism.[17]

---

17   Buckley, interview, *op. cit.*

Social Action Vignette
BOSTON LABOR GUILD: THE LABOR GUILD LIVES ON

Survivors get our attention and, if they've retained their core or essence, our respect. The Labor Guild of Boston, last of the old-time Catholic labor schools, is both noticed and respected by a wide circle of members and friends.

Among characteristics of an "old-time" labor school are total commitment to worker justice and a focus on the practical in course offerings and other activities. At the Guild, there are no exams and no grades. Skilled practitioners from labor and management share with worker-students principles and practices which each learner can apply to particular workplace situations.

The Guild was founded in 1946 as the Catholic Labor Guild, succeeding Archdiocesan/Jesuit labor schools which flourished during the Depression and in World War II. It struggled to develop a focus in the midst of postwar readjustments, but hit its stride in the 1950s thanks to an energetic nucleus of union activists, including John Cort.

Further strengthening of the Guild occurred in 1964, when Father Mort Gavin, SJ, a veteran of the Boston area's earliest labor schools, became the organization's chaplain and executive secretary. For 22 years, Gavin, a renowned labor economist and arbitrator, led the Guild in emphasizing cooperation among labor, management, and the wider community. Each year from 1967 on, the Guild has presented an exemplar of that emphasis with the Cushing (now Cushing-Gavin) Award, in honor of Richard Cardinal Cushing, the Boston Archbishop who strongly supported the Guild from its start until his death in 1970, and of Gavin, who died in 1984, at age 77. The award ceremony is a red-letter day on Boston's calendar.

After Gavin's death, Father Edward F. Boyle, SJ, who arrived at the Guild in 1970 as Gavin's assistant, directed the Labor Guild with great distinction. He died in 2007 (see Preface) and, although he is sorely missed, today the Guild keeps moving forward as a survivor with heart, the keeper of a worker-justice flame bright with history and promise.

CHAPTER FIVE
ED MARCINIAK (1918–2004)

Midway through the first term of President Franklin Roosevelt, as the President's initiatives to fight the Depression and restore confidence started to have real bite, Chicago high-school student Edward Marciniak was in a quandary. He was in his next-to-last year of Quigley Preparatory Seminary, a five-year Catholic high school for students heading towards the priesthood; and while he thought this calling might give him a way to help people in their lives, he wrestled with whether he could be equally helpful as a layperson.

Around that time two chance encounters lighted his way. First, he wandered through a Quigley schoolroom right after one of Father John Hayes' classes ended and found a copy of *The Catholic Worker* (*CW*), which Hayes was in the habit of leaving behind for just such a happening. Secondly, he attended a meeting of Chicago Inter-Student

Catholic Action, or CISCA, a group for high-school and college student activists in the Chicago area.

Ed Marciniak became intrigued with both the newspaper and the group, and was soon active in the Catholic Worker (CW) movement and in CISCA, which for him were just different aspects of the same message. The message was that personal reform and social reform went hand in hand, so that working for reform causes promoted both the common good and one's spiritual enrichment.

Marciniak coupled this message with something he learned from CISCA chaplain Father Martin Carrabine. The lesson was that, in Marciniak's words, "you didn't have to be a priest or religious [member of a religious order] to be the best Christian possible."[1] Between these two realizations, Marciniak's quandary over his calling was resolved and he went on to exercise his strong sense of both personal and social responsibility as an active Catholic layperson.

Although Marciniak gave up thoughts of the priesthood as a vocation, he saw the layperson's role as a vocation in itself, and threw his considerable energies towards developing that vocation, for himself and for the laity in general. His answer to the question "Are you a Christian?" was "I'm becoming one," and he immediately tackled the two tasks he saw as most critical at the time—helping workers organize and improving race relations.[2]

In CISCA, he and other young activists fought to open up Catholic colleges and high schools which were still closed to blacks. In the CW movement, he and fellow volunteers distributed *The Catholic Worker* at May Day parades, at union halls, and during union organizing drives at Chicago's steel mills and stockyards.

For his worker-justice activities, Marciniak paid a price. Chicago police generally frowned on them, so he was hauled off several times in a paddy-wagon. Also, spending a lot of time and effort in activism involved considerable sacrifice, since his parents ran a mom-and-pop grocery/butcher shop seven days a week and he was often needed. But, he says, "I had parents who, if anything had a Catholic connection, would let me do it."[3]

In fall 1936, Marciniak started his three years at Loyola University (his fifth year at Quigley equated to the college's freshman year), from

1 Marciniak, Ed, interview with author, July 5, 1995.
2 Ibid.
3 Ibid.

5 ❧ Ed Marciniak

which he earned a B.A. in 1939. While at Loyola, he worked on the student newspaper, so that when he got together later with two other young social actionists, John Cogley and Jim O'Gara, to establish a Chicago edition of *CW*, he became managing editor since only he could lay out a page. They were all great writers and committed activists, however, so from its first issue in June 1938 until World War II, *The Chicago Catholic Worker (CCW)* was a clear window into Catholic social action in Chicago. Marciniak set the tone in an early editorial:

> We remember last May Day, when we watched the workers' parade that filed through the Loop, how we were struck by the fact that so many of the loudest, noisiest Communists were speaking in English thickly accented with traditionally Catholic tongues—Irish, Polish, Italian, Mexican, and Lithuanian Catholics who had turned against their Church. Victims of exploitation on the part of Christians and Catholics—and some of these in high places—whose professions and doctrines seem to have no bearing on their lives, the fallen-away Catholics turned eager ears to the Communists who told of new doctrines, atheistic and materialistic, that "worked." The Communists point the practicability of their doctrines by acting according to them.
>
> For instance, Communists say that they consider Negroes as their brothers and often go on to prove it by their actions. We Catholics tell the Negro that he is our brother, a fellow member of the Mystical Body of Christ, and then go on to close our schools, our hospitals, and our organizations to him. We give this example to show that it is not always that these worker-apostates reject Christian doctrines as much as that they sometimes throw their lot in with the enemies of Christianity and the Church to show their contempt for the hypocrisy of Christians....
>
> We are all responsible for this apostasy, inasmuch as we have not gone to the worker. When the Pope told us to "Go to the worker" it was not mere papal persiflage. The Holy Father knew what he was talking about, and had good reason for issuing the general command. "Going to the worker" means just that, going to the worker—not just simply writing papers and listening to lectures that deal with workers from the comfortable, critical, safe vantage of scientific study. "Going to the worker" should become a matter of conscience for all of us in every station of life.
>
> The command of the Pope does not mean that all of us have to go marching on every picket line or addressing striking workers, although that would be desirable. Such activities must of necessity be limited to those who have the time and talent for them. However, a wide acceptance of the Holy Father's command can be genuinely, practically accepted by all Catholics.

> When Catholic employers, and here we include priests, religious and laity, are immediately spotted as Catholics because of the just treatment of people in their employ; when Catholic housewives are known to have influenced the tragic status of domestic help by their own treatment of servants; when Catholics, generally, are known—as Communists are known—to refuse to support any place of business unjust and unfair to the people in its employ; when Catholics, a formidable group of buyers, are known to eschew the low-selling product paid for by the sweat of exploited workers; when Catholics—twenty millions of us in America!—exert the full force of our number on the social order; when labor can look to us for enthusiastic support in its fight for recognition; when exploiters of human dignity can look to us for condemnation regardless of how much they may seem to be the pillars of our churches; when exploiters look at us with trepidation and the exploited turn to us for hope—then we will be on our way towards "going to the worker."[4]

These lines of Ed Marciniak in the March 1939 *CCW* indicate his belief that the two main non-governmental contenders for the role of worker-justice champion were the Catholic social actionists and the Communists, and that his group had more to offer workers. Indeed, at that time members of the American Communist Party (CP) were still in their Popular Front mode of muting revolutionary aims and working when possible with Catholic social actionists and other reformers.

John Cogley commented elsewhere in *CCW*'s pages that this stance of the U.S. Communists "leaves world revolution up to the Catholics—and that is how it should be, since the Mystical Body of Christ is the only International with any valid reality or spiritual significance. The only revolution that can come about without bloodshed and endure without purges, is the establishment of the Kingdom of God—Christ's Kingdom of Justice and Peace and Brotherly Love."[5]

The Marciniak passage demonstrates both his tremendous passion for social justice and his powerful sense of vocation. By "vocation," Marciniak meant a phase of daily life in which Christian social principles could be applied. That phase could be a person's being a unionist or relating to people of another race, but it could also be one of the person's many other roles: as a layperson, priest, member of an occupation (writer, personnel specialist, carpenter, farmer, etc.), husband,

---

4 Marciniak, "'Go to the Worker,'" *Chicago Catholic Worker*, Mar. 1939, 3.
5 Cogley, John, "Left Turns," *CCW*, July 1938, 2.

wife, young person, industry representative, civic activist, consumer, and so on.

Ed Marciniak was aware that the papal social-action encyclicals used "vocations" to describe groups of cooperating workers and employers, although Marciniak wisely cautioned that many of the encyclicals' descriptions had a European frame of reference and thus applied only loosely to the American situation. He also noted that the papal use of "vocations" outlined goals, not a specific road-map for reaching them. Such "crawling before you can walk," as he put it, might mean forming local labor-management partnerships before talking about groups at regional and national levels.

However, while Marciniak believed in and worked for the sharing of power represented by these partnerships, his priority was personal reform—not in the sense of one having to be personally reformed before he or she engaged in social reform, but in the sense of social reform resulting from an individual's striving to do his or her best in a particular vocation (or institution, or family, or group, or company, or union).

In a union, for example, an individual's striving to become the best unionist she or he could be made that union better, but the emphasis was on the individual enriching and fulfilling his or her spiritual life as a member of the vocation "unionist." At the heart of this viewpoint was the concept of the dignity of work, the subject of a Marciniak article in the March 1940 CCW.

> Pope Pius XI wrote: "Religion teaches the rich man and the employer that their working people are not their slaves; that they must respect in every man his dignity as a man and as a Christian; that labor is an honorable employment and that it is shameful and inhuman to treat men like chattels to make money by, or to look upon them as so much muscle or physical power."
>
> The Pope's words have many obvious implications, but we are mainly concerned in this article with the bearing they have on labor unions and the workers' right to organize. The popes have vigorously defended unionism. Many priests throughout the country are among the best friends the unions have. Why does the Church throw her support behind the trade union movement?
>
> The way we see it, labor unions are not just associations to bargain with employers for higher wages and shorter hours. The principle, the inspiration behind the union, is—or should be—something nobler, something more fundamental than mere bargaining. If wages were sky

high and hours of work were at a minimum, if working conditions were ideal, there would still be room for the labor union.

The popes defend the workers' right to join in associations because fundamentally it is a matter of human dignity. Today, of all the great world forces, only the Catholic Church refuses to lose sight of the dignity inherent in every man. Certainly the Communists have lost sight of this God-given innate gift. If you speak to them of the thousands of Russian peasants who were starved to death, they'll tell you blithely that these were sacrificed for the common good. They refuse to consider the right each and every one of these peasants had to life. The fascist and the nazi are willing to sacrifice anyone, should it seem best for the state....

The capitalist—now selfish, at other times benignly patronizing—has also forgotten the significance of human dignity. It is the "Christ a Worker" concept of human dignity that the trade unionist has to keep in mind. When workers join together into unions they should use their moral, unified strength to demand their rights to be treated as men, and not as so much muscle and bone....

When labor sets up as an aristocracy within its ranks and is indifferent to humbler, unskilled workers, then this idea of the dignity of man has been lost. Labor, itself, loses sight of the fact that the most menial work, the humblest toil, is an honorable employment.

When "scabs" are willing to sell their labor and betray their fellow workers in time of need; when they are willing to use their strength simply for higher wages, then they deem themselves simply as muscle and bone, chattels to make money by. They have forgotten their own dignity....

And so again we recall these fundamental facts about the dignity of the human person. Of course, this dignity implies rights and the rights imply duties. Workers, conscious of their own dignity and the honorable nature of their labor, will not have to be reminded that they have duties to their employers and to the consumers of their products. It is on this foundation, upon this Christian concept of man, that a new world will be built. Or else they who labor for a whole new order of things are building their houses on sand.[6]

Within the Catholic social-action movement, when there was a balance between this kind of emphasis on personal dignity and an emphasis on power sharing and industrial democracy, the movement gained strength. Absent that balance, the movement tended to weaken.

Marciniak positively influenced a wide array of critical issues and community forums throughout the Chicago area as he fought for de-

---

6 Marciniak, "The Dignity of Work," CCW, Mar. 1940, 2.

cades to improve labor-management cooperation, racial understanding, the quality of housing and urban life,[7] and religious toleration. However, as the breadth of these worthy struggles grew, one unexpected and unwelcome consequence was a looser focus on labor, a slower pace of labor activism, and a lack of staying power in worker-justice activities.

In the early stages of Ed Marciniak's activism, a broad approach to social justice was tremendously beneficial. When he and other Chicago Catholic Workers got together starting in October 1936 for their Jocist "see-judge-act" discussions at CW's West Taylor Street house (mentioned in Chapter One), the wide range of discussion leaders in the group made it seem like a social-justice diorama.

Among these featured guests were Father John LaFarge, SJ, editor of the Jesuit magazine *America*; Virgil Michel, Benedictine monk and liturgy reformer; Father Francis Haas, labor economist and skilled negotiator; and Walter Reuther, a young Detroit autoworker recounting his disenchanting experiences working at a car factory in the Soviet Union.

For the young Catholic activists of Marciniak's generation, this was a period when, in his words, "a whole new world opened up." Many, like Marciniak, were children of immigrants and members of the first generation of Catholics to attend college on a large scale. Above all, they were excited to find that their religion could be an instrument of social change and that they could help "right the wrongs of injustice." These weren't hard to find.[8]

Indeed, it was hard to miss among the victims of injustice in Chicago the jobless, homeless, hungry, and ill-clothed people wandering its streets. On Good Friday 1938, at 868 Blue Island Avenue, Marciniak, Cogley, Al Reser, and Marty Paul opened a Catholic Worker House of Hospitality in an old two-story factory, with a huge soup kitchen on the first floor and shelter space everywhere else. Soon, they fed 350 people and housed 50 of them every day and, when city relief funds

---

7   In Lakewood Balmoral, where he and his wife Virginia raised their four daughters—Francesca, Kate, Christina, and Claudia—in Edgewater, in whatever Chicago neighborhood where Marciniak lived, he was a tireless advocate of community improvement through grassroots activism. His book *Reversing Urban Decline* is a classic work on that subject.

8   Herr, Dan, "Chicago Dynamo," *Sign*, Sept. 1962, 12.

dried up, formed the Catholic Union of the Unemployed to help get the local relief office reopened.

The *Chicago Catholic Worker* was an outgrowth of the CW volunteers' various activities, as it enabled them to report outcomes, express ideas, and, of necessity, generate income. During labor strikes the paper printed extra editions for distribution on the picket lines.

When the United States entered World War II, Dorothy Day and many of her followers espoused pacifism, as they had done since the CW movement's inception, and other Catholic Workers supported American involvement. In Chicago some CW activists, including Cogley and O'Gara, went off to war and others, including Marciniak, declared themselves as conscientious objectors. He wrote, in one of his last *CCW* articles before the paper succumbed to wartime dislocations, that the root cause of war is "subordination of the human spirit to materialism"; and he dedicated himself to helping Catholic social actionists prepare for postwar and for what he felt would be an even greater need for reconstruction of the social order.[9]

Toward this end, he earned an M.A. in Social Administration from Loyola University in 1942 and from 1942-45 taught sociology at Loyola and researched at the University of Chicago's Committee for the Study of Social Thought. In 1943 he and a cross-section of Catholic labor activists in the Chicago area formed the Catholic Labor Alliance (CLA) and in July of that year published the first issue of the group's monthly magazine *Work*, which became highly influential in labor and reform circles.

The purposes and personnel of CLA reflect the "vocation" concept at the heart of Ed Marciniak's ideas and actions. For Marciniak, "Labor" in the organization's title meant all the vocations which composed the workforce, such as those of the unionist; the employer; people in particular occupations; and workforce groupings by race, gender, religion, and so on. Personnel were chosen with an eye towards fairly representing these vocations. Arthur Carstens, for example, brought to CLA the perspectives of both a U.S. Office of Price Administration investigator and a non-Catholic. John Yancey was a leading African-American in Chicago as well as an experienced unionist (Secretary-Treasurer of the United Transport Service Employees-CIO), while Frank Gillespie of the Dairy Employees Union expressed the AFL viewpoint. Visking Corporation Director Leonard Bajork, formerly a regional director of

---

9 Marciniak, editorial, *Work*, Nov. 1938.

the National Labor Relations Board, represented the employer vocation. Rita Clare Cooney, a *Work* assistant editor, and Sister Vincent Ferrer, an economics professor at Rosary College (River Forest, Illinois) provided the perspectives of women workers.

These and other core members of CLA taught courses in Catholic labor schools and also at the Sheil School (named for Bernard Sheil, auxiliary bishop of the Chicago Archdiocese and a leading social activist), an adult-education venture which featured a variety of courses on labor-management relations. Marciniak, CLA's Executive Secretary, taught almost every labor-related topic in the Sheil School catalog, including "Why Labor Unions?," "Trends in Collective Bargaining," "Grievance Clinic," "Jobs After the War," "Trade Unionism," "Unions and the Annual Wage," "Industrial Democracy," "Labor Looks at the Communists," "The Labor Press: Good, Bad, or Indifferent?," "Union Rights and Duties," and "What Is the Future of Organized Labor in the United States?"

CLA established a policy of openness to unionists (leaders and rank-and-filers), non-unionists, employers, women, non-Catholics, and minorities, a policy which for Marciniak went hand-in-hand with his concept of vocations. The concept's power for him was that "it brought into focus the liturgy, the church's interest in the labor movement, and personal responsibility—the initiative of lay people. We were to be self-starters, not merely followers. That's what excited me, probably more than anything else."[10]

When Marciniak first thought about an organization for Chicago's Catholic social actionists, in mid-1938, a chapter of the Association of Catholic Trade Unionists (ACTU) seemed the most likely possibility. Marciniak knew of the CW-inspired formation of an ACTU chapter in New York City and of the spread of the organization to other cities.

In the July 1938 *Chicago Catholic Worker*, he noted, referencing *Quadragesimo Anno*, that ACTU's twofold purpose was to instruct its members in Catholic doctrine and to apply doctrinal teachings in their labor unions. He added that "the future of labor in America lies in the CIO or at least in the principle of industrial organization, which is the CIO's basis."[11]

---

10 Troester, Rosalie Riegle, ed., *Voices from the Catholic Worker*, Philadelphia: Temple University Press, 1993.
11 Marciniak, "Wanted! Catholic Labor Leaders," CCW, July 1939, 4.

Of Catholic unionists he asked "Will they sit on the *outside* and watch the Communists sabotage the labor movement or will they be on the *inside* fighting with the rest of the workers for a stronger and better labor movement?" He invited interested readers to contact him so that he might put them in touch with those considering formation of an ACTU chapter in Chicago. Indeed, one was formed shortly thereafter, and Marciniak's perspective after CLA's establishment five years later traces what happened in the interim.

> *The CLA in Chicago was never affiliated with the ACTU. The CLA was formed in 1943, two years after the ACTU chapter here had folded for a whole variety of reasons. The Cathedral Chicago Chapter of ACTU was the Chicago ACTU. It [the chapter] was so-called because it had the hospitality of Holy Name Cathedral and its offices were located in Cathedral Square.*
>
> *When the Alliance was formed, there were several practical reasons and some theoretical ones why we did not call ourselves the Association of Catholic Trade Unionists. The practical ones were: 1) As a result of a long Newspaper Guild-CIO strike here [in 1938-39], ACTU had lost contact with most of the AFL leadership and had a CIO "name." In fact, one year there were two Labor Day Masses, one sponsored by ACTU at the Cathedral and another sponsored by AFL people at St. Peter's, a downtown church. 2) Just a few years prior to CLA's formation, the chaplain of Chicago ACTU [Father Bernard Burns] had mediated a dispute at one of the large department stores, and had gotten a strike settled, only to find that management went back on its word, creating one big stink. The new Archbishop [Samuel Stritch], who had just come from Milwaukee, walked right into this controversy, and was pretty sour on ACTU as a result of it. There is no question in my mind about ACTU's correctness in the controversy. It was just one of those things that can happen to an organization that is involved in trying to tangle with concrete issues. And 3) The people who were originally responsible for the formation of the CLA were principally not people connected with Chicago ACTU.*
>
> *Now for the theoretical reasons, which today perhaps do not loom as importantly as they did then: 1) We wanted to open our membership to Protestants and Jews as well as Catholics; 2) We wanted to open our membership to non-unionists, including employers; and 3) We did not want to get involved with the ACTU caucus/conference technique. We never had very much discussion in the 1943 days about affiliation with*

5 ❦ Ed Marciniak

ACTU. We were really trying to start something new, and the ACTU affiliation issue was not very important.[12]

The theoretical reasons Marciniak mentioned, particularly the third one, did loom more importantly in the 1938 discussions about the best form of organization for Chicago's Catholic social actionists, as he clarified in other comments made after CLA's formation in 1943:

> Another important difference between the ACTU and the Alliance raises a matter of policy: What role should a group of Catholics play in the affairs of a union? In New York, Detroit, Pittsburgh, and elsewhere, ACTU members have at times set up "ACTU conferences" in various industries to implement Christian social teaching. More than once these "conferences" have turned out to be ACTU caucuses for or against some candidate for union office. Caucuses have tended to create factionalism and sectarianism in a union, though ACTU members maintain that this charge against them is unfair.
>
> The leaders of the Alliance explain that the CLA is not against caucuses in the labor movement. In fact many of its members have been and are now active in union "caucuses." What the Alliance is trying to avoid, for the sake of Catholics and for the welfare of the union, is a Catholic "bloc" in the union. Such a bloc or faction would tend to isolate Catholics from the rest of the union and thus lessen their influence. Furthermore, it would split the union along religious lines, thus weakening the union's position in collective bargaining. Such a bloc, say leaders of the CLA, arises when Catholics are active in their unions <u>as Catholics</u> and not <u>as good trade unionists</u> who are Catholics.
>
> The difference can be illustrated by putting words into the mouths of two active union members, both Catholics: At a union meeting, the sectarian Catholic says: "At the recent national convention of the Association of Catholic Trade Unionists, a resolution was adopted supporting the Marshall Plan for European Recovery. <u>This</u> resolution, which I now read, contains some of the best arguments I have seen for the Marshall Plan. I move its adoption." The "good trade unionist" says: "I think that as union members we should support the Marshall Plan for these reasons.... I hereby move the adoption of <u>a</u> resolution in support of the European Recovery Program."
>
> In both instances the resolution presented is substantially the same, but the reasoning is different. The first unionist implies that his resolution is true and good because it is Catholic. The second assumes that his resolution is Catholic because it is good and true.

---

12   Marciniak to Richard Ward, May 15, 1954. [CHS]

> This is no minor problem. Upon its solution will depend in great measure the amount of influence that not only the Catholic "labor" groups will be able to exert but also the whole Catholic social movement.[13]

Obviously, the events leading up to World War II and the war itself contributed to significant changes, organizationally and otherwise, for Catholic social actionists in Chicago and throughout the United States. Another major catalyst for such changes was the American Communist Party's shift from reformism to obstructionism following the signing of the Nazi-Soviet pact on August 24, 1939. Marciniak disliked this obstructionism, but also disliked Catholic unionists (in ACTU or not) concentrating more on attacking Communists within their ranks than on building sound unions. "Catholic Union Leadership Must Be Earned: No Short Road to the Top," Marciniak headlined a 1940 CCW article.

> It is unfortunately true that the recent and overdue interest of some Catholics in their labor unions so often takes the form of a drive to oust the present officials who are suspected of being Communists or fellow travelers and to elect a slate of Catholics whose sole qualification for office is a hasty reading of a popularization of some of the papal encyclicals on labor.
>
> It is unquestionably a good thing to bring the Church's attitude on Labor to the attention of laborers but it is not necessary to have an official position in the union to do this or to influence the union's decisions. Any rank-and-file member who talks about union affairs with his fellow workers and who is alert at the meetings will be able to prevent the imposing of Communist-inspired policies and to turn the membership to constructive social thinking.
>
> But these Catholic leaders are obsessed with the idea of getting control of the unions, often through pressure and manipulations typical of political ward heelers. They explain, not apologize for, these methods by saying that "you have to fight fire with fire" and "you gotta use their own weapons."
>
> Their reasoning has at least two defects. In the first place, of course, the end, no matter how desirable, cannot justify such means. In the second place it is usually not by these means that the CPs, if they do control the union, secured such influence.
>
> The building of a union is a long, patient process, filled with heart-sickening disappointments and never-ended, unexciting, monotonous hard work. There are hundreds of individuals to be talked to carefully,

---

13 Marciniak, memo, "ACTU/CLA," Dec. 1950. [CHS]

5 ❧ Ed Marciniak

> thousands of postcards to be addressed, countless crankings of the third-hand mimeograph machine. There is night after night, not for weeks or months only, but perhaps for years, of planning and discussion. There are continued hours on the telephone and habitual meals of coffee and cigarettes to pay for the telephone and the mimeograph and the inadequate office. Heroic devotion, sacrifice, and plain unattractive drudgery are necessary to get the group together and to keep it together.
>
> And once you have a group, what? Crowded meetings with stimulating discussions of fundamental problems? Rarely. The members have to be nagged to attend the meetings and their grievances, more often than not, have to do with a badly-placed light, an untidy washroom, or some minor executive's unreliable disposition.
>
> There's nothing glamorous or splendid about all this detail but it is essential to the making and management of unions.[14]

Marciniak's call for Catholic unionists to become more active members of their locals took on added urgency as the Nazi-Soviet pact phase of the American Communist Party line was succeeded by the World War II phase, in which CP members echoed the dominant industrialists and their calls for speed-up. If enough Catholic (and other non-Communist) unionists had exercised their spiritual principles by becoming the best unionists they could be, Communist unionists putting their CP interests over labor interests would have been rebuffed by unionists themselves. Excessive government involvement in the situation, and excessive Red-baiting by the enemies of labor to harm it as much as possible, would have been stymied if not avoided.

Marciniak practiced what he preached in this regard. "Wherever there was a Communist-dominated union, we were active," he said of CLA members. "As a matter of fact, in one of the Communist-dominated unions at the time was a group of government workers who almost en masse joined CLA. They were concerned about how to deal with that domination."[15]

The run-up to World War II and the war itself affected Chicago's Catholic social actionists not only in terms of organization and of dealing with Communist adversaries within unions, but also in terms of priest-laity relationships. Father Daniel Cantwell, a member in 1939 of the last class of priests ordained by George Cardinal Munde-

---

14 Marciniak, "Catholic Union Leadership Must be Earned," *CCW*, Nov. 1940, 4.
15 Marciniak, interview, *op. cit.*

lein and an active participant in the Hillenbrand circle of priests, returned to Chicago in 1942 from his graduate studies in sociology and economics at The Catholic University of America, and gladly agreed to help with formation of the CLA and to become its chaplain.

Cantwell shared the Hillenbrand viewpoint of the priest-laity relationship as summarized by Marciniak, "that priests were basically there to assist laypeople in their calling, their vocation—that was the priests' job." This viewpoint didn't mean just that priests opened up leadership roles for the laity, though this was part of it, but also that through techniques like see-judge-act, laypeople made the choices involved. Marciniak again: "It wasn't as if you were going to some priest who said 'Here's the answer.' The priest would say 'Well, why don't you talk about it. Figure out what the answer is.'

"There were really two kinds of priest, two kinds of Catholic organizations at the time," Marciniak continued. "One approach was to set up a Catholic organization which was run by a priest, or which was Catholic Action under the direction of the hierarchy. But Cantwell's role was different. What he wanted to do was to develop a cadre of laypeople who would run the organization. You know, [Chicago Archbishop Samuel] Stritch thought Cantwell was running CLA, and Cantwell was willing to take the heat for what happened; but he gave the people the opportunity to assume the leadership, and that's a very different approach."[16]

CLA's results were mixed. It fought for social justice across a wide front, winning all of some battles and parts of most battles, and it reached a lot of people in many walks of life with the principles of the social-action encyclicals. Again, a tighter focus on the labor-movement perspective would have enhanced CLA; but even when it focused on labor it faced many of the same problems which had dissolved Hillenbrand's labor-school network.

These problems included low and/or irregular attendance and wartime dislocations—long and unpredictable shifts, travel difficulties, and less disposable income. Among postwar CLA problems were growing leisure time and affluence; other avenues for labor education, including unions, colleges, and adult-education programs; and decreases in union activism because of the Taft-Hartley Act, government red tape, and labor's internecine struggles.

---

16 *Ibid.*

5 Ed Marciniak

The labor classes at Sheil School (later called the Adult Education Center) continued into the 1950s, but fewer and fewer people attended and the classes tailed off rapidly. CLA then held neighborhood labor forums throughout the city, but interest waned, and that venture was discontinued in the mid-fifties.

Two CLA ventures, however, succeeded admirably—the Ryan Forum lecture series and the newspaper *Work*. The Ryan Forum, established in 1949, featured major addresses on important social and economic issues; prominent speakers; and cross-sections of Chicago as audiences. *Work*, with Marciniak as Editor and Bob Senser and Rita Clare Cooney as assistant editors, became, as we noted, a "must-read" on reform topics.

Marciniak estimated that labor was the focus of one in four Ryan Forum lectures, with speakers including AFL President George Meany; CIO President Philip Murray; Walter Reuther, his successor; U.S. Labor Secretary Maurice Tobin; President A. J. Hayes of the International Association of Machinists; and President Willard Townsend of United Transport Service Employees. In addition, CLA sponsored an annual Labor Day Mass, with the sermon by a prominent labor activist and as many as 1,500 dignitaries attending.

Work, however, was CLA's greatest contribution to Catholic social action and the labor movement, both locally and nationally. It had 15,000 readers per issue at its peak in the 1950s. They relied heavily on its thorough treatment of union conventions, collective bargaining, pending legislation, economic conditions, and "the news behind the news." The Taft-Hartley Act, passed in 1947, got a lot of coverage, as in these excerpts from the article "Taft-Hartley Law Looks No Better Than When Enacted," in the August 1950 issue:

> Since the days of Prohibition, no law has raised more blood pressure. When the Taft-Hartley Act was born three years ago, opponents called it a "slave labor law" and a lot of other names. Its friends blessed it and said all kinds of good things would come of it…. What facts about the law stand out above the smoke and heat of the argument?
>
> The federal government is now in the labor-management business more deeply than it has ever been before. The National Labor Relations Board shows the effect of this. It's swamped with work far beyond what it can handle even with its expanded staff.…
>
> Most union officers have signed the non-Communist affidavits which are required before a union can use the NLRB. But this T-H feature

has had little practical effect. The CIO cleaning out of Commies would have happened anyway. Besides, left-wing unions usually dodged the law's intent in two ways: they gave Commies different titles while letting them keep their old power; or else the suspected Communists simply signed the affidavits (T-H's wording makes prosecution against them almost impossible).

Since T-H's coming, union membership has dropped off an estimated half million or more. What size unions would be without T-H is anybody's guess. But this much is agreed upon even by business papers: the law has cramped labor's style in a big unorganized area—the South....

The United States is the only industrial country in the world using court injunctions against labor. Taft-Hartley continued this record. In the past three years the NLRB instituted injunction action against unions in 78 cases, against employers in two cases.

T-H forbids unions to spend money on political campaigns. But unions have set up separate "education" organizations....

T-H doesn't protect the right of supervisors to organize. Result: the law has taken the guts out of the pre-Taft Hartley's foremen's organizations and most of them have collapsed.

Back in December 1948, Business Week indicated ... "Given a few million unemployed in America, given an administration in Washington which was not pro-union—and the Taft-Hartley act conceivably could wreck the labor movement. These are the provisions that could do it: (1) picketing can be restrained by injunction; (2) employers can petition for a collective bargaining election; (3) strikers can be held ineligible to vote—while the strike replacements cast the only ballots; and (4) if the outcome of this is a no-union vote, the government must certify and enforce it."

Another frequent labor subject of *Work* coverage was workplace equality for women. In one of the first issues after World War II, the article "What About Women Workers?," by Sister Thomasine O.P., noted that (1) During the War, women often replaced men at equal pay and with equal skills, but men displacing many of these women after the War was a national problem and needed resolution; (2) Most women workers got jobs for economic reasons alone, and the questions of where women could find jobs and how had to be effectively answered; and (3) Church teachings recognize that many women have to work outside the home, and Catholic social actionists must cooper-

5 ❦ Ed Marciniak

ate with representatives from other religious bodies, industries, government agencies, and schools to help these women.[17]

Improving race relations, a Marciniak priority from his beginnings as a social activist, was another frequent topic. In 1944, *Work* covered an incident involving John Yancey, prominent Chicagoan, African-American, labor leader, and CLA member. The coverage displayed both Yancey's sense of worker justice and the American Communist Party's wartime relegation of worker and racial justice to secondary status when the Party's speed-up and win-no-matter-what modes took precedence. Marciniak reported on the incident in the article "Full Story Behind Smear: John Yancey, A Good Union Man."[18]

The background to the incident involved an action of Sewell Avery, executive-board chairman of Montgomery Ward and one of the nation's most vehement anti-unionists. When 7,000 of his employees voted for a union, it took two direct orders from President Roosevelt to get him to recognize it. In April 1944, he defied another direct order from Roosevelt to settle a strike and the President sent Attorney General Francis Biddle and a detail of National Guardsmen to the company's Chicago headquarters to redeliver the order.

When they attempted this, chairman Avery defied the order again, and Biddle asked two of the Guardsmen to carry Avery out of the building in his chair, which they did, with the chairman snarling away. An alert photographer snapped a picture of the outburst, and in the days following it was on view for thousands of newspaper readers worldwide, to their great glee or anguish. Yancey's reaction to Avery's defiance triggered what led to the Marciniak article.

> Readers of the letter columns of The Chicago Daily News were given a sample of Communist tactics in smearing a good union man. The labor leader was John Yancey, a nationally known figure in trade union circles....
>
> John Yancey is neither a Communist nor a Trotskyite; he has one, and only one, political allegiance: American democracy. Unlike some residents of the U.S., he is not tied to the apron strings of any foreign political system.
>
> As a citizen interested in the welfare of his country, John Yancey wrote the following letter which appeared in the Daily News on May

---

17 Sister Thomasine O.P., "What About Women Workers?," *Work*, Apr. 1946, 4-5.
18 "John Yancey, A Good Union Man," *Work*, June 1944, 5.

8th: "I am exceedingly alarmed by the number of letters that express a sympathy for the acts of Montgomery Ward through the chairman of its executive board, Sewell L. Avery. Many of the letters have indicated the thought that Avery is sincere in his convictions. This I seriously doubt. An individual who has reached the point of considering himself, his investments, and his personal interests paramount to the welfare of the people of this nation is either insincere or suffering from a severe neurosis.

"We cannot afford to have such an individual loose in our society. He should be confined by legal restrictions, and forced to observe these restrictions in as rigid a manner as imprisoned criminals or the padded-celled insane. Human rights at all times transcend the right of any individual to private property. This is a theme which must run through our thinking on all social and economic measures if we are to avoid a catastrophe both in our national economy and in the stable international economy which we hope to achieve." JOHN L. YANCEY.

To us on the editorial staff of Work, Mr. Yancey's views sounded pretty good. But a few days later the Daily News printed several letters in which Yancey was denounced as a Communist. The Red-baiting letters did not surprise us; anyone who puts human rights before property rights will invariably be called a Socialist or a Communist, as were Pope Leo XIII, Monsignor John A. Ryan, and others.

Then came the following letter in the May 19 edition of the Daily News: "I would like to correct an error of interpretation which has prompted a number of recent letters to the Views of Many Topics. A certain John L. Yancey is parading as a humanitarian. This stripe of 'radical' who hides his Trotskyite views behind revolutionary phrases is unfortunately not uncommon in the labor movement. The Trotskyites are opposed to our war effort and attack national unity. Mr. Yancey is affiliated with the Catholic Labor Alliance which publishes the paper 'Work' in Chicago. It is clear that he is no Communist and that his influence among trade unionists of the Catholic faith is, to say the least, negligible. The Communists in and out of the trade unions are working for the war effort, for national unity, for united nations solidarity. As a Communist, I ought to know." Chicago, OTTO WANGERIN.

Mr. Wangerin, who is a well-known Communist among railroad workers, is probably an authority on the activities of Communists, but nowhere in his letter does he offer one piece of evidence to support his wild charges against John L. Yancey. The explanation is easy: Mr. Wangerin offers no proof because no proof is possible. Nobody, not even Earl Browder [head of the U.S. Communist Party], can prove something which is not true.

5 ❦ Ed Marciniak

> The membership of the Catholic Labor Alliance is made up of Catholics, Jews, and Protestants, and its constitution bars Trotskyites from membership.
>
> Please note, Mr. Wangerin, that the only thing as bad as Red-baiting is Trotskyite-baiting.[19]

Whether through the pages of *Work* or in any other aspect of Ed Marciniak's activism, another hallmark of it, in addition to worker justice, gender equity, and racial equality, is religious ecumenism. In announcing CLA's policy of a membership open to Catholics, Protestants, and Jews, Marciniak cited the declaration of Pope Pius XI that he sought "collaboration with people of good will" in applying the principles of the labor encyclicals.[20]

An early postwar instance of ecumenical cooperation for social justice was the *Catholic, Jewish and Protestant Declaration on Economic Justice* signed in October 1946 by more than a hundred representatives of these religious persuasions. Among Catholic signers were Marciniak, Cort, Weber, and Fathers Hayes, McGowan, Monaghan, Hillenbrand, Higgins, Jerome Drolet, Donnelly, and Clancy, all social actionists already mentioned in this volume.

"[E]very phase of man's economic life is subject to the sovereignty of God and to the moral precepts which have their origin in God," the Declaration begins. The resources of the universe, it goes on, "are given in trust to man to be administered for the welfare of all and not for the exclusive benefit of the few. If follows, therefore, that the right to private property is limited by moral obligations and is subject to social restrictions for the common good" and that "the aim of economic life should be the widest possible diffusion of productive and consumptive property among the great masses of the people."[21]

Marciniak and other Chicago social actionists took an active part in several ecumenical efforts. These included the local branch of the National Religion and Labor Foundation, which worked for church/labor cooperation in a dozen cities; the James Mullenbach Industrial Institute, a Congregational labor school; and a CIO committee on relations with churches. Marciniak worked especially closely with Frank McCulloch, the Mullenbach Institute's director from 1940-46, head

---

19   Ibid.
20   Marciniak, "Memorandum on the Day of Action," 1947. [LUC]
21   "Catholic, Jewish and Protestant Declaration on Economic Justice," Oct. 16, 1946. [PR]

of Roosevelt University's Labor Education Division from 1946-49, and later a member of the National Labor Relations Board.

The ecumenical cooperation which took place around the issue of worker justice was concrete and effective. Father John LaFarge, SJ, a foremost leader in such cooperation, observed in 1953 that "Catholic social action, in its different manifestations, has made perhaps the most marked impression upon the non-Catholic world of any form of Catholic activity during the last few years, chiefly because it grappled with problems in which non-Catholics were already deeply interested."[22] Perceptive commentators in the two other major religious persuasions agreed.

Bpatist clergyman Stanley Stuber, in his *Primer on Roman Catholicism for Protestants* (1954), said "If anyone is inclined to feel that the Roman Catholic Church is reactionary, he should examine its position in regard to social and economic matters. It has pioneered in labor relations, both in principle and practice, for over half a century."[23]

In "A Jew Looks at Catholics," in the May 1953 *Commonweal*, Will Herberg notes "In an age disillusioned with the claims and pretensions of both individualism and collectivism, Catholicism is recognized as the long-time advocate of a 'third way', a society built on Christian responsibility, the society defined in the papal encyclicals and the 'social teachings' of the Church."[24]

Unfortunately, by the mid-1950s much of the social action and labor activism of every religious persuasion was "running on fumes," for a wide variety of converging reasons. The precipitating event was passage of Taft-Hartley, which, as labor historian Herbert Harris wrote in August 1947, "establishes a labor czar who can virtually dictate the size of pay envelopes."

Typically, a labor leader came out of World War II, Harris added, hoping "that the progress achieved in recent years in industrial relations was giving him and his adherents the rank of first-class citizens of industry" and "that the scope for joint management-union solutions of factory-floor problems would be enlarged." Instead, Taft-Hartley confronted the labor leader with "an attempt to segregate him and 15

---

22   Marciniak, "Catholics and Social Reform," *Commonweal*, Sept. 11, 1953, 558.
23   *Ibid.*
24   Herberg, Will, "A Jew Looks at Catholics," *Commonweal*, May 22, 1953, 174.

million other unionists from the rest of American society, and compel them to operate within an economic set-up that is a diluted but perilous imitation of the totalitarian."[25]

Even after the American labor movement expelled 11 Communist-dominated unions from the CIO by late 1950, following years of gut-wrenching struggles within these unions, the labor movement couldn't gain its rightful place in the economy. That expulsion was followed by a wave of extreme anti-Communism, with Senator Joseph McCarthy riding its crest. (The expulsion and the postwar anti-Communism are explored in the next chapter.) Factor into the equation Pope Pius XII's pro-business papacy, the military-industrial complex, the Eisenhower Administration, and a society characterized by affluence, complacency, and uniformity (characteristics sharply etched in Herberg's 1955 book *Protestant, Catholic, Jew*), and you're on the road to understanding Catholic social action's mid-1950s collapse.

The collapse was gradual and shrouded in denial. As willing as some of the movement's leaders were to tunnel under obstacles or to work around them, by and large they were a devout and dutiful bunch, and it was hard for them to believe the decreasing receptiveness to their message among both their superiors and the Church faithful, including many Catholic employers. The activists' search for a supportive papal quote was easy before Pius XI died in 1939, but thereafter became something of a "needle in a haystack" pursuit.

After World War II the signs of decline increased and accelerated. The encyclical-based Industry Council concept gained labor a semblance of equality in New Deal legislation and in wartime labor-management maneuvering. In the postwar period, however, the concept was often used defensively by the CIO and Catholic social action in the face of corporate interests' unwillingness to share power.

In addition, the concept became, for many conservative Church and business leaders, a vehicle for making the Catholic social-action movement more conservative. They pointed to instances of labor-management cooperation in the movement (such as in labor schools) as reflecting an American labor-management relationship characterized predominantly by partnership, not as examples of how labor and management could relate in American society if true partnership really did predominate. Movement activists increasingly refused to take

---

25 Harris, Herbert, "What Taft Taught Labor," *New Republic*, Aug. 18, 1947, 21.

part in a shift which pretended labor-management equality when little of it existed in the workforce.

A shift in the identity of a movement's foes is a sure sign of change, as when Marciniak, Cantwell, and many other Catholic social actionists started seeing secularism as a greater enemy to their movement than the rugged, or selfish, individualism still dominating American capitalism. Marciniak defined secularism as "the opinion that religion should be kept locked in the tabernacle."[26] This had been American Catholicism's traditional viewpoint, and in the 1950s he saw it returning after an all-too-brief hiatus in the late 1930s and early 1940s.

A significant part in this return was played by Protestant author Paul Blanshard, who in *American Freedom and Catholic Power* (1949) took the Catholic Church to task for stepping outside of what he asserted was its only proper sphere—"devotional life." Reviewers of all faiths objected vigorously that in making that assertion, Blanshard placed himself, in Marciniak's words, "not only at war with the Catholic Church but with every Protestant and Jewish person who tries to put his religious principles into practice at the office, in politics, or among his neighbors."[27]

Blanshard and his works heightened defensiveness among some Catholics and diverted attention and energies from Catholic and interfaith social action, at a time when it had proved its value in strengthening American labor, and when labor showed signs of renewed weakness. What labor needed more than anything else, according to Will Herberg in 1950, was "a labor conscience—or, as it has sometimes been called, a labor public opinion." Its lack was, Herberg added, "the basic problem of American trade unionism, and is closely linked with its lack of a philosophy or long-range perspective."

Herberg, with both a labor and social-action background—he was an educator for the International Ladies' Garment Workers Union—then noted that ACTU, praiseworthy as it was, faced "bitter opposition" from Catholic labor leaders; that Protestants and Jews in the labor movement hardly ever related labor to their religions; and that socialism's service as such a conscience had, unfortunately, declined. "If labor is really to fulfill its vocation," Herberg concluded, "it must redeem itself, and be redeemed, from its intellectual narrowness and spiritual torpor. It must develop a philosophy and a civic morality that

26 Marciniak, "Blanshard, Again!," *Work*, June 1951, 2.
27 *Ibid.*

will enable it to use the power it possesses in a responsible and creative manner."[28]

The decline of many movements features an episode which shows why that decline is rapidly becoming a fall, and so it was with the Catholic social-action movement. As usual, Ed Marciniak was on the case, with "Why Catholic Businessmen Tangled with an Archbishop," in the August 1954 issue of *Work*. Two months previously, Marciniak reported, New Orleans Archbishop Joseph Rummel denounced a right-to-work bill before the Louisiana legislature as "a mockery of the Constitutional right to organize for the common good," prompting 66 local businessmen to take out a newspaper ad accusing Rummel of "injecting a non-existent moral issue" into a labor matter.

The episode, reporter Marciniak revealed, was the tip of the iceberg of a national movement among Catholic businessmen to organize against the social encyclicals and their applications, a movement buttressed by the book *Christianity and American Capitalism*, by University of Notre Dame professor Edward Keller, CSC, whose mission, wrote Marciniak, "was to explain to businessmen that the Church's social teaching is not as radical as it sounds." The *Work* article concluded with an observation from the editor of *The Catholic Transcript*, Hartford, Connecticut: "Rummel's action serves to inform similarly-minded Catholics anywhere that they are wrong in maintaining that it is out of order for a bishop to declare a social and economic measure to be morally unacceptable."[29]

At the time of this episode, Ed Marciniak was well aware that those "similarly-minded Catholics" were playing a large role in Catholic social action's impending demise. He explored with John Cort and others the idea of a new national organization (decline proved to be too far along for such a step), and in Chicago CLA broadened its focus by creating groups for more vocations and by changing CLA's name to the Catholic Council on Working Life and *Work*'s name to *New City*. Little revitalization resulted.

Simultaneously, however, Marciniak became more politically active, and this was a move of greater promise. In "Catholics and Social Reform," a September 1953 article in *Commonweal*, he spoke of performing "tasks of economic, political, and international reconstruction"

---

28 "Notable Remarks," *Social Action Notes*, SAD, 1950, 12.
29 Marciniak, "Why Catholic Businessmen Tangled with an Archbishop," *Work*, Aug. 1954, 1.

with "the unstinting cooperation of Protestants, Jews, and Catholics."[30] Also, in a letter somewhat earlier to business columnist Robert Vanderpoel of *The Chicago Sun-Times*, Marciniak asserted that "measures like compulsory arbitration and the Taft-Hartley law ... sharpen class consciousness on the political level, by shifting some of the economic warfare from the economic battleground to the political one."[31]

This was a difficult transition for Marciniak. Ed Willock, another activist who got his start in the Catholic Worker movement, acknowledged in an October 1953 issue of *Commonweal* that the movement displayed "a certain ineffectuality in social areas where organized cooperation is of the essence." He included politics as one such area.[32]

Marciniak made the transition, however, and made it successfully. He was always active in the American Newspaper Guild, but in 1953 became an international vice-president. In 1960, Chicago Mayor Richard J. Daley appointed him director of the city's Commission on Human Relations, a position he held until 1967. In 1977 he helped found the National Center for the Laity, which proclaimed in its charter that "the church is present to the world in the striving of the laity to transform the world of political, economic, and social institutions."[33]

Had "Mr. Outside" suddenly become "Mr. Inside"? "I think I'm just the same guy playing a different role," Marciniak said after his 1960 appointment. "It's in the nature of the political process that you engage in a sort of give-and-take to get things done. But let me emphasize that this way you <u>do</u> get things done."[34]

Many members in the closing phases of the Catholic social-action movement—both members able to stay active in the movement and those pursuing related paths—shifted their energies to the political arena. Many of them, for example, could name you the 16 "right to work" states through 1955 (Alabama, Arizona, Arkansas, Florida, Georgia, Iowa, Mississippi, Nebraska, Nevada, North Carolina, North Dakota, South Carolina, South Dakota, Tennessee, Virginia, and Utah) and could describe the efforts to prevent states from being

---

30   Marciniak, "Catholics and Social Reform," *op. cit.*
31   Marciniak to Robert Vanderpoel, Aug. 26, 1952. [LUC]
32   Willock, Edward, "Catholic Radicalism," *Commonweal*, Oct. 2, 1953, 633.
33   *Chicago Declaration of Christian Concern*, National Center for Laity, 1977.
34   Cook, Bruce, "Outsider on the Inside," *Chicago*, Jan. 20, 1965.

added to that group. (The states added since are Kansas, 1958; Wyoming, 1963; Louisiana, 1976; Idaho, 1986; Texas, 1993; and Oklahoma, 2001.) Those activists' efforts inspire today's activists to repeal, or roll way back, the Taft-Hartley Act—one of the worst pieces of legislation ever enacted in the United States.

Why "one of the worst"? Because it creates and sustains the "open shop," an anti-worker entity if there ever was one. And why "anti-worker"? Ed Marciniak, writer, editor, and Catholic social actionist extraordinaire, answered that question definitively by devoting his editorial space in the July 1946 issue of *Work* to a master of American political humor.[35]

> **On the Open Shop: Mr. Dooley Expounds to Mr. Hennessey**
>
> "What is the open shop?"
>
> "Sure, 'tis a shop where they keep the door open to accommodate the constant stream of men comin' in t'take jobs cheaper thin the min that has the jobs. 'Tis like this, Mr. Hennessey, suppose one of these free-barn American citizens is wurkin' in an open shop for the princely wages of one large dollar a day for tin hours. Along comes another free-barn American citizen an he sez to the boss, 'I think I could handle the job for ninety cents.'
>
> "'Sure,' sez the boss, an' the one dollar man gets the merry jinglin' can, and goes out into the crool world t'exercize his inalienable rights as a free-barn citizen and scab on some other poor devil. And so it goes. And who gets the benefits? Thrue, it saves the boss money, but he don't care no more for money than he does for his roight eye. It's all principles wid him. He hates t'see min robbed of their independence, regardless of anything else."
>
> "But," said Hennessey, "these open shop min ye minshun say they are fer the unions, if properly conducted."
>
> "Shure," said Mr. Dooley, "if properly conducted. An' there ye are. And how wud they have thim conducted? No strikes, no rules, no conthracts, no scales, hardly iny wages, an' damn few members...."
>
> Finley Peter Dunne
> American political humorist, 1897–1936

---

35 Dunne, Finley Peter, "On the Open Shop," *Work*, July 1946, 5.

Social Action Vignette
DENNIS COMEY: "HONEST & EARNEST & FAIR"

Dennis Comey grew up in downtown Philadelphia, two blocks away from St. Joseph's College Preparatory School, where he graduated in 1914. His parents, Dennis and Catherine, Irish immigrants, represented both labor and management, son Dennis often remarked, since his dad was a locomotive fitter and his mom managed the household.

Linking labor and management was the dominant note of Comey's illustrious career as a Jesuit priest. In 1943, with a decade as a teacher and high school president behind him, Father Comey returned to St. Joe's Prep to teach and to serve as director of the labor school Father Richard McKeon, SJ, established at the prep school seven years earlier as St. Joseph's College School of Social Service. As director, Comey emphasized (like Father Gavin in Boston) that the key part of labor-management relations was the hyphen, because it joined the two sides.

Under Comey, the school, renamed St. Joseph's College Institute of Industrial Relations, became a model for labor schools which taught labor and management representatives together. It worked because Comey insisted upon a total commitment to "honest and earnest and fair" collective bargaining, and because he was honest and earnest and fair himself. These traits made him a vital force especially on Philadelphia's rough waterfront—as did his tallness, ruggedness, and direct gaze.

So effective was Father Comey on the docks that the shipping companies and longshoremens' union agreed on his becoming their binding arbitrator, a position he held from 1951-8. He had reservations about it, since, in his words, "I am not too keen on arbitration as a substitute for good bargaining." However, he made the position work.

In 1963, the Institute moved to St. Joseph's College (now University) and is still, as the Dennis Comey IIR, a crucial part of its curriculum. Comey retired in 1981 and died in 1987, at age 91. The one-time spinning-mill worker was buried, at his request, with his work-boots on.

CHAPTER SIX
THOMAS DARBY (1907–1992)

The decisions were made. The teachers were ready. Pastors announced the opening date at the Masses on the Sunday previous. Parish societies and trade union halls heard the idea from priest speakers. The religious and secular papers gave it space. Under the sponsorship of the Association of Catholic Trade Unionists (ACTU), a laity organization recently founded, the Labor School was launched. The first session was held on the first Thursday in October 1938. Over 100 trade unionists and their friends were present. Monsignor Francis W. Walsh, P.A., then President of the College of New Rochelle, presided. The opening address was given by Father (later Monsignor) John P. Boland, the Chairman of the N.Y. State Labor Relations Board. Thus was very auspiciously launched, to the high credit of the Ursuline nuns, the only Labor School in an American women's college.[1]

---

1 Darby, Thomas, *Thirteen Years in a Labor School*, St. Paul: Radio Replies Press, 1953, 6.

So wrote Father Thomas Darby in *Thirteen Years in a Labor School*, one of the few published memoirs of a Catholic labor school teacher/administrator. It gives us a close-up look at a labor school's inner workings.

New Rochelle Labor School's first year, Darby recalled, though full of ups and downs, ended with largely positive results. They proved to school director Joseph Moody and assistant director Darby the effectiveness of the type of adult education they pioneered. The results were especially gratifying to Darby and Moody, both instructors at the College, in light of their recollections of sitting for hours "on the outer rocks of an island in Long Island Sound" making plans for the school's first term.

The school started with 102 students, men and women, unionists and non-unionists. The 75 unionists, some officers and some rank-and-filers, represented 19 unions and were a diverse lot, including members of the International Brotherhood of Teamsters-AFL who had already joined together in Yonkers to oust racketeers in their midst; clerical utility workers seeking recognition of their union, some of the earliest U.S. white-collar employees to do so; and unionists in a wide variety of other trades looking for ways to increase their wages and improve their working conditions.

To Darby, one of the labor's school's greatest achievements was enabling experienced unionists to mingle and chat with less-experienced unionists and with non-unionists, thus creating a channel of practical advice on the benefits of joining a union and of keeping a union strong. Darby highlighted other achievements as well.

> One of the several interesting achievements of that first year proved the wisdom of not restricting the attendance to trade unionists. A comparatively young Catholic businessman quietly presented himself for each session. He never said a word nor offered a proposal but obviously was enjoying every moment. When the school closed for the Christmas recess and everyone was extending the Season's Greetings to the Director and teachers, he added in his words to Father Moody: "Keep up the fine work, Father. You'll never realize all the good you are doing." Later on, one of the teachers suggested that the remark, while excellent in itself, might also have a valuable cryptic meaning. It was decided that the Director should ask, in January, the gentleman from the business world whether he would care to elaborate on his encouraging words.
>
> After the first class of the new term, Moody drew the businessman aside and told him the reaction to his remark. His response was enlight-

ening: "I'm the Auditor of a national organization with plants in several cities, including New York and Philadelphia," said the executive. "While I was making up a very important report for our Board of Directors, I could not keep out of my mind one remark that was made in the Labor School class on 'The Just Wage.' Our firm employs many women, mostly young, as machine and assembly line operators. In the class discussion, it was brought out that if a business can afford to pay a just minimum wage and does not, then someone else, usually the family, must help the worker to meet the minimum expenses of keeping alive. It is at least possible in such cases that corporation officials and investors are expecting such families to subsidize them free, <u>gratis</u>, and for nothing when they will not pay young women enough to live on, though they must do a fair day's work. Now I knew that in our plants there is a small chance for not doing a full day's work. I also knew from that class discussion what the N.Y. State Department of Labor estimate was for a just minimum wage for a working young woman, either living at home or by herself. I knew, too, that our firm was far under that figure. What to do?

"Our board of directors has some high caliber members, but they are not the type that would tolerate direct advice from an auditor. I had to use some diplomacy. Before the meeting I spoke to a few of the important members and tried to unfold the problem in such a way that they might feel that they were doing the original thinking themselves. To make a long story short, I think I succeeded. Some 3,000 people as a result will be nearer a just minimum in all our plants."[2]

This example shows the advantages to a labor school not only of welcoming non-unionist students but also of exploring the pre-World War II era's widening horizons for women workers and students—and not just women labor-school-students, but women students attending the College of New Rochelle. They were encouraged to register for the labor school and each year a half-dozen or more did so—including Helen Haye, John Cort's future wife. In addition, the labor school attracted and mentored a large number of women telephone workers.

The first, Margaret Feldhaus, never thought she would have the courage to bargain with her superiors, and yet ended by achieving election as a union official and becoming a very capable negotiator. The second, Marie Bosch, was the first woman to be elected an officer in her union and developed a technique that won her the highest respect of management. In class she would carefully underline all pertinent passages in the encyclicals of Pius XI, keep the marked copy in her handbag, and then, dur-

---

2   Ibid., 8-10.

ing negotiations and discussions, produce her copy when Catholic executives advocated positions contrary to their own principles. The method was so effective that management finally offered her an executive rating. Marie accepted, a step no member of the Labor School would quarrel with her taking as long as she remains faithful to her own principles.[3]

Few worthwhile ventures are easy, and New Rochelle Labor School was no different. Father Darby outlined several challenges and how the school responded: 1) The Communist Party's Tom Paine Labor School in New Rochelle characterized its Catholic counterpart as mere opportunism yet boosted publicity for the CP school; New Rochelle Labor School simply kept up its steady support of sound unionism. 2) Westchester County residents who refused to believe that "Catholic" and "labor school" could be part of the same phrase discouraged interest in the school; staff and students increased their outreach to the community. 3) Some residents turned critics after a visit or two and made such allegations as that the school taught workers their rights but not their responsibilities; Darby pointed out to these critics that supporting the rights of workers gained their understanding and that no school year ended "without an extended treatment of labor's responsibilities." And 4) A serious problem arose with the AFL, as Father Darby explains:

> At the very start of the second year there was a noticeable decline in registration. In attempting to uncover the cause, the teachers learned that human apathy was not the only factor. Some of the decline originated partly in a whispering campaign in all the ranks of the A.F. of L. That year, at the annual convention of the N.Y. State Federation of Labor, word somehow flitted around that Catholic Labor Schools were to be blackballed. It seemed, said the rumor, that such schools, at their best, would divide the American labor movement along religious lines and, at their worst, would lead by design to the formation of separate Catholic unions. It took about five years to lay this canard to rest. Only when several Labor School directors carefully explained to him [Frank Fenton of the A.F. of L.'s national office] just what the encyclicals taught about how Catholic workers in non-Catholic countries should organize, about the validity of neutral or secular unions (the type in the United States) and the situation in other countries, did he begin to see that the position of many in the A.F. of L. was unjustified....
>
> There was another cause for the reluctance of A.F. of L. members to attend the New Rochelle School. In these years, many Catholic Labor

---

3   Ibid., 19-20.

> Schools were designated "pro CIO" and the peculiar circumstances of the time lent some color of truth to the label. These were still the days when the original organizing drive of the CIO retained its enthusiastic spirit with the result that more "students" appeared at the various schools with interest in and inquiries about the CIO. Since the A.F. of L., by and large, had no provision for these workers, mostly unskilled, the Catholic labor schools assisted them into the CIO, always at the same time, endeavoring to save them from any Communist domination that might exist in particular CIO locals. Thus the lot of many "low-paid" working people decidedly improved. Time eventually cleared the New Rochelle Labor School of the accidental accusation of biased favor to the CIO.[4]

"The best and most important achievements of the labor school," Father Darby asserted, "were non-material, in the realm of ideas and philosophy, in the mind and heart and soul. Clear thinking in the social question was beginning to appear."[5] Darby made this assertion at the end of New Rochelle Labor School's first year of existence, but its truth was not confined to that time period.

> Despite difficulties and [lower] numbers, the Labor School began a second year whose results were proportionately as good as those of the year before. A non-Catholic machinist born in Scotland read about the school in his Mt. Vernon [N.Y.] newspaper and brought his Catholic fellow workers. Jim Lyon had served his apprenticeship in a trade union atmosphere and when he came to this country wondered why so many shops were unorganized. When the decent though paternalistic management of the plant in which he worked began to change to that of the driving efficiency kind, he recalled the value of union organization and persuaded his co-workers to see what the Labor School had to offer. None of them wanted the Communist or racketeering brand of unionism and the School was able over the years, with legal and practical advice, to coach the men in establishing a bona fide trade union. The first constitution, modest in its objectives, was written in a New Rochelle Labor School classroom and has been gradually strengthened each year at the school. All the other necessary details have been successfully handled as occasion arose so that the machinists involved never cease from expressing their gratitude.[6]

---

4   Ibid., 16-7.
5   Ibid., 10.
6   Ibid., 19.

Margaret Feldhaus, Marie Bosch, and Jim Lyon were typical of the rank-and-file unionists whom the school helped motivate to become more active as members of their locals. Such unionists played key roles in the adjustments which World War II and its aftermath required of both the labor schools and the entire labor movement. For Darby, the war meant not only replacing Father Moody as school director after Moody was called to service as a Navy chaplain, but also facing new challenges for the school.

Darby remembered one night in February 1943 when, because of a black-out required by wartime regulations, a class had to be held in a basement room. Only six students attended the class because gas rationing, the dislocations of work schedules and locations, and many students or potential students going into the military, had substantially decreased the number of registrants. "While the main objective of the school, to promote industrial peace, was never overshadowed," recalled Darby, "special meetings were held on the topics of wage-freezing, labor hoarding, voluntary arbitration, labor-management committees, War Labor Board regulations, and postwar problems. In this last category, the school can claim it was ahead of its time because it explored the problems of returned veterans and housing long before such matters became major issues." Darby gave an example:

> In at least one instance, the happy spirit of give and take between teacher and student gave birth to an idea that proved a decided boon to two unions and many returned soldiers. The teacher of Public Speaking and Parliamentary Procedure during the war years was Mr. William C. McGill, then head of the Bronx Home News chapel [unit] of the Printers' Union and one of the many members of the "Big Six" typographical union who have been trying sensibly to meet the problem of new technological inventions without injuring either progress or workers. In class one evening with the discussion subject on the post-war world, Jim Lyon, who had served with the British Forces in the Middle East during the first World War, described the system that his amalgamated union devised for British veterans. So sound and fair did it seem, that Bill McGill proposed it to the New York local of the printers. The "typos" not only adopted the suggestion with suitable modifications, but also placed McGill in charge of that entire important committee....
>
> The story of this achievement reached the ears of Michael Papalardo through the director of a Labor School in New York City [Phil Carey] with the result that Papalardo's union, a local of the United Association of Journeymen Plumbers, also adopted the plan. So successful was

the procedure that a positive and constructive group in the local rallied around Mike and eventually, in 1951, elected him delegate.[7]

The school welcomed several other important innovations in the postwar period. A course on economics was established because of its increasing importance in the workplace. John Fenton, a U.S. Conciliation Service commissioner and a brother of AFL's Frank Fenton, introduced the school to a "grievance clinic," whereby six students from labor and six students from business, under the guidance of an expert leader for each team, studied and negotiated for the "other" side (the labor students for management and vice versa) of a real-life grievance issue; the grievance had to be settled, the settlement was compared with a real-life settlement, and non-participating students discussed the results. And one class night each week was set aside to hear from officials of member unions of the Westchester County Federation of Labor, a feature established through John Acropolis, Federation president.[8] Among those officials were Louis Rieff of the Ladies Garment Workers, Jim Bowe of the Electrical Workers (CIO), George Grimm, Jr. of the Plumbers, Mike Nugent of the Moving Picture Operators (returning to the school where he had been a student), and Gareth Fitzgerald of the Bricklayers; each speaker gave a history of his union and explained its objectives and procedures.

Another of the many New Rochelle Labor School students who went from excellence at the school's lessons to excellence in a union local, was Henry Sturmer. Darby told his story:

> Sturmer, a very active member of the International Brotherhood of Electrical Workers (IBEW-A.F. of L.) and a non-Catholic, had for years urged his local union to widen its educational program for apprentices. When, after World War II, the influx of new applicants rightly increased, the union officials finally saw the wisdom of Henry's constant request. And they handed the whole proposition to him to work out in detail and reality. He was ready for this situation because, having heard about the New Rochelle Labor School and having been impressed by

---

7   Ibid., 21-2.
8   John Acropolis was President of Teamsters Local 456, a union he and a rank-and-file insurgency cleaned up after years of corruption. The insurgency was helped by ACTU lawyers John Harold and John Sheehan and by the New Rochelle Labor School. Acropolis was murdered in 1952 because, friends say, "he could not be bought." The case is still unsolved. See John Cort's *Dreadful Conversions*, 116-7.

the basic common sense of Catholic Social Doctrine and the School's presentation of it, he had the outlines of a course almost ready. When he was finally presented with the task, he sat down with the teachers at the Labor School and hammered out the final form for his apprentices....

During this time, Henry, chatting with his barber one afternoon while taking a haircut, mentioned what he was doing. The barber, a Catholic active in his own parish Holy Name Society, determined that his fellow parishioners ought to learn about the Labor School and Catholic social teaching. The barber spoke to his parish priest, the pastor agreed, and Henry asked the Director of the School to check his speech. Hence, one fine Sunday morning at a Holy Name Communion Breakfast in White Plains, Henry Sturmer, a non-Catholic, in rather classic language, told a group of Catholic men, most of them hearing it for the first time, about the grand Social Doctrine of their own Faith. Further, at his own expense, he handed every man a Paulist Press pamphlet explaining the correct relationship of a Catholic to whatever union he might belong.[9]

With postwar also came increased registration and a drive to attract and assist other workers. It reached out, for example, to white-collar workers, both those employed in the County and those who commuted to New York. This outreach failed because clerical workers in offices and department stores, in Darby's words, "had not yet awakened to the most effective practical means for bettering their conditions, though they continue to grumble on their jobs, in their homes, in local pubs, and over the bridge table."[10] The drive triumphed in another area, however.

The night of February 28, 1946 was snowy, blustery, freezing, and, because of previous bad weather, still quite slushy underfoot. The Labor School classes were in session and a small group was quietly chatting around the table of pamphlets and books in the warm corridor. The peculiar sound that accompanied the opening of the large door on a windy night and the stamping of snow-covered feet indicated the arrival of a late-comer. The late-comer proved to be a new-comer, a short, sturdy fellow on the youngish-looking side, with a very straightforward approach.

"Is this the New Rochelle Labor School?" were his first words. When assured that it was and after the Director of the Labor School was pointed out, he said: "I'm John Page, member of the Executive Board of Local 453, UE [United Electrical Workers-CIO], and I work at the

---

9   Darby, *op. cit.*, 24-5.
10 *Ibid.*, 27.

Otis Elevator plant in Yonkers. I'm looking for help and I think I can get it here."

He then told how the Otis Elevator shops had to be and were organized by UE. Only after organization had been well-established did some of the union members begin to realize that their local had been gradually "captured" by the Communists. The usual story had been repeated here: most of the 1,700 members, after the union had produced satisfactory results, did not attend meetings or did not sit them out, while a small group (how small he could not tell) little by little achieved control. As a matter of fact, this condition was only clear after a multitude of instances of Communist propaganda and CP techniques like the never-ending proposals of resolutions favorable to Russian policy. And it was clear only to a few, who, fortunately, recognized their duty in the situation. These had wisely banded together, met secretly in their homes, and effectively in the American democratic way acquired a few seats on the union Executive Board. The more they progressed in their attempt to break Commie control, the more they realized that they needed training and advice.

Page then said: "I'm not a Catholic, Father, but most of the fellows are. Some of them saw the way you and Father [John] Byrne and Father [Joseph] Hammond pulled the rug out from under Harry Sacher, the Commie lawyer, at the UAW strike rally in Tarrytown that Sunday in December and when they found out about the Labor School, delegated me to ask you if we could come over here for some special coaching."

"How many are you?"

"Oh, we could get 15 to 20 here every Thursday. Maybe more."

"Well, John, if you can get that many together, I think we could find some place in Yonkers, perhaps a school or parish hall, to set up a special Labor School with your own special staff. It would be easier to have three teachers go to Yonkers than to have 25 men come over here. Especially in this weather. Besides, the teachers could concentrate on your own problem while giving you more general information."

"Father, that gives me an idea. If you can get us a set of teachers, what would be wrong with setting the School up right in the union hall and throwing it open to the membership?"

"There wouldn't be anything wrong with it, but it would mean some difficulty and a little delay. We couldn't and wouldn't go in there without an invitation, a very official letter invitation post-marked from the local itself. The School here, each year, has been involved in any number of industrial or trade union difficulties. Always an invitation was in some way extended so that the charge "intrusion by outsiders" (a charge often made, by the way) has never been and never can be substantiated.

'Outsider' the school was, but someone with a right to do so, perhaps an employer, perhaps a union official or a union faction, or especially a rank-and-file committee, sent the invitation."

"Well, that fits in with my idea. I'd like to bring the proposition up and battle it through the Executive Board and then bring it to the membership. More would learn that way."

"That's fine, John, if you can do it. But don't risk it yet unless you can win."

"I think we can win. I don't see how the CP's can oppose the idea of education for the membership."

"Don't worry, they won't oppose it. They'll try to appropriate it or twist it to their own uses. Here you will run up against one of the fine points of CP strategy. Never oppose someone else's basically sound idea. Education for the members is a sound idea. They will probably try to use it for their own purposes. Do you think you can meet that situation?"

"I think so, Father. I'll get our boys together and start the ball moving. Is that all right with you?"

"Of course it is. I'll get a staff together and we'll be ready when we hear from you."

"Here's another idea, Father. See what you think of it. You write a letter to the 453 Executive Board. You can say I told you. Offer to form a school for the members. I'm on the Board and will be watching for the letter. It will save some time and they'll have to answer. It will also take them by surprise and give us right-wingers [union 'left-wingers' are Communists, 'right-wingers' are nearly everyone else, from Actists to socialists] a good talking point and a good issue. What do you think, Father?"

"It looks good to me. But, John, be prepared for that 'outsider' argument. Remind them that if such 'outsiders' as lawyers, mediators, arbitrators, labor relations experts, and public figures can be invited to help unions, certainly the Labor School teachers could rightly receive an invitation without being regarded as 'intruders.'"

"OK, Father, you'll send the letter then?"[11]

The letter went out March 1, Father Darby further recalled, and the meeting was held in an upper Manhattan apartment on March 3. Thus began what Darby described as "the most important and interesting of the many problems met by the school." Its response proved, he added, "how wide an influence a labor school can wield and how patriotic a

---

11 Ibid., 29-32.

service it can render. Through it New Rochelle Labor School aided the country as well as the county."¹²

On March 13 the mail brought an invitation to the Director to appear at a meeting of the Executive Board of Local 453 and describe whatever courses the Labor School had to offer.... On Friday evening, March 15, the Director ... arrived at the union hall. Already present were representatives of the CP Jefferson School in New York, the CP Tom Paine School in New Rochelle, the CP Booker T. Washington School in Harlem, and perhaps for respectability's sake, Sarah Lawrence College.... Each of these told, in a rather vague way, what could be done to educate the local's members, and fortunately all the others mentioned that it would cost money. The New Rochelle Labor School offered three specific courses: Industrial Ethics, Public Speaking, and Parliamentary Law. When each course was explained in detail and when it was mentioned there would be no tuition or fees because the teachers wished in this way to make their contribution to the solution of the social problem, the meeting was thrown open for discussion.

The consensus of the Executive Board members seemed decidedly in favor of the idea of learning Parliamentary Procedure and of having free courses (the 453 treasury was low). The consensus was not achieved easily, however, since the CP leaders, in the question period, charged the New Rochelle School with being _only_ anti-Communist, and not having done anything constructive for labor. The work of the school for Yonkers alone was then cited. When the members of 453 heard what had been done without cost for their own Yonkers neighbors, the teamsters and textile workers and moving-picture operators, their favorable opinion was evident.... John Page later reported that, although a great gain had been made, the battle for the School had only begun. The Executive Board had yet to vote directly and decisively on the School....

The CP's in Local 453 displayed intense determination to block the approval of a membership school connected in any way with ACTU. They first argued for close ties with the Sarah Lawrence College efforts and finally stood firm for UE District 4 classes at the Palisades Avenue CIO Headquarters in Yonkers. The 453 Executive Board referred the school question to the membership with the result that the CP's staged a typical filibuster at the next local meeting in mid-April. No decision resulted but actually the filibuster itself was the cause of their defeat. Word spread around the Otis shops and the next meeting had standing room only.

---

12   Ibid., 32.

> After a long and heated session, with everyone staying to the final motion to adjourn at 12:55 a.m., a vote was taken which the right-wingers won by 6-1. The school was in. On May 25, the Director of the New Rochelle Labor School received an official invitation from the Secretary of UE Local 453 to start classes in the local union hall at 8:00 P.M. on Wednesday, May 29, 1946.
>
> The classes began on schedule.... After three weeks, it was democratically decided to recess, because of vacations, until the fall. In September, the classes were resumed and continued regularly through 1946 to June 1947....
>
> Through the slow educative efforts of the 453 school, the membership, fortified with a knowledge of right principles and an acquaintance with sound, legitimate trade union tactics, finally ousted the controlling CP's and chose a completely rightwing, pro-American slate of officers in the next regular Local election.[13]

The struggle between Catholics and Communists has a long history in America. From the mid-19th century onward, the great majority of American Catholics opposed revolutionary Marxism (first revolutionary socialism and later Communism), but differed as to how best to do so. Most Catholic social actionists emphasized fighting for social justice and thus eradicating the ills which bred Communism, while a small grouping emphasized fighting Communism regardless of what effect their battles had on social-justice objectives. Worker justice and sound unionism were obviously in the forefront of UE Local 453's struggles with the Communists in its ranks.

The more-negative brand of Catholic anti-Communism, however, rose sharply coming out of World War II, a trend given impetus by a January 1946 report entitled *The Problem of American Communism in 1945*. It was prepared for the National Catholic Welfare Conference's Administrative Committee—the American bishops meeting in executive session—by Father John Cronin, a professor at St. Mary's Seminary in Baltimore. As a labor school director/teacher, a noted speaker, and the author of economics texts for Catholic schools (including labor schools), he was active in Catholic social action locally and nationally.

The genesis and development of his report reveal much about Catholic anti-Communism, particularly its differing emphases within Catholic social action. On March 7, 1936, U.S. Apostolic Delegate

---

13 Ibid., 32-7.

(the pope's liaison with American Catholics) Amleto Cicognani informed NCWC Secretary Father John Burke of Pope Pius XI's "serious preoccupation" with "the communistic propaganda now spreading over the world," specifically with Communist attempts to recruit Catholic sailors and immigrants in American seaports. The letter was dated five days after such an attempt in San Pedro, California.[14]

Because of these attempts, Cicognani wrote, Pius XI wanted the American bishops to provide him with a full report on all Communist activities in the United States and on Catholic measures "to protect the faithful, especially the laboring classes, against the enticements and false mirages of communism in this present hour of crisis." The Pope was especially concerned about Communist efforts "to insinuate their doctrines among the ranks of Catholics, especially among the young, under the pretext of pursuing high humanitarian aims, for example, of protecting the working classes against the oppression of capitalism, elevating human dignity, promoting a more just distribution of wealth, etc."[15]

The papal encyclical *Divini Redemptoris*, also known as "On Atheistic Communism," appeared a year after this letter. At the end of 1937, NCWC published the pamphlet *Communism in the United States*, an abbreviated version of the report provided to Pius XI in answer to his request.

The American bishops had responded to it by directing NCWC to survey Communist activities in 53 dioceses. Part I of the two-part pamphlet summarized the survey's findings, excluding data from specific dioceses. Part II suggested steps dioceses could take to develop programs of social action and anti-Communism.[16]

The bishops' discussions about this initial report, and about subsequent agenda items regarding anti-Communism, bring to light a clear division among the bishops in terms of which approach to anti-Communism they favored. Generally, they favored the more-positive

---

14   The attempt involved Joseph Curran, a Catholic and East Coast sailor aboard the intercoastal liner *California*. He led shipmates in refusing to sail unless they got the higher wage of West Coast sailors. Curran's union, the ISU, said he was under CPUSA influence. He broke away to lead the NMU, which was Communist-dominated until Curran broke with the Party in the late 1940s.

15   Cicognani to Burke, Mar. 7, 1936. [CUA]

16   *Communism in the United States*, NCWC, 1937.

approach, in large part because of Archbishop Mooney's leadership. A vocal minority, however, favored the more-negative approach—including a few bishops skeptical of or indifferent to Catholic social action's value.

In the years following the initial report, the information-gathering network behind the report's findings took on a life of its own, as such things do in large bureaucracies. As it did, Father Cronin, backed by Archbishop Michael Curley (whose archdiocese included Baltimore and Washington, DC), became prominent in the information gathering.

Cronin's involvement is significant. For one thing, he spearheaded a wartime increase in the more-negative anti-Communist approach. Also, by World War II the Federal Bureau of Investigation (FBI) recruited him to serve as a conduit and coordinator between the Bureau and the labor and Catholic social-action movements—roles infrequently advertised to those affected by them.

Few people in the Catholic social-action movement applauded Cronin's extremist anti-Communism, many in the movement opposed it (at least privately), and many ignored it or went about their business. In October 1945, Cronin furnished a draft of *The Problem of American Communism in 1945* to economist Francis Haas, after 1943 Bishop of Grand Rapids.

Haas, one of the most eminently-respected figures in the movement, replied that "the whole Report does not, as it ought, breathe and demand social justice. If this judgment is valid, the Report as an outline of recommendations on Communism, fails, in my opinion, in one very fundamental respect."

Haas added that numerous details in the draft are "loose and even ambiguous in meaning." He forwarded a copy of his reply to Archbishop Mooney with the comment "I am sending it to you for what I hope will be more than your curiosity."[17]

Mooney finished his term as NCWC Episcopal Chairman at the end of 1945. On December 4, NCWC's Social Action Department informed the American bishops that the report was ready for distribution to them, but that a bishop must first indicate a desire for the document. That bishop must then agree not to quote from it, cite names mentioned, or give a copy to a layperson. Priests who were "edi-

---

17 Haas to Mooney, Oct. 9, 1945; attached is Haas to Cronin Oct. 8, replying to Cronin to Haas Sept. 29. [AD]

tors, teachers in labor schools, and the like" could see it, but only with approval of a priest's diocesan bishop.[18]

According to *The Premier See*, however, Thomas Spalding's history of the Baltimore Archdiocese, the report was leaked by several bishops to important Catholic laypeople in government and business.[19] Eventually it served as raw material for Congressman Richard Nixon, the House Un-American Activities Committee, and Senator Joseph McCarthy.

Even Paul Weber, definitely an anti-Communist hard-liner, took issue with Cronin's *Confidential Report on Communist Activities*, April 1943, saying it adopted "a rather dangerous procedure." Among the report's proposals was to have priests take the lead in organizing and mobilizing counter-minorities within unions, a clear example of clericalism.

"You will note," Weber commented, "that he [Cronin] proposes that the counter-minorities in each union should be started with interviews with parish working people, 'either by the priest or by zealous Holy Name, Knights of Columbus, or St. Vincent de Paul men.' I am afraid that if this were carried beyond the most elementary efforts to get Catholic people interested and active in their unions, it would inevitably be discovered and be used most strongly against us. I know, personally, I would be inclined to resent a visit by a 'zealous Knight of Columbus' questioning me about the affairs and leadership of the American Newspaper Guild."

Father Cronin also proposed, Weber added, that the priest "take charge of a given industry" in terms of anti-Communist activism, call meetings, "and then work out a plan to organize a plant against Communism." Observed Weber, "I am afraid that at about the second time such a meeting was held, it would become public property...."[20]

Cronin actually applied these methods in local unions in wartime Baltimore, with decidedly mixed results.[21] He taught the methods in

---

18 Cronin, John, "The Problem of Communism in 1945," SAD, Dec. 4, 1945. [CUA]

19 Spalding, Thomas, *The Premier See: A History of the Archdiocese of Baltimore, 1789-1989*, Baltimore: Johns Hopkins University Press, 1989, 387.

20 Weber, Paul, untitled memo on Cronin's *Confidential Report on Communist Activities, April 1943*. [Report at WSU, memo at CHS]

21 Cronin, "Communism in Baltimore" series, *Catholic Review*, Apr. 7, 14, 21, 28, 1944. Freeman, Joshua B., and Steve Rosswurm, "The Education

the Institute of Catholic Social Studies at Catholic University, a summer school he initiated in 1941 and operated for a decade thereafter—although it must be emphasized that the teaching of these methods was a small part in the overall curriculum of an institute which generally provided a quality educational experience to many Catholic social actionists.[22]

In October 1943, Father Cronin even set up and held an FBI-recorded meeting with two leading communists, Roy Hudson and Albert Lannon, inside the walls of St. Mary's Seminary. The meeting indicates the disturbing extent to which Cronin allowed his "handlers" to direct his activities.

Another indication was a November 1942 letter in which Cronin sought advice from Chicago's Father Hillenbrand. Cronin told Hillenbrand that he wanted to establish and publicize labor schools in the Baltimore area to recruit helpers for his wartime union activities there, but said "My advisors, with long experience in handling subversive groups, disagreed strongly with my proposal. They advocated the much harder method of discovering leaders through personal contacts and interviews, rounding up these selected men for unadvertised study, and a soft-pedaling of the ultimate purpose of our schools."[23]

At some point Cronin went so far in his anti-Communism that he lost sight of worker justice, and basically went over to the side of the rugged (selfish) individualists. He came out of World War II praising Friedrich Hayek's *The Road to Serfdom*, with its abandonment of the search for a middle way between capitalism and totalitarianism. Publication of Cronin's anti-Communist report in 1946 led to his being hired on a secret basis by the U.S. Chamber of Commerce to ghost-

---

of an Anti-Communist," *Labor History*, Spring 1992, 217-247. Cronin's series, with its rationale for his activities, contrasts intriguingly with an article which primarily reflects Communistic viewpoints yet provides much useful information.

22   SAD files on the Institute show that Cronin clashed often with CUA Summer Session director Dr. Roy Deferrari and Sociology Department Chairman Paul Furfey. Issues ranged from Institute competition with regular departments to deep philosophical differences. Furfey, for example, as in *Fire on the Earth*, 1936, linked the living of Christ's message with radical social reform, while Cronin was skeptical of that approach. The Institute ceased in 1950, but Higgins ran a summer institute after he became SAD director.

23   Cronin to Hillenbrand, Nov. 17, 1942. [UND]

write a series of three publications based on the report and its FBI data.[24]

Given the postwar anti-labor drive, and the Catholic Church's growing conservatism, it is no surprise that when Father John Ryan died in 1945, Cronin was tabbed to join Father George Higgins as an assistant director of NCWC's Social Action Department, under the titular leadership of Father Ray McGowan. Higgins (see Chapter Ten) provided most of the day-to-day leadership and ensured continuance of strong support for labor schools and other worker-justice activities, while Cronin worked with anti-Communist crusaders and in the 1950s served as a special assistant and speechwriter for Vice-President Richard Nixon.

Father Cronin's curious journey presents us with a very cautionary tale, not only in terms of how far Cronin departed from his original intentions, but in terms of how neglectful he was of his duty to protect the Church from undue interference by the State. Specifically, he forgot these words of Pope Leo XIII in *Rerum Novarum*: "Let the State watch over these societies of citizens banded together for the exercise of their rights; but let it not thrust itself into their peculiar concerns and their organization; for things move and live by the spirit inspiring them, and may be killed by the rough grasp of a hand from without."

Cronin was important enough in Catholic social action for Communist critics of the movement to portray him as a prototype of it, whereas his extremism was largely atypical in its ranks. On the other hand, today's Catholic social actionists tend to belittle or ignore the anti-Communist buccaneering of Cronin and a few others. Both misrepresentations prevent us from adding to our knowledge of such extremism's harm to the causes of social justice.

It's very instructive to contrast those extremists with Father Darby and the many other social actionists whose anti-Communism was positive, constructive, and effective. So effective was New Rochelle Labor School in helping its UE worker-students, for example, that by the time Local 453 turned itself around, the skirmish to get labor-school classes into the local's union hall had become a battle of nationwide proportions.

---

24 Irons, Peter H., "American Business and the Origins of McCarthyism," in *The Specter*, eds. Robert Griffith and Alton Theoharis, New York: New Viewpoints, 1974.

The Annual Communion Breakfast of the Association of Catholic Trade Unionists was scheduled that year for Sunday, March 31. [On March 15 Darby had briefed UE Local 453's Executive Board on what the labor school could offer the local.] *The ACTU had always been in touch with the UE problem, particularly through one fighting right-wing local of typewriter repairmen, Local 1237 in New York City. Ed Timmes, Bill Boulton, Tom Bell and others had never allowed their local to get into CP hands. This local was a nucleus, and the ACTU Breakfast seemed a fitting occasion to use to bring together all right-wingers so far discovered in UE. The result was that all who could attended the Mass and Breakfast. Afterwards, in St. Agnes' Hall in mid-town Manhattan, members of 1237, 453, 456 (Jersey City), 404 (Hastings), and 419 (Mt. Vernon) held a caucus, became fully acquainted, and outlined a program....*

The caucus had one important consequence: the decision of those present, Catholic and non-Catholic, to stay together and work together. The men quickly realized that they all faced the similar complex problems of membership apathy, employer opposition, strikes in progress, known CP's, and the "smoking out" of suspected CP's. They also sensed that, to meet these problems, their still small group already contained a fund of experience which each could draw upon by trading ideas and comparing methods. A schedule of weekly Saturday afternoon meetings was arranged. ACTU offered the hospitality of its New York Headquarters until the group grew and solidified enough to have its own center. Some later meetings took place in the offices of Local 1237.[25]

On that first day, also, the plan of campaign became clear. The UE had a majority of local unions that required "cleaning up." All the locals the men were familiar with belonged to UE District 4 (Southern New York and Northern New Jersey), and this District was Red-controlled On these two levels, local union and district, they knew the battle must be waged.

The Saturday meetings began on April 6 with delegations from six locals: 1237, 1202, 456, 453, 419, and 404. The Director of the New Rochelle Labor School was asked to open with a few words, and briefly stressed two points. He commended the members for deciding to "cleanse" the union without harming the economic protection needed by the rank-and-file and their families.... Secondly, the Director suggested that they adopt the practice of selecting a different chairman for each meeting until each one had had some practice and the men knew one another better. The system of rotating chairmen was adopted. Then a member of each local reported on the situation in his own organization.....

---

25 Darby, 35-6, 39-40.

6 ❦ Thomas Darby

The following Saturday, April 13, another local, 475 (Mergenthaler Co. in Brooklyn), joined the caucus. These men reported that they too were on strike and that, while it had been difficult to achieve it, all Commie influence had been prevented by the shop's strike committee....

By far the best result of this April 13 meeting was the unanimous decision to issue a paper (mimeographed it had to be) for District-wide distribution. [The name of the paper was *The Searchlight*.]

The father of the idea for a newspaper was Jim Conroy of UE Local 419 in Mt. Vernon. As a young man, Conroy joined the Communist Party in New York because, he said, "at the time, it seemed to him Party members were the only ones doing anything materially concrete for the poor of the Depression." Over the years, however, he became increasingly disillusioned with the CP's techniques and ultimate goals, publicly repudiated the Party, and became active in ACTU and its "right-wing" caucus.

Conroy's former Communist affiliation furnished telling information, specific and pointed. The Searchlight first appeared on May 1, 1946 under the aegis of "The UE District 4 Committee for Rank-and-File Democracy," the name which the caucus had finally adopted. So effective was it that the caucus soon doubled its strength. So feared was it that the Communists would not even use its correct title (Spotlight, they called it) when trying to warn the members against it as a sheet influenced by "unprincipled outsiders." No other factor in the UE battle was more productive than this hard-hitting and lively paper. Its greatest asset was that it consistently supported and publicized the legitimate aims of sound American trade unionism while simultaneously exposing CP goals and strategy. In the typing, mimeographing, and distributing of The Searchlight lasting gratitude goes to Roger K. Larkin, for years Executive Secretary of the ACTU, who was always available as a kind of central clearing house and nerve center in the UE struggle, taking and transmitting from group to group and person to person messages, information, ideas, and whatever else was necessary for intelligent action....

A May 11 meeting welcomed from Long Island City UE Local 425 (Ford Instrument Co.), a contingent which included the impressive Ken Peterson. The Searchlight, which had been sent to 34 locals, was having its effect.... Another encouraging item was the news that the District 4 leaders were in real pain from exposures in The Searchlight.

The most crucial and memorable decision at the May 11 meeting was acceptance of the proposal by Ed Timmes of UE Local 1237 that since the UE national convention was coming up in Milwaukee that September, the newly-formed UE District 4 Committee find delegates to the convention and send them there. The proposal was accepted, Darby reported, because it was felt that "the experience would broaden those who went. The convention could be used as a test of strength, could help them become acquainted with more right-wingers across the country, and could give them issues to capitalize upon even at home in their own locals."

When Bill Boulton informed the caucus that he had already compiled from former conventions a moderately satisfactory list of anti-Communists in other districts and had their addresses, it was thereupon decided that he and everyone else should write to all potential sympathizers, send them the May 15 Searchlight, and urge their continued cooperation. The priests and the ACTU were requested to aid in getting countrywide "leads" and support....

And the reports did come in. Bill Boulton received a reply from Local 101 (Philco) in Philadelphia where Harry Block, an aggressive Jewish lad, had never ceased to oppose the Reds since they gained control in 1941. Joe Vicinanza, a G.E. worker in the White Plains Local (428), and Father Joseph Donnelly of New Haven put the Committee in touch with workers in the Bridgeport G.E. plant and, eventually, throughout New England (District 2). Father Leo G. Brown, SJ, of St. Louis persuaded two men from Local 1102 to write to and finally to visit New York. These men, Jim Click, a non-Catholic, and Bill Drohan, a Catholic, both shrewd and worldly-wise idealists, had consistently fought the CP's all along and were finally to clean up District 8 in the Mid-West. James B. Carey, Secretary-Treasurer of the National CIO and former UE President, was told of the right-wing revolt and agreed to support it. Through Father Charles Owen Rice of Pittsburgh [see Chapter Eight], a whole group from various locals there joined the movement [UE Members for Democratic Action] and out of the Pittsburgh group came John M. Duffy, who, practically single-handedly and after long effort, broke the Communist control of District 6 and influenced subsequent victories in other places. Similar developments grew out of replies during June and July from Dayton, Schenectady, Detroit, Buffalo, Rochester, Baltimore, Milwaukee, Camden, and Cleveland.

Some of the caucus, Tom Bell, Bill Boulton, Jack Garvey (Local 428), Joe Vicinanza, and Bart Enright, traveled far and wide, paying their own way, in order to inform old acquaintances of the mind of many in the UE and to increase, through them, the forces of the right-wing. The result of all this correspondence and activity was that a pre-convention conference was set for August 11 in Pittsburgh....

6 ❧ Thomas Darby

The Convention opened on September 9. The right-wingers (how relative the term is!) staged a more-than-satisfactory performance. On the test votes, they garnered from 525 to 687 delegates. More important for the future, they recruited new followers, shook the complacency of some of the "innocents," made an impression on some of the working committees, and "smoked out" many a previously unknown Red. Despite the expected loss by approximately six to one, all returned to their homes with honorable scars and a taste for battle. They knew they had taken the accurate measure of President Albert Fitzgerald, who "fronted" conveniently for the CP's, as well as of Secretary-Treasurer Julius Emspak ("Comrade Juniper" in the Party's code) and Director of Organization James Matles ("The Bessarabian" in the code of the right-wingers)....

The end result in the UE was that Murray finally realized he had to expel it from the CIO and to appoint Carey to found a new union, the International Electrical Union (IUE). Most of the "UE Members for Democratic Action" transferred easily to the new IUE.... [26]

In August 1950, CIO expelled nine Communist-oriented unions, bringing the total expelled to 11, but the action meant only relief for the American labor movement, not resurgence.[27]

In the beginning of that year, Joseph McCarthy, a U.S. Senator from Wisconsin, sought an issue on which to base his reelection campaign. He observed both that Red-baiting of labor had worked well, and that Russia's foreign adventurism was creating much anxiety among Americans. So he expanded Red-baiting to encompass both international relations and the entire American scene, and the strategy succeeded beyond his wildest imaginings. Labor never had a chance to resurge.

McCarthyism cast its sinister spell over much of the nation, including people from all religious groups. The Senator used his Catholicism to gain a wide audience among Church members, but *Commonweal*,

---

26   Ibid., 43-5, 47.

27   UE—the United Electrical, Radio and Machine Workers of America—and the United Farm Equipment and Metal Workers of America were expelled in 1949. The nine unions expelled in 1950: Mine, Mill and Smelter Workers of America; Food, Tobacco, Agricultural and Allied Workers of America; United Public Workers of America; United Professional and Office Workers of America; American Communications Association; International Fur and Leather Workers Union; International Longshoremen's and Warehousemen's Union; International Fishermen and Allied Workers of America; and the National Union of Marine Cooks and Stewards of America.

the well-regarded liberal Catholic magazine, strongly opposed the Senator's tyrannies from their earliest days. Leading the magazine's charge were John Cogley and Jim O'Gara, veterans of Catholic social action from the movement's pioneering paper *The Chicago Catholic Worker*.

In June 1950, a few months after Senator McCarthy's smear tactics started, *Commonweal*'s lead editorial described him as "a reckless, irresponsible bogey-man." Nearly four years later, with McCarthy at the height of his recklessness and irresponsibility, Chicago's auxiliary bishop Sheil contributed to the demagogue's demise with a speech written with Cogley's help and delivered April 9, 1954 to a United Auto Workers conference in Chicago.

"Now, while we are free," Bishop Sheil declared, "is the time to cry out against the phony anti-Communism that mocks our way of life, flouts our traditions and democratic procedures and our sense of fair play, feeds on the meat of suspicion, and grows great on the dissension among Americans which it cynically creates and keeps alive by a mad pursuit of headlines ... As you can see, I take a pretty dim view of some noisy anti-Communists—one in particular, the junior Senator from Wisconsin."[28]

It's tragic for Americans when pressing domestic needs become entangled with foreign concerns to the detriment of the former. When Communist unionists pushed resolutions praising the Yalta Conference or denouncing the Marshall Plan, they demonstrated that their primary objective was to support Soviet empire building, and ignited battles between extraneous resolutions. Also, when McCarthy and other extremist anti-Communists played on Cold War fears by attacking Communism around the globe, they contributed to Americans ignoring the crying need for a stronger U.S. workforce.

In addition, extremist anti-Communism adversely affected Catholic social action's cooperation with reform socialism. Such cooperation reflected a long-lasting natural alliance (Catholic social action, as this volume has frequently noted, blends reform socialism, industrial and political democracy, and an intense and practical spirituality), but coming out of World War II extremist anti-Communists—within and outside of Catholic social action—either stirred up a more-grudging

---

28   Sheil, Bernard, speech, UAW conference, Chicago, Apr. 9, 1954, NCWC News Service, 2, 4.

attitude among those cooperating with reform socialists, or replaced cooperation with conflict.

American Communists welcomed this development, since they often opposed socialism as much as they opposed the selfish capitalism whose overthrow they sought. Too many in the Catholic social action movement failed to recognize the extent of Communist opposition to socialism, or lumped together all Communists and socialists as "Red" enemies of the movement.

With the growth of extremism, more Catholic social actionists co-operated with socialists only for the purpose of expelling Communists, with cooperation declining or disappearing when that goal was reached. There were numerous instances of such corrosion of cooperation.

For example, many of the UE insurgents whom Father Darby worked with became so critical of the socialists within UE Members for Democratic Action that one marvels that it held together as well as it initially did. In Detroit, after its lively ACTU chapter helped Reuther win the UAW presidency and longtime leader Paul Weber left for other pursuits, the chapter carried on fitful battles with socialists and ended up concentrating on non-labor causes. Finally, Catholic social actionists at a Cleveland conference in 1955, discussing what pieces of their dissolving movement were left, decided to cut back on cooperation with Protestant and Jewish social actionists because some conference participants questioned their motivation or saw little future in working with them.

The corrosion of natural alliances played a major role in the dissolution of the Catholic social-action movement, but the underlying cause of the dissolution was a corporate domination which yielded little of its rigidity. Presiding over the Cleveland conference was Monsignor Joseph Donnelly, Director of the Diocesan Labor Institute of Hartford, Connecticut, and he put his finger right on that cause when he said "we have won little cooperation and respect from management."[29]

At its beginnings, the movement had to emphasize labor, since the labor-management relationship was so unbalanced in management's favor; yet there were great hopes for true harmony later. Such hopes were largely unfulfilled, for reasons explored throughout this history of America's labor apostles.

29 Donnelly, Joseph, "What Is the Labor Schools' Future?," *Work*, Dec. 1955.

Nevertheless, the Catholic social actionists who tried hard to increase constructive harmony deserve affirmation, as do the management representatives involved in their efforts. Father Thomas Darby, as effective in this area as in his anti-Communism, described New Rochelle Labor School's outreach to management.

> [E]very year, at least one inquisitive and good-willed management official or owner would enroll in the School. On the master list of all attending will be found the names of the owner of a small factory, the managers of two plants, several executives of large corporations, and a Wall St. broker and a banker. Paul Cunningham of New Rochelle is the small businessman. The others are John H. Armstrong, Edward A. Helgans, Robert Lawrence, Albert Leibfred, James A. Mulvey, W. J. Niederauer, J. Victor Stockell, and T. A. Walsh. One sign of the fortunate change in American thinking is just such a list as this because it was formerly generally feared that big business was not "big" enough to risk mentioning executives' names without fear of reprisals upon the individuals concerned....
>
> From the moment of the establishment of the New Rochelle school for working people, it was the intention and hope of the priests involved to form a businessman's group as a complementary activity. This idea was based primarily on the sage words of Leo XIII in <u>Rerum Novarum</u>: "The great mistake that is made in the matter now under consideration, is to possess oneself of the idea that class is naturally hostile to class.... Each requires the other; capital cannot do without labor, or labor without capital." The Moderator and the teachers realized that attaining industrial peace required the reaching of some ground common to both employers and employees and that Catholic businessmen and Catholic workers already had that common ground in the Faith and its social teaching. However, in the late thirties most Catholic business executives quite openly admitted timidity or fear or suspicion of the venture of founding a Management forum....
>
> This reluctance began to change during the War years.... In 1949, such a forum was started by Helgans and Clarence Keeley. Twenty-nine letters went out and, from the five surrounding communities, 21 men appeared in the College of New Rochelle library. The Director outlined the work of the following five Tuesdays, which saw an average attendance of 16 each session. The sessions became almost exclusively study and discussion of Industrial Ethics with <u>Quadragesimo Anno</u> serving as the textbook.... After a general introduction to the history of Catholic Social Doctrine, the men easily absorbed the encyclical items of "Self-Help by Self-Organization," "The Just Wage," "The Industry Council

Plan," "Capitalism," "Socialism" (in its full Marxian sense), and "The Call for Moral Renovation," by means of a practically paragraph by paragraph analysis of the Papal letter. While only a few of the participants underwent any radical change in their own previous personal views, all did admit that they learned there is great common sense in the Church's social doctrines and program....

The name Westchester Management Forum was eventually adopted.... Along with reviewing briefly the subject matter of previous sessions, the Forum explored topics such as: "The Taft-Hartley Act," "The Closed Shop," "Pius XII's Address to European Businessmen," and "The West German Co-Determination Movement," and several books by Catholic and non-Catholic authors explored them all in the light of Catholic Social Doctrine.... It is worth nothing that ... as was clearly brought out to the genuine surprise of all during one session on "The Catholic Press and Catholic Social Teaching," businessmen do not read widely or enough outside the daily newspaper of their choice and the trade journals of their own particular field....

The Secretary's weekly notice became a resume of the chief points of the topic to be discussed. The member was expected to arrive at the meeting with a definite opinion on the moral rightness or wrongness of the subject in the light of Catholic Social doctrine. During the session each member in turn had an opportunity to express his own or modify another's idea. When necessary, the Moderator closed by correcting an erroneous aspect or by citing a reliable Catholic authority in the matter....

One guest speaker, the Reverend Joseph Hammond, Assistant Director of the Social Action Department of Brooklyn Catholic Charities, both charmed and informed his audience with a review of the thinking on the social question among non-Catholic lay leaders and businessmen, stressing two items: that many outside the Church have been slowly groping their way toward the position the Church has always held on the social problem and that, if Catholic laypeople do not themselves initiate sound programs based on their own solid philosophy, they will discover rather embarrassingly that non-Catholics have done their work for them.[30]

John Q. Adams, a refrigeration industry executive and, with Father Darby, a partner of ACTU throughout the New York City area, was a foremost exemplar of the kind of initiative Hammond encouraged. Adams, a devout Catholic and a student of the labor encyclicals, told members of the Catholic Business Education Association in October

---

30 Darby, *op. cit.*, 51-6.

1950 that "Labor and management are inextricably bound. The prosperity of one determines the prosperity of the other; the misery of labor undermines the position of management. To deprive labor of its just rights is a sure way of eliminating management's rights."[31]

Adams practiced what he preached. In April 1948, he wrote Francis Cardinal Spellman urging him to support the Wall Street strike. The appeal failed, but Adams was able to state his rationale: "We feel it to be a matter of Christian duty to champion and carry out the difficult teachings of the Church even though it be against a natural inclination to let the other fellow take care of himself.... Hence my troubling you to prevail upon them [Catholics], as you alone can, no longer to lag behind their fellow-citizens, but to take the lead in social questions for which our Holy Father has so earnestly appealed."[32]

Adams also practiced what he preached in his workplace. His firm, Manhattan Refrigerating Company, had seven separate union contracts and established labor-management councils. At Chicago's celebration of the 60th anniversary of *Rerum Novarum* and the 20th anniversary of *Quadragesimo Anno*, Adams asserted that these councils "have greatly increased our production and enhanced the spirit of our whole organization."[33]

Two years later, in his memoir of New Rochelle Labor School, Father Thomas Darby expressed satisfaction in the success of the school's outreach to management, and in its overall record. By that time, Darby had received a PhD from Fordham University and passed the halfway point of a 20-year career teaching history at Cathedral College, then the minor seminary of the New York Archdiocese.

The labor school lasted into the mid-1950s, after which Darby went on to pastor two churches, including Holy Trinity in Mamaroneck, Westchester County, from which he retired in 1976. His career was diverse and rewarding, but he counted no reward higher than his days as one of America's labor apostles.

---

31   *Xavier Detail*, Oct. 25, 1950.
32   Adams to Spellman, Apr. 22, 1948. [FU]
33   Adams, speech at 1951 Ryan Forum, Chicago.

CHAPTER SEVEN
KARL HUBBLE (1912–2005)

In downtown Detroit soon after World War II, returning Navy veteran Tony Kaiser leaned on a counter of Walter Romig's Catholic bookstore in the basement of the National Bank Building.

"What's happening to our country?", the intense young man asked Romig. "It looks like a revolution's gonna break out."

Romig, like Kaiser, scanned the day's headlines, which proclaimed labor strikes here, there, and seemingly everywhere. "Yeah, it looks bad," the older man said.

"Has anyone come up with a solution to all this mess?"

"Yeah."

"Who was it?"

"The popes."

The vet laughed. "What the heck do the popes know about it?"

Romig pulled down two pamphlets, ten cents each, and handed them to Kaiser. They were the 1891 papal encyclical *Rerum Novarum*, by Leo XIII, and the 1931 encyclical *Quadragesimo Anno*, by Pius XI. Kaiser plunked down two dimes and waved goodbye, reading as he did.

"What those two dimes started!", Kaiser exclaimed to Romig a week later, and was still exclaiming a half-century later as he described this episode.[1]

Kaiser, a product of 14 years in Catholic schools and a plant worker in 1941 and 1942 before he joined the Navy, had never read those two documents before the episode started. Indeed, in pre-War years he opposed a Congress of Industrial Organizations (CIO) drive to organize his plant and, when he heard a priest was to speak at an organization meeting, said "What's he doing here? He ought to be back in his parish saying Mass and hearing confessions."

By the time he read the encyclicals, however, it was in the context of the labor lessons he had learned in wartime. He had learned, for example, that wartime workers chafed under the no-strike pledge, that their legitimate grievances piled up as unrestrained capitalists piled up power and excess profits, and that wage hikes lagged way behind price hikes.

Postwar, he had learned that workers were tremendously anxious about their futures. He had learned that they struck to let off pent-up steam and make up for lost time, and that their bosses conspired to blame them for high prices and strikes—and expensively achieved their dubious task. Above all, he had learned that these outcomes were not part of the American economic democracy he and his mates thought they had been fighting to defend.

So when he picked up the first pamphlet and read from Leo XIII's *Rerum Novarum*, he recalled feeling like he had been jolted awake: "Working men have been given over, isolated and defenseless, to the callousness of employers and the greed of unrestrained competition." The further Kaiser read, the more awakened he felt.

When Kaiser returned to work, at the R. P. Scherer Corporation, he joined and became active in Local 155, United Chemical Workers-CIO. So effectively did he apply encyclical principles in the local that he was elected its president, became a vice-president of the state CIO council, and joined the Detroit chapter of the Association of Catholic

---

1 Kaiser, Tony, interview with author, July 13, 1995.

7 🐝 Karl Hubble 171

Trade Unionists (ACTU). Kaiser was a dynamic speaker, and campaigned tirelessly throughout the city encouraging workers to unionize or, if they already had, to become active in their unions and join ACTU.

For that group, Kaiser's arrival was a shot in the arm. Chapter Three detailed how several years earlier, ACTU partnered with socialists and others in the United Auto Workers' "right wing" as that coalition made Reuther union president in October 1946. A year later, it helped put his candidates into the union's top offices.

One result of those victories was that they were acclaimed by many as a validation of Detroit ACTU's basic approach—establishing and operating ACTU "conferences" within unions and shops. At the same time, however, the victories uncovered a serious organizational weakness.

The chapter's conferences were so single-minded in pursuing the political objective of electing Reuther and his slate that when this objective was attained, there seemed little left for Actists to do. Consequently, many of them became inactive or drifted away from the organization, so that those who remained welcomed the energy of Kaiser and other new arrivals. These included a new chaplain, Father Karl Hubble, whose positive impact on Detroit ACTU was also a welcome development.

Old or new, chapter members in this period were unsure what path their organization should follow, an uncertainty compounded by leadership crisis. Paul Weber, who in 1948 had been Detroit ACTU's president for a decade and whose impressive leadership skills we explored earlier, left office that year to become press secretary for G. Mennen Williams, a Democrat just elected Michigan governor.

The titular head of Catholic social action in Detroit was Father Raymond Clancy. An archdiocesan network of approximately 40 labor schools was established under his direction in 1939 but few of them took root, and they were replaced in 1943 by an ACTU-conducted basic training course.[2] It was given sporadically, however, as

---

2   In January 1939, schools were established at eight parishes: Centerline; St. Clement; St. Florian; Holy Name; Holy Rosary (replacing an ACTU-Catholic Worker school established in November 1938); St. Luke; Nativity of Our Lord; and Vincent DePaul, Pontiac. In September 1939, schools were added at 31 parishes: Annunciation; Assumption Grotto; St. Augustine; St. Bernard; St. Catherine; St. Cecilia; St. Charles; St. Da-

the ACTU chapter's involvement in union politics eclipsed its educational efforts. Not only that, but Clancy's many responsibilities as an assistant to Archbishop Mooney left him little time to devote to labor education.

Fortunately, Clancy put his responsibilities in this area into the capable hands of Father Clement Kern. Clem Kern was a caring and well-loved parish priest who made worker justice a priority. He gained considerable understanding of worker interests from his father, an auto-industry painter.

Kern was ordained in 1943, and over the next decade was assistant pastor at two blue-collar Detroit parishes, St. Leo's and St. Edward's. There, he taught in labor schools and supported the organizing and development of industrial unions. His parish after 1943 was Holy Trinity, which he served as pastor from 1947 until his retirement in 1977.

Holy Trinity was in Corktown, an aging, inner-city neighborhood on Detroit's west side. Corktown's residents were poor, diverse (with Hispanics, Maltese, Southern blacks, and Appalachian whites), and with a strong sense of community nourished by Father Kern and the parish's complex of ministries. These included a school, labor and English classes, medical and legal clinics, a work-experience program for alcoholics, a homeless shelter, and co-op housing for seniors.

Somehow, Father Kern found time both to serve his parishioners and to engage in labor activism. This meant training the Archdiocese's social-action priests, conducting regional labor schools after the parish schools folded, cooperating with Catholic labor activists throughout the country, and even picketing with Playboy Club bunnies on strike. The latter bit of activism was displayed in many a news photo and soon came to the attention of Archbishop Mooney. When he asked Kern about it, he replied "Well, they asked me to join them and, you know, they do need to buy new costumes."[3]

---

vid; St. Dominic; St. Edward; St. Francis de Sales; Gate of Heaven; St. Gertrude, St. Clair Shores; Holy Redeemer; St. Hyacinth; St. Ladislaus; St. Leo; St. Mary, Rockwood; St. Mary, St. Clair; St. Mary Magdalene, Hazel Park; St. Martin; St. Matthew; St. Patrick; St. Philip Neri; Precious Blood; St. Rose; Sacred Heart, Roseville; St. Stanislaus; St. Stephen, Port Huron; St. Theresa; and St. Thomas the Apostle.

3 Casey, Genevieve M., *Father Clem Kern: Conscience of Detroit*, Detroit, Marygrove College, 1989, 95.

7 ❦ Karl Hubble

As time went on, it became obvious to Father Kern that he needed help with his labor duties. He persuaded Archbishop Mooney to put Father Karl Hubble in charge of archdiocesan social-action efforts and to appoint him as Detroit ACTU chaplain.

Hubble had been one of the best teachers in the first year of Clancy's short-lived labor-school network, at Guardian Angels Church in northeast Detroit. Mooney then appointed him to the faculty of Sacred Heart Seminary, but Kern frequently enlisted him in labor-related tasks and thus helped prepare him to assume his new roles. These took effect on the last day of 1948.

Hubble was an excellent choice to fill them. He was articulate and knowledgeable yet possessed a common touch, all as befits a seminary professor who taught Latin, Greek, and religion yet also coached basketball. In addition, he wrote well.

This talent came in handy as he and others tried to fill the huge hole Weber's departure left at *The Wage Earner*. Among Hubble's colleagues there were Actists Joe Sullivan, later a judge; Bob Forbes, circulation director, *Michigan CIO News*; Norm McKenna, later a labor reporter for the U.S. Information Agency; and Bill Ryan, President of UAW Local 104 and later a Speaker of the Michigan House of Representatives.

Father Hubble was wise enough to admit that he didn't have a worker's perspective—his dad was a Customs officer—and to seek input from Kern, Clancy, Weber, Kaiser and others who either came from worker families or were active, skilled unionists themselves. Back at the Guardian Angels labor school, for example, Hubble had called upon parishioner Ralph Novak, an activist in his local, to be the school's parliamentary procedure expert. In Hubble's new role as ACTU chaplain, he continued to rely upon such reality-based advice.

It's a good thing he did, because he came into that role right in the middle of a sharp clash between leading figures in the national Catholic social-action movement, a debate which affected Detroit ACTU's search for renewal. The debate unfolded in the pages of *Commonweal*, an influential journal widely read by Catholic social actionists nationally and locally.

The topic was whether ACTU as an organization was, or a significant number of its chapters were, engaging too much in sectarian, even religious, factionalism in the labor movement. Varying views on that topic have been undercurrents throughout this entire volume.

Detroit's name often came up when the topic was discussed. While many observers acclaimed the UAW victories of 1946 and 1947 as validating Detroit ACTU's "conference" approach, others maintained that the victories happened despite that approach or would have been even greater with another approach.

In 1948, the conference approach and others were summarized in *Catholic Social Action*, by Father John Cronin.[4] Summarizing the conference approach, Cronin stated "It has been argued that outside intervention [in unions], whether by clergy or by ACTU, is an unhealthy innovation. The reason cited is that these activities, however well-intentioned, give color to the charges that we [Catholics] are forming a Catholic bloc within unions." The author was not stating this argument as his position.

Nevertheless, Cronin's summary of approaches triggered Father George Kelly, a priest active in New York-ACTU (see Chapter Four) to come to ACTU's defense in a December 1948 *Commonweal* article.[5] Why the summary triggered Kelly to write this article is unclear.

Cronin was not an ACTU priest, so perhaps Kelly felt that this fact detracted from Cronin's understanding of the organization. Another possible factor is that some of Cronin's activities in unions in wartime Baltimore (alluded to in Chapter Six) are classic examples of inappropriate clerical interference, although Kelly makes no mention of these activities.

Primarily, though, the article seems to stem from Kelly's feeling that the Social Action Department in Washington did not understand how it was for Kelly and others in the "front lines" of the Catholic labor apostolate—the old field-versus-headquarters complaint. Cronin and Father George Higgins (the focus of Chapter Ten) were SAD's assistant directors.

Indeed, Kelly starts his article by recalling a Higgins letter *Commonweal* published more than four years earlier.[6] Higgins wrote then that he knew of instances of labor activism where ACTU chapters "interfered in local disputes in which the issues were not patently as black-and-white as they were alleged to be," that chapters should confine themselves "scrupulously to sustained religious and technical edu-

---

4 Cronin, John. *Catholic Social Action*, Milwaukee, Bruce, 1948.
5 Kelly, George, "ACTU and Its Critics", *Commonweal*, Dec. 31, 1944, 298-302.
6 Higgins to *Commonweal*, Apr. 3, 1944, 24.

cation," and that if they, "acting as organizations, insist in doctrinaire fashion on their solution as the unique solution in the practical application of their admittedly excellent principles, they may expect to be charged with sectarian factionalism." Some "very decent labor groups," Higgins noted, regarded ACTU and similar efforts with some degree of suspicion.

Kelly answered that letter in the 1944 pages of *Commonweal*, and in 1948 restated the thrust of his response. Insufficient credit, he said, was given to educational activities of ACTU, including labor schools and newspapers, and he affirmed that its other activities—joining picket lines, priests speaking at strike meetings, legal aid, "conferences" helping with strategy planning—were constructive.

As for charges of outside interference by ACTU, Kelly maintained, as did Father Darby in Chapter Six, that ACTU members, teachers, and chaplains were unionists or were activists who supported labor. One reason they helped keep labor's house clean, Kelly added, was to keep the government from unwisely intruding into union affairs.

Amplifying Kelly's point were the results of the multiplying labor bureaucracy of war and postwar: more red tape and an increasing lean towards management. "The Taft-Hartley Act has interfered with the internal affairs of good labor unions as well as bad ones," Kelly asserted. "The good unions have been regulated precisely because the bad unions have remained bad."[7]

Kelly's 1948 letter was weakest in defending ACTU against charges of divisiveness. ACTU chapters which restricted membership to Catholics, including Detroit ACTU, created division right off the bat, since the labor movement is based on democracy.

Kelly approved of such restriction because "the program of the ACTU is based on Catholic social principles." The genius of these principles, however, was Catholics, Protestants, and Jews cooperating for justice for all workers on the basis of the common good of society. Openness in every respect is essential to social justice, as many other Actists, and Catholic social actionists generally, proclaimed vigorously.

Finally, Kelly alleged that many Catholic critics of ACTU listened too sympathetically to powerful and affluent labor leaders who saw the organization as interfering with their activities. Much of the job of George Higgins was liaison with top labor leaders, but he said his criticism of ACTU did not come from them. Also, Higgins said, in his

---

7 Kelly, *op. cit.*, 300.

Commonweal reply to Kelly in January 1949, "some of the most intelligent 'critics' of ACTU are humble priests and laymen" who are "allergic to the blandishments of affluent labor leaders."[8]

Detroit-ACTU was not mentioned specifically in this round of exchanges, but criticisms of ACTU similar to those made in the debate were frequently aimed at the chapter. In the chapter's uncertain state at the end of 1948, the *Commonweal* controversy touched sensitive nerves.

Certainly Archbishop Mooney, who expressed reservations about the divisiveness of ACTU before its Detroit chapter even started, was very much aware of the controversy. His response was to direct Father Hubble, whom he had just appointed as Detroit ACTU's chaplain, to explore the controversy's implications for the chapter. Here's Hubble on this exploration's findings:

> There has been no change in the concept of the purposes of Detroit ACTU as defined both by the articles of its Constitution or by His Eminence [Mooney]. There has never been any serious disagreement, even between various ACTU chapters, about these purposes. The differences have been with regard to the means or methods of attaining the ends agreed upon by all.
>
> All concerned (even New York) agree that the basic method and activity of the organization is <u>education</u>. In New York, ACTU established labor schools to do this educational work. In Detroit, this work was made the responsibility of the Archdiocesan Labor Institute composed of priest directors and teachers. The president of ACTU was on the Archdiocesan Labor Institute's Board of Directors, and ACTU members assisted some parish priests who directed the labor schools.
>
> But, again, all concerned seem to have agreed that education was not enough. <u>Organized</u> action by ACTU within unions was thought to be necessary. His Eminence has maintained that the Labor Institute should teach principles but ACTU should put them into effect, saying "The prime purpose (of ACTU) is to make the Catholic membership in the unions an <u>organized force</u> for sound unionism."
>
> In New York, Father George Kelly argued that "Labor school work is only the first step in ACTU's educational program—the beginning of education, not education. The workers needed help which spoke louder than words. What kind of help? When a group faced a difficult problem within their union, ACTU established a 'Conference.'" In Detroit the "Conference" method was adopted originally as an anti-Communist

---

8   Higgins to *Commonweal*, Jan. 2, 1949, 376.

> tactic. The conferences were described as "permanent counter-minorities ... a permanent core of leadership to give successful opposition to the CP."
>
> The full story of the successes and failures of these conferences has not been put together. They were certainly not "permanent". An important reason for the demise of some at least was disagreement among the members in making judgments about personalities and political strategy within unions.
>
> In 1947-48 efforts were made to revive the conferences but these were almost entirely fruitless. The conference within the AFL Teachers Federation was formed at this time, flourished briefly, and foundered on the usual shoals.
>
> It was and is the considered judgment of the present chaplain that these conferences not only provide a target for the criticisms of other unionists, but have inherent weaknesses and dangers that lead to real justification for such criticism. It is impossible for such conferences to avoid the aspect and, to some extent at least, the actual function of a political-religious caucus.[9]

Before Detroit ACTU could move in a new direction, Hubble told Cardinal Mooney, the Archdiocese and the Actists needed to understand the reasons for the demise of the Clancy labor schools. Mooney had asked Father Hubble to address this, and Hubble identified the primary reason as too much dependence on the priest-directors of the schools in view of the "rather superficial" training they received and of the numerous demands on their time and effort.

At the time of the schools' heyday, Hubble added, he and others tried to persuade Detroit ACTU that it would have to assume responsibility for the schools if they were to last. The only result had been the chapter's short-lived basic-training course, followed by several years of preoccupation with chapter "conferences" and UAW's intense, internecine struggles. Hubble again:

> During these years the Executive Board [of Detroit ACTU] has carried out the educational function of ACTU through <u>The Wage Earner</u> and lectures, discussion forums, talks to non-member groups, etc. These latter have reached a very small fraction of the Catholic unionists in the area and at the same time, the number of active members has continued to dwindle.
>
> ACTU indeed stands at the crossroads. The direction that it will take is a crucial decision that must be made now. Having thought the thing

---

9 Hubble, Karl, "ACTU Report to Cardinal Mooney", 1950. [WSU]

out in terms of long-range objectives and of attainable ends, it is our judgment that the only salvation lies in reorganization on the basis of parish or (in some localities) inter-parish units or conferences.

What could a parish ACTU conference hope to accomplish? There is solid hope that it could give some permanence to the good effects attained by the labor schools in their brief history, but we do not think of a parish conference as a labor school. The term "school" suggests a temporary place and process of learning, and, after a number of courses, a graduation. The labor schools were perhaps too ambitious, plunging the students into the middle of the woods of encyclical doctrine and economic problems without sustained emphasis on more fundamental attitudes of mind for motivating and directing Catholics, both into and in union activity.

The ordinary active unionist, even in a position of leadership, does not <u>need</u> to be well-versed in Catholic social doctrine. He does need some basic convictions and principles of action which, added to the basic goodness of a good Catholic, will equip him to be a good unionist.

The implanting and developing of these attitudes, convictions, and principles in the minds of more and more Catholics should be the fundamental work of ACTU. This job can best be accomplished by association with people who have these convictions and principles. The place where more minds can best be reached with religious inspiration and motivation is the parish. Experience has shown that without the points of contact through many small units, educational efforts are wasted on empty seats.

Nor is a pulpit sermon enough to motivate Catholics to union activity. Even if a talk would be so inspirational as to prompt one or another to make an effort, few would persevere long. Does Father Doakes know what he is asking? Does he appreciate the heartaches, headaches, grief, frustration, discouragement, enmities, bewilderment, time away from home, sacrifices, weariness, that he is asking the activated unionist to undergo? ...

A parish unit would provide a forum for the discussion, a promulgation of these ideas and ideals.... Realism, born of experience, indicates that such activity will be that of a small group. This fact is no handicap if there are enough groups. This activity whereby the few try to bring these fundamental principles to the minds of the many will result in some truly well-formed Catholic leaders for the union movement locally. Those who have worked the hardest in the ACTU educational program have become the most influential in their own unions.[10]

---

10   Ibid.

Archbishop Mooney supported Hubble and Detroit ACTU in their reorganization plans and programs. It was a major shift in direction, involving considerable down-scaling in size, ambitions, and operations. The lowering of expectations boosted morale, however, enabling the chapter to build a cadre of both longtime and new members, the goal set by Hubble.

Detroit Actists other than those already mentioned included: Tom Doherty, Secretary, Chrysler Local 7-UAW (and Weber's key aide as chapter executive secretary); Mike Novak (Ralph's brother), president, Dodge 3-UAW and CIO Council; Mary Ellen Riordan, President, Detroit Federation of Teachers; Mike Lacey, Director, UAW Region 1; John Tracey, President, Buhl 772-UAW; Ann Pastuszka, UAW Local 29, state CIO executive board; Pat Hamilton, United Chemical Workers international representative, Region 6, under Actist Chet Adamczyk; Dorothy Haener, UAW international representative; Henry McCusker, Ford 600-UAW, head of UAW's aircraft unit; Marguerite Gahagan, Detroit Newspaper Guild; Tony Oleksinski, Chrysler 490-UAW; Lloyd LaChapelle, Communications Workers of America; Helene Barwick, community services chairman, Wayne County CIO; Al Chisholm, counsel, Local 705, Hotel, Bar, and Restaurant Workers-AFL; and Joe Ptaszynski, Dodge 3-UAW and executive assistant to CIO members of the Regional Wage Stabilization Board.

Most of these unionists became participants in one or another of Detroit ACTU's parish conferences, which at one point in the early 1950s were held at eight locations in or near Detroit: St. Joseph's, Port Huron; St. Vincent's, Pontiac; St. Gregory's; St. Catherine's; St. Francis Xavier, Ecorse; St. Thomas's, Ann Arbor; and sites in Hamtramck and Hardy. Topics discussed ran the entire gamut of applying the encyclicals in a chapter member's life, as both a Catholic and a unionist.

Father Hubble felt that the chapter's members and potential members were unionists who could get into leadership positions, "effective, balanced people, people who knew what they were doing and how to relate to other, non-Catholic trade unionists. They became responsible members of their unions, their parishes, and the community at large."[11] Also, Actists extensively circulated *The Wage Earner*, which contin-

---

11 Hubble, interview with author, July 14, 1995.

ued to be an influential newspaper in labor and Catholic social-action circles locally and nationally.

Paul Weber didn't have time to watch over the newspaper full-time after he became Governor Williams' press secretary in 1948, but he kept an eye on things and made sure the paper stayed faithful to his policy of not being a paper of Detroit ACTU news but rather of labor news, both in Detroit and throughout the country. A good example is *The Wage Earner* standing up to Westbrook Pegler, a nationally syndicated columnist who from the 1930s through the 1950s continuously attacked all unions as needless, corrupt, and/or tools of Moscow.

As Activist Joe Sullivan described it, on a slow day at *The Wage Earner* office and with some space to fill, he inserted into the October 1949 issue a brief, boxed item calling for October 31 to be "Pray for Westbrook Pegler Day." "Once a very promising liberal," the item began, "Mr. Pegler exhibited intervals of brilliance which might have carried over to his socially-conscious days had not some unforeseen event intervened. Prayer, coupled with patient explanations, may once again restore the gifted writer to his normal place in society."[12]

Pegler, unsurprisingly, used this call as another excuse to go on the attack. In his next syndicated column, he described the box as "a piece of pietistical cant" and concluded "Inasmuch as I am in the right and *The Wage Earner* is in error, I will not be needing those prayers on Pegler Day for the purpose specified."[13] It was definitely a case of "Methinks he doth protest too much," and media around the nation had a field day covering all aspects of it.

In a response to Pegler's response, for example, Father Hubble was quoted by *The Detroit Times* as follows: "To decline to be prayed for is rather an idle gesture. If anyone resists the graces of truth, justice, and charity, which prayers would obtain for him, God will no doubt see that someone else gets them. Good prayers are always answered in one way or another. We will continue to pray that all those who are influential in the labor movement, as well as those who hate it, will be guided by the principles of truth, justice, and charity."[14]

---

12 "Pray for Westbrook Pegler Day", *Wage Earner*, Oct. 1949, 1.
13 "Pegler Raps Prayer Day Asked for Him", King Features Syndicate, Oct. 1949.
14 Pickering, Jack,"Chide Pegler for Declining Day of Prayer", *Detroit Times*, nd.

7 ॐ Karl Hubble

As for the parish conferences, the most successful was the one at St. Joseph's Church in Port Huron, Father Hubble's home parish. Father Ron Heidelberger, a priest just a few years out of seminary, directed the school with energy and with an understanding gained from his father, a waiter who often told his son of dad's activism (including leading a strike) for Local 705 of the Hotel, Bar, and Restaurant Workers union. Heidelberger also remembered the 1939 labor school at St. Leo's in Detroit, which he had attended as a high-school student.

Father Clem Kern, whom Heidelberger recalled from those St. Leo days, came to Port Huron to help him start the parish conference at St. Joseph's, as did Tony Kaiser and Father Clancy. The conference developed into a well-attended forum for discussion of such topics as Organized Labor in Politics; Catholic Workers and the Organized Labor Movement; Organized Labor and the Community; Pensions, Health Insurance, and the Guaranteed Annual Wage; the Taft-Hartley Act; Strikes; Parliamentary Procedure; Public Speaking; and Organized Labor's Gains within the Past 15 Years. Detroit ACTU had shifted to a direction which was less organization and more spirituality, but as these topics indicate, Father Hubble and conference moderators placed a high priority on practicality.

This priority stemmed from Hubble's days as a labor-school teacher, when, as he recalled of his students, "these were workaday people, and we'd be talking about the encyclicals' industry-council idea and things akin to it—things which were theoretical."[15] From those days forward, Hubble was aware that when theory was discussed, it needed to be placed into a practical context. In the case of industry-council ideas in the encyclicals, he felt, they needed to be related to wages, prices, and profits.

Perhaps because of his awareness in this regard, Hubble contributed significantly to the national debate which grew up, in World War II and postwar, around the encyclicals' industry-council ideas. After the war, some Catholic social actionists continued to proclaim them, and Phil Murray and others in the labor movement continued to proclaim the CIO Industry Council Plan, but many of these proclamations were less clear about their meanings, and more distant from reality, than they had been earlier. Hubble's perceptive wrestling with industry-council issues, in the pages of *The Wage Earner*, had a tonic effect.

---

15   Hubble, interview with author, *op. cit.*

The anniversary celebrations of the social encyclicals of Popes Leo XIII and Pius XI have served to focus public attention to some extent on what Cardinal Mooney has recently called the core of the encyclicals, i.e. their program for the establishment of an organic socio-economic order.

It is anybody's guess as to the possibility of such a program being carried out in this country within the foreseeable future, and the point of this piece is to make a few comments on that possibility.

It seems to me that one favorable condition exists in a kind of common denominator of current social thought, for it is more or less generally admitted that a nation's economy will not serve the common good without some kind of intelligent planning.

What divides those who bother to think about it is, on the one hand, to what extent can and must economic competition be restricted and, on the other hand, who will formulate and execute the restrictive plans.

There can still be found, of course, some honest-to-goodness, unreconstructed individuals who remain convinced that unrestricted competition would serve the common economic welfare.

But the less doctrinaire and supposedly "enlightened" individualist admits that unrestrained competition leads to monopoly for the few and bankruptcy for the many.

That is why a study of the history of the legal restrictions on economic enterprise in this country shows that they almost invariably resulted from the demands of one or another trade or manufacturing association that the Government "pass a law" to save their industry from the evil consequences of unrestrained competition.

Many of the current members of the U.S. Chamber of Commerce might be surprised to hear that in 1932, 90% of their membership felt that some kind of economic planning was necessary.

In 1933 the USCC was proposing that "government permit business through its own organization to set up standards of fair play, to agree on fair wages, fair hours of work, even fair prices.... How will business accept this regimentation of business by itself? The majority will accept it gladly."

The socialists and Communists have their plans, of course, for social control of the economy.

The latter must follow one plan and, while they prate of democracy, practice dictatorship.

The former seldom agree among themselves except in giving the planning function to the state and, if they are of the "democratic" variety, in electing the planners by a democratic process.

7 ❦ Karl Hubble

> *The crises of the last ten years have highlighted the need of planning for war production but with it the everlasting dispute as to who should have the authority to make and execute the plans.* [16]

Favorable conditions for at least a consideration of the Industry Council plan, Hubble maintained, also included what he called "wider acceptance of the plan's most basic principle—that Christian morality has relevance for socio-economic relations." Both labor and management, he observed, increasingly accepted that principle, as difficult as it often was to detect it in their day-to-day operations.

The Hubble article then focused on obstacles facing the plan.

> *Not the least of these is that those who expound it seem too often to take what is generally called the "doctrinaire" approach.*
>
> *Perhaps too much emphasis is put on the authority of the source and not enough on the feasibility of the program.*
>
> *The average American is an empiricist even if he can't define the word.*
>
> *For this reason the American variety of free enterprise developed as one that was a far cry from that in Europe.*
>
> *And so when you talk about the "industry council" plan or "occupational group" plan, the first question that springs to mind is "Will it work?" and the second is "How will it work?"*
>
> *The practical-minded American just will not buy untested the theory that a socio-economic group can effectively order the company of a whole industry for the welfare of a whole industry.*
>
> *He wants spelled out the specific function, the exact purpose, the limits of jurisdiction, etc., that such a group would have in order to limit the freedom of enterprise of individual companies so as to make them contribute to the economic health of the whole industry.*
>
> *For the same reason, it needs to be spelled out in economic terms how representatives of all industries and professions could order the national economy for the common good.*
>
> *The "pat" answer, of course, is "that would have to be worked out" by those concerned; an answer which only lends credence to the assertion that it is just another unrealistic ideal.*
>
> *By and large those with the "know how" are disinterested in the principles and untouched by the motives in the papal encyclicals.*
>
> *After all, a man has to make a living, and if you are a skilled economist or an experienced and successful industrialist, you will not help*

---

16 Hubble, Karl, "What Are the Chances for Industry Councils in America?", *Wage Earner*, nd. [AD]

your advancement in management circles by preaching the socio-economic ideas of Quadragesimo Anno.

By the same token, if you work for a labor union, you will not make yourself popular by advocating in union halls the papal ideal of "cooperation" with management.

The disinclination of the industrialist and the labor leader to comprehend and apply the "core of the encyclicals" finds a kind of counterpoint in the disability of those familiar with the principles to think them out in terms of current economic conditions.

This results in a general misunderstanding of the whole idea on the part of most everybody.

It is confused with the fascistic syndicates of Mussolini, the co-management plans currently in vogue in parts of Germany, and any and every type of socialism.

It is viewed with alarm by representatives of management as an invasion of their rights and prerogatives and a threat to individual initiative and freedom of enterprise.

It is dismissed with scorn by the Marxists in the labor movement as well as the battle-scarred type like John L. Lewis, which considers labor-management conflict as hopelessly inevitable and, in a day when most everyone else is looking for a formula of industrial peace, calls for $50,000,000 with which to carry on the eternal fight.

Even the CIO Industry Council Plan—a specific and practical proposal for labor-management-government collaboration on both the industry and national levels—receives only lip support from CIO leaders everywhere, who make little or no attempt to understand and advance it.

In short, now that the echoes of the polite applause accorded the encyclical anniversary speeches have died away, we can get back to the stark realism of the fact that little is being done by people of influence to bring to realization the idealism of the "core of the encyclicals".[17]

This was candid commentary. Hubble recalled that when he gave the same message to a regional Catholic social-action conference in Columbus, Ohio in March 1953, SAD's Father Higgins seemed unpleasantly surprised with Hubble's candor. Hubble attributed the reaction to frustration, since Higgins and others supportive of the CIO Industry Council Plan faced tough sledding in the midst of a laissez faire U.S. administration and widespread public apathy. Higgins and Hubble agreed, however, that although encyclical appliers had made

---

17 *Ibid.*

little progress, at the heart of it was a push for stronger collective bargaining.

> *Collective bargaining seems to me to be the hope for approaching the industry council plan, especially industry-wide bargaining and bargaining in large enterprises like General Motors. Cooperation will come after mutual respect acquired at the bargaining table. That, I think, is what has happened and is happening.*
>
> *The collective-bargaining story of UAW and GM bears this out. That is where Reuther won his place. Those victories, together with the victories of Murray, have done more than futuristic, idealistic planning.*
>
> *Idealism must have its place, but the common economic good, like the common political good, will come more out of the debate of equal groups than a fanciful peaceful cooperation.*
>
> *If more workers had the collective-bargaining gains of the well-organized, the common economic good would be more served.*
>
> *In this sense we could twist [Charles] Wilson's "What's good for GM is good for the country" to "What's good for wage earners is good for the country."...*
>
> *I think that cooperation is more likely to be the inevitable outcome of collective bargaining than the result of ideological pressures and legislative sanctions.*[18]

Hubble recognized "where Reuther won his place." Detroit ACTU's partnership with socialists helped Reuther win the UAW victories of 1946 and 1947. Why, then, did the ACTU chapter not continue in partnership with the socialists as supporters of Reuther's leadership?

Granted, Weber, quoted earlier on the value of cooperating with socialists, left the chapter's top job for the political arena in 1948. But he continued such cooperation himself, and still significantly influenced the chapter and *The Wage Earner*. Too many people had moved on, however, and there was not enough development of lay leadership within parishes for the parish-conference approach to become solidly grounded.

In the process of retrenchment, Catholic social action in Detroit missed an excellent chance to revive a coalition of natural allies, since commitment to a power-sharing industrial democracy united Actists, socialists, and others supporting Reuther. If this coalition had rebounded and made a concerted effort to reduce factionalism (some-

---

18   Hubble, Karl, speech, Social Action Conference, Columbus, O., Mar. 3-4, 1953, 7-8. [AD]

thing both the ACTU chapter and Reuther realized was necessary), there's a chance it could have bucked the prevailing anti-labor tides and the rise of anti-Communist extremism.

What prevented that from happening was primarily that too many Actists and their leaders, including Father Hubble himself at times, saw the primary value of cooperation with socialists as being to help get Reuther into the UAW presidency. That achieved, the ACTU chapter largely ignored the socialists or quarreled with them.

Too often, chapter members and leaders failed to distinguish between revolutionary socialists and reform socialists, but rather lumped all socialists together and coupled them with Communists. As extreme anti-Communism and McCarthyism escalated throughout the early fifties, this careless categorizing also increased, and played a key role in reducing labor reform and Catholic social action to a low level.

Failure to renew coalitions or make distinctions facilitated Communists' isolating socialists or Actists, then attacking one group by exploiting its differences with the other. Reuther's Communist foes did not admit defeat, but fought back for years, especially through the union newspapers they controlled.

Many socialists weren't active in coalition renewal either. Some were extreme secularists opposed to alliance with Catholics, and the fact that many Actists followed a Catholics-only policy in classes and conferences didn't help. In addition, Catholic social actionists frequently got caught up in American echoes of European clashes between Social Democrats and Christian Democrats. During much of the late forties and early fifties, Catholic activists and socialists devoted too much effort to lining up patronage positions or to seemingly endless debates in their newspapers on relatively insignificant topics.

Another consequence of Catholic social actionists failing to renew coalitions or make distinctions was these activists' sometimes treating friends as foes. Consider the relationship of some Catholic social actionists with Americans for Democratic Action (ADA), an organization formed in early 1947, with Walter Reuther as one of its founding members. The group promoted economic reform, civil rights and liberties, and responsible anti-Communism.

The group was a great friend of labor, but around 1950, in Detroit and elsewhere, some Catholic social actionists aimed socialist-baiting criticisms at it. Father Joseph Donnelly, Director of the Hartford, Connecticut Diocesan Labor Institute (and an ADA executive committeeman) reminded the readers of his nationally-disseminated *Social Action Bulletin* that "in social reform, if we follow the teachings of the Church we would lead our members into an area of change far more radical than the ADA and its stalwarts will subscribe to for decades."[19]

Yet another consequence of the failures we're discussing is that Catholic employers who opposed the organizing and bargaining efforts of their employees found it easier to do so when such efforts did not have the broadest base of support possible. A classic example surfaced during this period in Detroit and occupied a great deal of time and attention throughout the last half of Father Hubble's first year as Detroit ACTU chaplain.

> Archbishop Mooney took exception to something we were going to print in The Wage Earner *about the University of Detroit* [a Jesuit institution] *and its opposition to professors having a union. They were chartered by the Detroit Federation of Teachers. They appealed to ACTU for help after some of them didn't get contracts. The Archbishop was rather unhappy because we were going to print a story about that and he wanted me to kill it.*[20]

Not only that, but he wanted to deliver his wishes in person. Karl Hubble, new to the Detroit ACTU chaplaincy, appeared before Archbishop Mooney with a fair degree of trepidation.

"The Jesuit fathers had given him to believe," Hubble paraphrased Mooney, "that union teachers, under the guise of academic freedom, would possibly teach something contrary to Catholic dogma or morals. He also termed ACTU 'threats' to the University of Detroit 'a kind of blackmail.' He also said he might take the name 'Catholic' off *The Wage Earner*."[21]

Hubble, Clancy, and Kern had already met with the President and the Chancellor of Detroit University, with few positive results. So Hubble bravely replied to Archbishop Mooney that he could not agree to kill the story, but that he would convey the Archbishop's feelings to the Detroit ACTU Executive Board that evening. As he left, Mooney

---

19   Donnelly, Joseph, "That ADA", *Social Action Bulletin*, Diocese of Hartford (Connecticut), Nov. 15, 1950, 3.
20   Hubble, intvw., *op. cit.*
21   Hubble, Karl, "Additional Information", Mar. 21, 1990, to "ACTU Brief", Hubble to Mooney, Nov. 23, 1949. [AD]

asked him to let the Board's members know that he was willing to appoint Clancy as a mediator in the dispute.

The Board, after a tough overnight session, agreed that in view of that willingness it would drop the planned *Wage Earner* story. Hubble's back-and-forth shuttle continued—Archbishop Mooney was at the other end of Washington Boulevard from ACTU-*Wage Earner* offices. The next day he briefed the Archbishop on the meeting's answer, and Mooney promised to meet later with Hubble, to accept his written report on the chapter's position regarding the controversy, and to read the report.

> By that time it was late in the afternoon, I think it was Holy Thursday of November 1949. You have to understand: I wasn't that old in the priesthood, and I've just gone around and around with the Archbishop. Anyway, I get back to the Seminary, flat tuckered out, and my telephone rang. I picked up the phone and it was Archbishop Mooney. Of course I was surprised.
> He asked "How do you feel?"
> "All tied up," I said.
> He replied "Keep your fists at your side."[22]

The meeting Mooney promised Hubble never happened. "Eventually," Hubble concluded sadly, "the whole thing was permitted to die on the vine."

> I think this incident made him feel that we were being a pressure group, in this case pressuring the University, and he asked us "What happened to you? What you used to do in the labor schools was more educational." For a long time after that, the galley sheets of what we were going to print were pinned on the wall of The Wage Earner office, as souvenirs.[23]

The injustice revealed by this episode discouraged the members of Detroit ACTU. *Detroit Times* ace reporter Marguerite Gahagan, who replaced Paul Weber as chapter president, was especially discouraged. Not only was she a graduate of the University of Detroit, but at the request of its president, Father William Millor, SJ, she had helped it to establish a workers' education program. It was hard for Gahagan to believe that Millor opposed a union for the University's teachers, and even harder to believe that Mooney let the University get away with its stance.

---

22 Hubble, intvw., *op. cit.*
23 Hubble, *ibid.*

7 ❦ Karl Hubble

Gahagan was no stranger to opponents of union organizing. She was a leading Detroit Newspaper Guild organizer at the *Times* years before, and for that the paper demoted her to the lowly recorder's-court beat for 12 years. She responded by turning the beat into a huge plus for the paper. In the University situation, however, she felt powerless, as did Hubble and the others.

With this kind of postwar start and with its drastic organizational shift, Detroit ACTU wasn't able to find a strong sense of purpose again, nor to keep enough parish conferences alive to make the chapter's new direction viable. The chapter's labor-related activities barely made it into the second half of the fifties, and in 1958 Father Hubble left the chapter chaplaincy and resumed a full schedule as a teacher and administrator at Sacred Heart Seminary.

"What might have been" is an inescapable question in the case of Detroit ACTU. The most intriguing "road not taken," as already noted, is the road of continued coalition among Actists, socialists, and others supporting Reuther.

Reuther's course after 1947 was a perilous one. It took him through a 1948 assassination attempt, CIO's expulsion of its Communist-dominated unions, his accession to the CIO presidency in 1952, McCarthyism, the 1955 merger of AFL and CIO, and his uneasy years as number two to George Meany before Reuther took UAW out of AFL-CIO in 1968 [UAW reaffiliated with the federation in 1981]. He died at 62 in a 1970 plane crash.

At every step of his perilous journey, he was watched like a hawk to see how socialistic he would be. He had been thus watched ever since he left the Socialist Party in 1938.

He was watched by the FBI, conservative politicians and industrialists, Catholic social actionists, Communists, socialists of every stripe, UAW members, other unions' leaders, the public, you name it. Through it all he remained a dynamic leader and a true industrial democrat, improved the working lives of his members in pioneering ways, and helped them determine their destinies in workplaces dignified by their labor.

He always worked closely with Catholic social actionists, and would have welcomed Actists' remaining in the coalition which put him in office. Detroit ACTU could have been a positive force in his struggles with the capitalist crusaders who shadowed him so closely.

Nevertheless, Reuther did very well as it was. In an era short on heroes, his record shines brightly, in worker justice and in social justice generally. The same spirit which drove him is available to American workers and their allies today.

This is not a time to keep our fists at our sides. Rather, it's a time for us to channel our constructive anger and our passion for social justice into renewed organizing of workers—supervisory workers, manufacturing workers, "knowledge industry" workers, white-collar workers, all kinds of workers—and into renewing unions as a vital partner in industrial-strength democracy.

CHAPTER EIGHT
CHARLES OWEN RICE (1908–2005)

No American labor apostle spent more time as a Catholic labor activist and was more in the front lines of the labor movement's triumphs and tribulations than Father Charles Owen Rice (made a monsignor in 1963). He was feared by his foes, loved by his friends, and respected by all. This chapter focuses on his labor leadership, but his passion burned and his voice thundered for racial justice, peace, and the whole panoply of social-justice causes.

Rice was born in Brooklyn, but when he was four years old, his mother Anna died in childbirth and his father Michael sent him and his older brother Pat to Ireland to be raised by the boys' grandmother. By the time Charlie returned to the United States seven years later, his father was remarried, to Anna's older sister Jennie, and lived in Pittsburgh with Michael's brother Joe, later a CIO organizer.

Charlie Rice's Irish experience flavored both his speech and his political development, for he lived through the Easter Rising of 1916, the start of the insurrection which eventually led to Irish independence. After graduating from Duquesne University in 1930 and St. Vincent Seminary in nearby Latrobe in 1934, he looked for ways to apply the social teachings of Pope Pius XI's *Quadragesimo Anno* encyclical and of Dorothy Day's *The Catholic Worker*—powerful influences on him as a young priest—to get justice for workers in Depression-era Pittsburgh.

After ordination, Father Rice was assigned as assistant pastor at St. Agnes Church. Soon he began to actively and articulately address social and economic issues, whether in the newspaper *The Pittsburgh Catholic*, on local radio stations WWSW and WJAS, or in discussion groups for priests and laity.

In 1937, he and Fathers George Barry O'Toole and Carl Hensler, with several laypeople, formed the Catholic Radical Alliance (CRA). From the beginning, Catholic social actionists knew that if they didn't fight for workers against capitalism's rugged individualists, Communism's world revolutionists would move to the fore. The founders of CRA felt that the "Radical" in its name, an adjective suggested by O'Toole, was perfect for the two-front war they faced, because it let both capitalistic and Communistic exploiters know that Catholic social teachings are truly radical in the sense of going right to the root ("radix", in Latin) of the American society and economy. This message is clear in a paper Rice presented to the group's nucleus on April 18, 1937, and in Rice's account of the presentation's aftermath.

> This paper set forth a four-fold plan with tactics for reaching workers, the poor, the intelligentsia, and employers and the rich. The plan followed the Catholic Worker movement's plan to a great extent. The workers would be reached by a chapter of the Association of Catholic Trade Unionists [ACTU] and with aid in strikes and picketing; the poor, by a house of hospitality where they would be received as guests and where there would be friendship, material help, and instruction; the intelligentsia, by a literature-distribution campaign, counter-demonstrations at Reddish meetings, and bureaus of information on local campuses; and the rich and bosses, by instruction in their duties....
>
> With the workers our plans are going great guns. This is what has attracted attention to us. To start this part of the plan into operation is duck soup. The procedure we followed is this: We called the local CIO offices and told them what we were and how we could help them. The

CIO may not take you up right away as they are terribly disorganized as yet. Anyway they sent me to Aliquippa to talk there the day before a union election. I took a thousand <u>Catholic Workers</u> and passed them around to the crowds I talked to. We were then invited to Youngstown [Ohio] and with Bishop Schrembs' permission we went and talked to the strikers.

If that plan of attack fails of entrée, try this: Pick out a local strike or labor dispute. (We picked the Heinz trouble.) Make out signs saying that your organization supports the justice of that strike. Get a few lay members of the group and go down to join the picket line. It will be necessary before doing this to get in touch with the union leader of the trouble. Offer your services to him and he will be delighted to accept them. Tell him that you can supply him with picket signs, with pickets, with speakers for rallies, and with a statement supporting the justice of his cause....

The priest will be used chiefly for talking at rallies. The union is practically always right, unless it is an old-line racket one. But it is the best policy to talk to the management and get its side, even though you know beforehand just what sophistry it will be. You will find that you generally have to go after the union; they are not used to clerical aid, and generally stay away from priests when they have strike trouble. We have not bothered consulting the local clergy in strike troubles; that way, you save time and you avoid embarrassments.

I and Fathers Hensler and O'Toole have engaged in strike talks and picket encouragement. Our policy towards Communists in the ranks has been courtesy and friendliness. When we see <u>The Daily Worker</u> going around, we speak quietly to the union heads but we don't raise any squawk. We help AFL or CIO impartially but favor the CIO. However, we are most careful to stay out of the union civil war.

A tremendous thing happened in Pittsburgh when Father Tom Lappan, priest director of the local St. Vincent de Paul, offered aid to strikers, and in the Loose-Wiles dispute, actually gave it. That made a splendid impression. [Lappan fed 200 strikers for two weeks; the strike was won.] We have found that the anti-clericals and Communist-minded are first distrustful and then agreeably surprised beyond belief when they find there is no catch to it, but that priests really are with the People.

When we are opposed by reactionary clerics we follow no rule in particular. We speak softly to the people about the thing, explain how the others are being fooled and are not really of the people. On occasion, we have publicly cracked back at the opposition when they made public anti-union statements. We have met with a good bit of misrepresentation and attack but we rather welcome that.

> My advice to any one wishing to start something like this is to just start it. Don't try to get too many priests into the thing—take the ones who are so-minded, but don't try to get the prestige of big names. Get a hall, call a meeting—announcements in dailies and Catholic sheets—get a name for the outfit, make out a plan, get *The Catholic Worker* and some NCWC pamphlets, start in with action of some kind, and dodge the brickbats. You will be amazed what the Roman Collar and a little brass can do.[1]

The "Heinz trouble" Rice referred to as CRA's first labor activism was an AFL Canning and Pickle Workers' June 1937 strike at a huge food factory of the H. J. Heinz Company. The CIO had just formed and was energetically organizing, and its youthfulness and vigor inspired some unions of the more-lethargic AFL. Full-page ads appeared in Pittsburgh newspapers denouncing the strike and praising the company.

> This was the time for action and our CRA following was ready. So I rallied a contingent of them, including some nice-looking young women, and the two other priests, and with our Catholic Radical Alliance signs simply went down and joined the pickets. Some of the pickets were a bit timid and didn't like our use of the word "Radical", but we held firm and kept the signs. I saw to it that the newspapers covered our foray. There was an uproar. Priests had not picketed before anywhere, to my knowledge. We were denounced from pulpits and in the papers by a few of the clergy. Heinz was a paternalistic company and had helped neighboring parishes.
>
> Father James R. Cox, a great radio priest, had supported labor in the darkest days of the 1920s and early 1930s, but he was a Republican, albeit a stormy and rebellious one, and was AFL-minded. For him, the CIO was a bunch of Communists. He said there were Communists involved in organizing Heinz. Indeed there were, although I wasn't sure of it at the time, and stoutly denied the allegation. Even if I had known, I, and I am sure the other priests, would have supported the strikers anyway since their cause was just, and we were not about to abandon them to the Communists or to fate. We addressed many meetings, and I was very vocal and rhetorical. (The owner of Heinz, grandfather of the

---

1   Rice, Charles, "Catholic Radical Alliance", *The Work of the Priest*, Washington, D.C.: Social Action Department, 1938.

Senator, told a confidant later on that I had made the difference. I hope that was true.) This action even made the pages of *Time*.[2]

A CRA member took part in settlement negotiations, which resulted in agreement by both parties to an NLRB-supervised election. Fathers Rice, Hensler, and O'Toole urged the plant's workers to vote for the union, and it won the election.

The labor-management situation was tense in Pittsburgh and across the nation. In March 1937, U.S. Steel had signed an agreement with the Steel Workers Organizing Committee (SWOC) without a fight, but the "Little Steel" companies fought unions bitterly. Chicago's Memorial Day massacre of workers at Republic Steel, one of those companies, took place just days before the Heinz strike, and right after its settlement, the Steelworkers union asked CRA to help in its strike against another Little Steel company, Youngstown. "I got the other two priests [Hensler and O'Toole] in my little Chevy," Rice recalled, "and we hit the picket lines there."[3] Here's part of what Rice told the steel strikers:

> If you men organize and stay organized in a strong and just union, this will be good not only for yourselves, but for the country at large and for your employers themselves, though at the moment they can't see it. The principle of union and cooperation is a good one and we can only regret that it is so lacking in American life today. You men, organized and loyal to each other, to your country and your God, have a chance to bring that principle of unity and cooperation into our life; and I hope, and know, that you will not let that chance slip by.
>
> Because I have come here at this moment I shall be accused of injecting religion into the labor issue, and I reply: It is about time that religion was introduced into that issue. The reason we have labor strife today, the reason we have had it for generations, the reason six men lost their lives in Illinois last week, is that religion and religious principles have been kept out of the labor question. Because religion was forgotten, no, not forgotten but deliberately thrown aside, too many industrialists have conducted their affairs as if Christ had never lived and died, as if there were no just God in heaven, and have tried to rule like the absolute Pagan Emperors of old, forgetting that they were dealing with human beings, endowed with human rights by the God who made them.

---

2   Rice, "America's Darkest Decade", *The Critic*, 1987, in *Fighter with a Heart*, Charles J. McCollester, ed., Pittsburgh: University of Pittsburgh Press, 1996, 27.

3   Ibid.

> If Christianity were injected into the labor issue, and if the Charity of Christ reigned there rather than the naked greed of Hell, laborers would long since have been treated as partners and cooperators, to be helped and loved, not as wage slaves to be exploited and kept down; all employers would have given decent wages, decent working conditions, security of employment, and common human liberty to their workers. But the Charity of Christ has been absent from the hearts of the great mass of these rulers of industry and trade, and the result has been the class war, rather than class cooperation. Sad to relate, many of the malefactors, who in practice were flouting the straight doctrine of Christ, have brazenly masqueraded as Christians of the holiest kind.
>
> There are those who today view the march of labor with alarm. Some do this because they have been fooled by false cries of Communism, directed at labor leaders, others do it out of sheer white-collar snobbery, and others still because they fear the laborer whom they have exploited and can exploit no longer. Let them put their fears to rest. The laboring man in this country does not demand a Godless soviet system, the SWOC does not demand it; but they do demand, and we all demand, that the Godless features of our own system cease and give place to an order that recognizes God, and human rights and duties, and justice for all....[4]

The Little Steel companies together were a huge and unyielding force, and eventually broke that strike. But the three Pittsburgh priests won many converts to unionism in Youngstown with their bravery and forthrightness in the face of numerous obstacles. The rally they addressed took place in the midst of a driving rain, and Rice spoke from under an umbrella. Cars drove back and forth, revving their engines to drown out speakers. Some local clergymen denounced the strikes, with a few entering a mill to say Mass for scabs. Youngstown's establishment opposed the steelworkers, as did the city's newspapers and even a few local AFL leaders.

The next two years were busy and challenging ones for the versatile Father Rice. In November 1937, St. Joseph House of Hospitality opened, with Rice as administrator, and soon it was feeding and sleeping several hundred needy people daily; Rice became residential director in February 1940, guiding the caring efforts of scores of volunteers.

Labor still occupied much of Rice's agenda, although versatility prevailed there too. He gave the opening prayer at CIO's founding

---

4   Rice, "Speech to Little Steel Strikers in Youngstown", June 6, 1937, in McCollester, 35-6.

national convention, held in Pittsburgh on November 14, 1938. He organized and directed CRA labor schools, which became ACTU labor schools in fall 1938 with formation of a Pittsburgh chapter of that organization. In the next year schools started at the North Side and Oakland branches of Boys' Catholic High School; these schools extended into mid-World War II, with no enrollment limitations and an average enrollment per school of about 70 men and 30 women per term.

Among the courses in Pittsburgh's Catholic labor schools were labor history, legislation, logic, parliamentary law, public speaking, labor ethics, simplified economics, organizing and operating a union, workman's compensation, and time study and rate-setting. Teachers included Rice; Father Hensler; diocesan adult-education director Cyril Vogel; ACTU executive director Frank McCabe; and Father Michael Faidel, organizer of the ACTU national convention held in Pittsburgh in September 1941. Texts included the NCWC pamphlet *Toward Social Justice*, by Father Ray McGowan, and books on a special shelf maintained at Carnegie Public Library.

Pittsburgh's labor schools, as other labor schools we've highlighted, had plenty of real-life examples for study and involvement. In an article in *The Pittsburgh Catholic* announcing the 1940 fall term, McCabe of ACTU reported speaking on its schools to union audiences nearly every weekday, Saturday, and Sunday. In addition, he noted Father Rice's speaking at Local 424 of the Retail Food Stores Employees Union and at Local 590 of the Amalgamated Meat Cutters and Butcher Workmen of North America. The Local 424 meeting discussed contract provisions, including overtime, minimum-wage rates, and dues and insurance payments of draftees.

McCabe also pointed out how much picketers at Childs Restaurant and Whelan's drug store appreciated Actists joining picket lines and carrying signs showing their support. Hubbard strikers, he added, thanked Actists for the bread and vegetables they distributed and remarked upon support coming from both CIO and AFL unionists. "Members of the rank and file in labor are still pulling together," McCabe concluded.[5]

In 1939, as Europe rearmed, the U.S. economy started to regain strength but not necessarily labor peace. Companies wanting to win war-related contracts and avoid strikes suddenly became more coop-

---

5 "ACTU, Pittsburgh Chapter", *Pittsburgh Catholic*, Oct. 10, 1940, 12.

erative, while unions increased their aggressiveness to get the kind of agreement they felt they should have gotten all along.

Also, the coming of war prompted far-sighted labor observers to ask tough questions about the long-uneasy man-machine relationship. Rice, for example, in "The Machine and Society" in *The Pittsburgh Catholic*, acknowledged that the steel industry's replacement of hand mills by continuous strip mills meant that 15,000 workers produced an output previously requiring 125,000 workers, and that one result was much higher profits. However, he added, in a non-robust economy price decreases and jobs for those displaced might very well not accompany such a technological development.

> *The important thing is not the making of profits. It is not the turning out of more products which are cheaper and better. No, it is the proper sociological and moral use of the instruments of industry. The machine must serve the common good. When debating whether or not to install new machinery, the decision should hinge on the welfare of the workers and the community as a whole. There are no inevitable laws of economics left—the depression has repealed them all.*[6]

Stimulating speculation about economic morality was not the order of the day in that era, although it was the order of the day several decades later, and Father Rice was right in the middle of it then too (see pp. 213). But the pace of the early 1940s was too fast for much reflection, and too often generated by events foreign to America and thus outside of its control.

The rapid rise of CIO and the accession of Phil Murray to its presidency gave many friends of labor a real cause for rejoicing—"it [CIO] fired the imaginations of millions of workers," Rice enthused, "and gave them their first delicious taste of industrial liberty!"[7]—but rejoicing had to be brief. The "fly in the ointment" was the heavy influence of CIO unions' Communists at a time when their priorities were determined by Party-line gyrations: first the reformist masquerade of 1935-39, then disruption of industry in the Nazi-Soviet pact era, then being industrialists' echo after Hitler invaded Russia and throughout World War II.

---

6 Rice, "The Machine and Society", *Pittsburgh Catholic*, June 22, 1939, in McCollester, 48-52.

7 Rice, "Lewis, Murray, and the CIO", June 2, 1960, in McCollester, 63.

8 ❦ Charles Owen Rice

From the beginnings of the Catholic social-action movement, affirming social justice and opposing Communism were linked priorities. Father Rice represented the positive approach to these priorities, the approach predominant in the movement. He was one of its staunchest anti-Communists, but in so open and forthright a manner that he gained the respect of many of his Communist foes, as when, on October 10, 1938, he vigorously but respectfully debated Clarence Hathaway, editor of *The Daily Worker*, in front of 2,000 listeners. In a 1937 speech to Canton, Ohio, strikers, Rice articulated his anti-Communism.

> *The twin evils of Fascism and Communism have grown up across the water and they have been brought into being and nourished by the injustices of the social and economic setup. These horrors have been worse than the disease they set out to cure and we in America want none of them. We have it in us, I believe, to avoid these excesses, but if we are to avoid them and keep intact our country and our traditions, we must overcome the things that breed Communism and its reaction. Here is where labor unionism comes in. The labor union is a middle-of-the-road attempt to cure certain of the more flagrant abuses in current history.... The labor union, the CIO in particular, has been called everything from Communist to Fascist, but it is none of these things. It is a normal American, Christian attempt to right certain unbearable wrongs, and in my mind it may well serve as the first step toward the building of a new, just, Christian, United States of America.*[8]

Openness and forthrightness were important in Rice's anti-Communist stance, but certainly didn't preclude his competing fiercely with Communists in Pittsburgh's unions when occasion arose. In 1941, when Communists took over the leadership of the huge Westinghouse Local 601 of the United Electrical, Radio and Machine Workers of America (UERMWA, or just UE), Rice worked with members who sought to regain control. For example, he organized a labor school for them in St. William's parish, and in elections later that year the leadership switched back, although it reversed again at the end of the war.

Father Rice was appointed federal rent-control director for Pittsburgh during the war, and between that position and the House of Hospitality directorship, he had much less time for labor activism. The Communists, behind their camouflage of patriotic proclamations,

---

8   Rice, "Speech to Canton, Ohio Strikers", Aug. 20, 1937, in McCollester, 38.

kept burrowing into CIO unions with considerable success, much of which they squandered with another abrupt shift of strategy late in the war and in the postwar period.

As Stalin moved to dominate Eastern Europe, Communists everywhere took a hard line in support—a line which in America took the form of opposition to the Marshall Plan and allegiance to the Progressive Party. This group ran former Secretary of Agriculture Henry Wallace for President in 1948 and was resoundingly defeated.

Rice, fearing for the labor movement if Communists were able to push it away from its Democratic Party base, returned to full-time labor activism in 1947. Locally, he resumed work with members of UE Local 601 to try to again unseat its Communist leadership, and nationally he helped mobilize unions and their locals to fight Communist influence and control. His major vehicles for this mobilization were his *Pittsburgh Catholic* columns; a series of articles in the nationally-distributed Catholic publication *Our Sunday Visitor*; and his *How to De-Control Your Union of Communists*, a practical manual for unionists. His 1947 article "Philip Murray and the Reds" is typical of this output.

> *Philip Murray, president of the CIO, is a Catholic and a good man. He is also an extremely loyal, patriotic American citizen, and a clean, honest trade unionist.*
>
> *These facts are known to a great many, who ask, "Why, then, are communists tolerated in the CIO?" They are not exactly tolerated, but they are in a position of some strength in CIO unions because they have been there for a long time....*
>
> *The CIO is a congress of unions. Each of the international unions which comprise it is in theory and in fact independent.... Murray could arrange to expel from the CIO those unions which are Red-tainted or dominated; but that would not extirpate the communists. The Red bloc of unions could operate independently. There would be no check on them at all....*
>
> *The CIO convention [the 1946 annual convention in Atlantic City, N.J.] and its aftermath are important. Two very important things happened there. A change was made in the rules and regulations governing state and city industrial-union councils; and a resolution was drawn up and passed....*
>
> *The state and city central bodies are merely clearing-houses. They permit the various CIO unions in a locality to meet regularly and consider common problems. The councils have little power. However, the commu-*

nists put them to good use. Their voting and representation rules were such that "paper" unions could club together to gain control. In many cities and states these councils became sounding boards for communist propaganda. The change in the voting rules automatically weakens the Red stranglehold on such bodies.

Furthermore, restrictions were placed on the councils as to resolutions that could be passed and organizations that could be supported and financially aided. This second provision has had the immediate and continuing effect of closing down those bodies completely as sounding-off devices for the communists. That move has definitely worked, and the communists are puzzled. Also, Red-dominated international unions which could not be put under the ban have been more careful about their party-line sputterings....

In some ways this [the ban] is not a bright idea, because all worthy organizations could not possibly be listed and some good ones are omitted along with the bad. But the idea was to exclude the bad, and that is done. The omissions of worthy charities can be corrected.

During the convention, a committee of six, consisting of an equal number of right- and left-wingers, was instructed to draft a resolution condemning communism. After terrific squabbling, a resolution "condemning and resenting communist interference" and not mentioning any other systems or organizations was voted out of committee and passed by the convention unanimously.[9]

Many feared that this resolution was a weak compromise and would have little practical effect. Results, however, proved otherwise. The resolution, according to Rice, spurred the house-cleaning of CIO's central bodies, permeated internationals and locals, and heartened Murray to keep up the pressure.

Harry Bridges [President, International Longshoremen's & Warehousemen's Union] has been removed as director from more than half the West Coast unions. Others of "leftist" leaning have been restrained. The southern CIO drive remains clear of the Reds in spite of the screaming by the Red-controlled internationals which must contribute to it.

Ferment within the communist-dominated United Electrical Workers has been quickened. The enormous (18,000) Westinghouse local in Pittsburgh rejected a communist-favored slate of officers and installed professed anti-communists. The large Dayton, Ohio local followed suit. And in New York, New England, and elsewhere, UE locals have thrown off the Red yoke. [See Chapter Six.]

---

9   Rice, "Philip Murray and the Reds", The Catholic Digest, May 1947 (from Our Sunday Visitor, Mar. 23, 1947), 97-101.

In Pittsburgh, Detroit, Chicago, and St. Louis, unions of postal employees withdrew entirely from the Red United Public Workers and are demanding a separate CIO charter. Ten locals of the Mine, Mill and Smelter Workers, protesting that the Red slate of international officers was elected by fraud, have withdrawn from the International and demanded a separate charter. Joseph Curran, president of the National Maritime Union, formerly safe in the Red camp, is fighting the communists more openly every day and has smashed the Red-dominated Committee for Maritime Unity. There is a stirring in Michael Quill's Transport Workers Union. [In a year's time, Quill broke with the Communists, tearing up his CP membership card in front of 2,000 TWU members.] *In this winter's elections in Murray's own United Steel Workers, the few communists who stuck their heads above water were smashingly defeated....*

Lewis Merrill, in the most surprising move of all, had his union, the United Office and Professional Workers of America, pass a resolution even stronger than the official CIO version. He personally withdrew from the staff of the Thomas Jefferson Labor School and New Masses, both communist outfits.

But is it necessary to proceed in this relatively roundabout way? Could not Murray blast away at the Reds, expel their unions and raid them? The answer is No, for several reasons.

The direct-assault method would certainly split the CIO. Some unions would drop out, or be forced out. In others, the Steelworkers for instance, the communists, through certain entrenched positions which they hold by rank-and-file vote, could wreak havoc. The communists have enough of the rank and file bamboozled to cause serious disruptions in many unions which they do not actually control.

The CIO is not firmly enough established to withstand a bitter civil war such as would certainly eventuate if a direct assault were made to clean out the communists. Even if John L. Lewis' District 50 and the entire AFL were not standing by to pick up stragglers and perhaps start wholesale raiding, it would be risky business to plunge the organization into an internal pitched battle.

Philip Murray is not one to destroy but one to conserve. He is reckoned about the greatest cohesive force organized labor ever produced. He ranks right with [Samuel] Gompers [AFL's founder] *in this faculty*. Before Murray became CIO president, his genius for holding people together saved the Auto Workers Union from destruction. It is agreed that no one else could have saved the CIO at the time he took over.

Is the CIO worth saving? It certainly is. It is doing a job for the workers in mass-production industries that was not being done until

CIO came on the scene. It has made a contribution to the welfare of hitherto-unorganized millions of Americans that entitles it to a bright place in history.

The CIO is a good organization. Philip Murray has done a good thing in saving it and keeping it together. He is fighting a good fight, in the way he judges the most effective.

It behooves all Catholics and other men of good will to aid him in the battle. Catholics in Red-dominated CIO unions have an obligation to learn the facts and cooperate with other men who are trying to drive the communists out by the only effective means, democratic action.[10]

As much as Murray and Rice disliked the "direct-assault method," eventually it had to be resorted to. CIO's Communists knew they were on a collision course with Phil Murray. The Communists in UE knew they were on a collision course with the union's "right wingers" and their Catholic social-action allies. In both cases, however, the Communist laborites were too committed to the Comintern's agenda to adjust their behavior. Rice heard one veteran unionist's summary of the results: "Once again, the Communists have succeeded in capturing themselves."[11]

The critical moment was expulsion of UE and the Farm Equipment Workers union at the November 1949 CIO national convention in Cleveland, a move that preceded expulsion of nine other Communist-dominated CIO unions the following year.[12] The Communist leaders of UE barely managed to retain control at that union's national convention two months before the Cleveland action, even though Pittsburgh's huge Local 601, for the first time, sent a right-wing slate of delegates. "We have cleaned our house," Murray said after the last of the 11 expulsions.[13]

Murray, Rice, and many others in labor and Catholic social action greeted this necessary step with a sense of loss over the departure of former colleagues and their vital if misguided energies. As Rice mentioned above, he and his allies had wanted to go the real "democratic

---

10   Ibid.
11   Rice, "That's All Brother", *Pittsburgh Catholic*, Nov. 3, 1948, in McCollester, 88.
12   The 11 unions are listed in footnote 27, Chapter Six.
13   McAuliffe, Mary Sperling, *Crisis on the Left: Cold War Politics and American Liberals, 1947-1954*, Amherst: University of Massachusetts Press, 1978, 58.

action" route of restoring soundness and democracy to locals and unions from within, from members who always made labor's agenda their top priority and who cared enough and worked hard enough to move that agenda forward. Sadly, there were not enough members of that type to follow the "democratic action" route all the way through. Also, too many companies took advantage of unions' internecine warfare to keep labor down.

> It is enough to make any good union man's heart sick, and very angry, the way certain unions are breaking up. Unions that under clean leadership could have lasted indefinitely and could have done a splendid job are slipping every day. Some of these Communist-controlled unions during the war got into small open-shop towns where unions had never existed before. They got in under the magic name of the CIO and now they are breaking up.
>
> Anti-Communists do not want to destroy these unions. They want to reform them. They want to force the Communist officers to sign the Taft-Hartley affidavits so that they can at least get on the ballot and defend themselves. But the members are taking matters into their own hands. Instead of the hard job of clearing out the Reds, they do the easy job of just dropping out of the union. Anti-labor companies are having a field day. In many cases they just will not deal with the union and it melts away. In some places there is a fight, as in the Univis at Dayton, or a long bitter struggle, as with the Hoover Company in Canton, but the end is the same, unless the union is cleaned up and rescued.[14]

The Taft-Hartley Act required a union's officers to sign non-Communist affidavits before that union could use the National Labor Relations Board to call elections and for other purposes. Since UE officers refused to sign (until it was too late), thus putting the union at risk of being decertified, some anti-labor companies moved for decertification.

> The viciously anti-union Remington-Rand Corporation has moved to de-certify the UE in six of its plants.... The Remington-Rand has a bad labor record. Even though the UE has its Communists I don't wish the corporation any success in its drive against the UE. Communists can be cleaned out through rank-and-file action. That is the way ACTU likes to see it done.[15]

---

14 Rice, "Sickening", *Pittsburgh Catholic*, Aug. 26, 1948, in McCollester, 82.
15 Rice, "UE Troubles", *Pittsburgh Catholic*, Nov. 27, 1947, in McCollester, 81.

Many Communist officers, as noted in a *Work* article cited earlier (see p. 131-32), signed the affidavits since the Act's "wording makes prosecution almost impossible." Rice was against keeping the affidavits.

> A solution for Communism in unions, that destroys unions, is no solution at all. For example I personally would deeply regret the wrecking of the United Electrical Workers union. [This was written the year before expulsion.] I want a solution for Communism that will keep the union but get rid of the Reds. Such a solution will take years but it is the only way. The members have to be assisted in doing a democratic job of house cleaning. It is slow and hard, but it is the only worthwhile way.
>
> This type of reasoning is what has kept Philip Murray from issuing a duplicate charter in the CIO to Electrical Workers and opening an all-out war on the UE. It would probably at this time mean a vicious fight of uncertain outcome, but with a real risk of destroying hundreds of local unions which are functioning passably at the moment.[16]

Rice continually made clear that he opposed unions which were Communist-dominated, not unions which had strong internal opposition. He repeatedly emphasized his view that locals where members fight vigorously for their principles and positions are among the best locals. He saw a local's greatest enemy as indifference, which in his opinion caused more locals to fold than anything else—50 had done so, he estimated, by September 1948.

> They [Communists] use the unions, those they now control, to supply jobs and training for worthy Communists; to dribble amounts of money to various Communist front organizations; and to issue endorsements and pass resolutions favorable to the Party Line and Soviet Russia. This type of misuse of a union does not annoy the ordinary rank-and-file member. This all important citizen is fair game for the Communist propaganda that his particular Communist-controlled union is doing a wonderful job for him and there is nothing to get excited about. That is the anatomy of Communist labor control as I see it.
>
> At any rate, we have seen the spectacle of a large union of American working men, made up of delegates elected with a reasonable semblance of democracy, endorsing Russian foreign policy at the moment of the most acute crisis between Russia and America; and at the moment

---

16 Rice, "Effects on Communist Unions", *Pittsburgh Catholic*, Nov. 11, 1948, in McCollester, 85-6.

when the cleavage between Russia and America has been most clearly established. That is a real Communist victory.[17]

Rice was always amazed at the indifference which enabled such a triumph, but occasionally he got letters which were rays of hope, such as this one from a woman worker in a UE plant:

> Dear Father Rice: I was surprised and felt very shy when I was nominated to the executive board last summer but I attended the meetings very faithfully. The Communist propaganda I heard made me sick. I tried to tell the girls what I thought and a few of us got together, elected a new steward in our department, then started attending a Catholic labor school. Two of the girls had some of your literature. We read that and passed it around, then started to fight. So far we have elected a new president and one other officer. We made peace with the state CIO and voted down the local edition of *The Daily Worker*.[18]

After UE's expulsion, the union which replaced it, the International Union of Electrical, Radio and Machine Workers, or IUE, became a thriving union in its own right. The cheers of constructive anti-Communists were short-lived, however, for on February 7, 1950, U.S. Senator Joseph McCarthy emerged from a plane in Wheeling, West Virginia waving around a sheaf of papers which he said carried the names of 205 card-carrying Communists who supposedly had burrowed their way into the deepest recesses of the U.S. State Department. Ahead lay four years of McCarthyism and its damages in every direction—to constructive anti-Communism, to labor, to Catholic social action, to fairness, and to America society generally.

Father Rice fought McCarthyism vigorously, but at the same time it was the beginning of an eye-opening educational experience for him, a passage in his life which led him to a deeper and broader exploration of social justice. Another 1950 prompt for this passage was the replacement of longtime Bishop Hugh Boyle with the more conservative John Dearden. Boyle, who as a young priest had picketed with the 1919 Homestead strikers when corporations had enlisted most churches as strike opponents, was a supporter of Father Rice's labor activism, but Rice had not endeared himself to Dearden.

---

17 Rice, "Not Weakening", *Pittsburgh Catholic*, Oct. 14, 1948, in McCollester, 85.
18 Rice, "The Struggle for UE", *Pittsburgh Catholic*, Oct. 2, 1947, in McCollester, 80.

Dearden had been in the Youngstown area at the time of the Little Steel strike and, according to Rice, "is said to have carried a not-too-favorable impression of your humble correspondent, who had dared to make fiery speeches in a time of turmoil."[19] Dearden wasted little time distancing himself from Rice, in 1952 reassigning him to serve as pastor of St. Joseph's Church in Natrona, Pennsylvania. In 1955 Dearden took over *The Pittsburgh Catholic*, which previously was independently published, and relieved Rice of his column.

Rice struggled to adjust to the prevailing conservatism of those times, in the Pittsburgh Diocese as well as in national politics during the Eisenhower administration and the rapid expansion of the military-industrial complex. Philip Murray's death in 1952 was a real blow to Rice, and gradually his focus shifted from labor to the alleviation of poverty and, in the 1960s, to civil rights activism and to protest against the Vietnam war.

Bishop John Wright replaced Bishop Dearden in 1958 and Rice's situation improved considerably. He got his *Pittsburgh Catholic* column back; served as pastor of Immaculate Conception Church in Washington, Pennsylvania from 1958-61; and was assigned, at his own request, as pastor of Holy Rosary Church in Pittsburgh's Homewood, an African-American neighborhood where from 1965-76 he helped guide his parishioners and the city through a time of racial discord and civil unrest. In 1976, at age 68, he became pastor of St. Anne's in Castle Shannon, a parish just south of Pittsburgh and the place where Phil Murray is buried.

In the 1970s and beyond, after a generation's worth of diverse and challenging spiritual and social-justice missions and experiences—starting with the jolt of McCarthyism—Charles Owen Rice reevaluated his life and career in ways which challenge all of us to deepen our understanding of him. He looked back, for example, on the Army-McCarthy hearings.

> He [McCarthy] made the mistake of picking on those who could fight back, which is always bad. Too many strong folks felt threatened and the powers went after him. They had all enjoyed him for a while and they used him, but he got too big for his britches....
> The powers had set McCarthy up in the hearings. They put him on trial, him not the Army, and they closed ranks against him. The betting

---

19   Rice, "Memories of a Union Strike", *Pittsburgh Catholic*, Sept. 4, 1981, in McCollester, 40.

was that he could not act with restraint but would knock himself out; he did.

There lay his fault (a happy fault for the sake of decency), no inner censor to tell him when he went too far. You see it was all right for him to smear Democrats, liberal Republicans, the colleges, actors, bureaucrats large and small (others were doing the same and getting by), but President Eisenhower was out of season, so was our grand and glorious military, and so were a variety of respectable men and institutions, which McCarthy did not fear but would have been wise to.

McCarthy destroyed people, most of them little people, and he seemed to enjoy the work.

McCarthyism was an era and a malignancy and it had an effect on liberals of a certain type who became ultra anti-Communist; even some who had been sensible and tolerant began proclaiming that their anti-Communism was as strong as anyone's. They would think that they were correct because they were careful to be hostile only to real Communists, or, at most, fellow travelers, but bad laws were passed, some of which were sponsored by liberal legislators, and freedom suffered.

It annoys me that I was one of those bad liberals, my only virtue being that, unlike others, I had not played up to the Communists when they were strong and could help one. I deeply regret that I did not fight to have their rights fully respected. Communism seemed almost irresistible and certainly irreversible; it is only a step from regarding the enemy as superhuman to regarding him as unhuman.[20]

As for his anti-Communism within labor, Rice regretted some aspects of it and affirmed others. Of the dangers posed by American labor's Communists having primary loyalty to the Comintern and secondary loyalty to labor, Rice still believed that these dangers had been very real, but looking back he felt he'd exaggerated them. On the other hand, he held firm to his conviction that a Communist takeover of the labor movement "would have been a disaster."[21]

> A persistent question is, what would have happened if their [the Communists'] control of unions had increased, or even been solidified, and if Phil Murray and the CIO had not turned on them? I still believe that the resultant reaction would have been bad, if not disastrous, for labor; more and worse repressive legislation and a hobbling of all unions. The

---

20   Rice, "The McCarthy Era", *Pittsburgh Catholic*, Aug. 31, 1973, in McCollester, 107-8.
21   Rice, "Confessions of an Anti-Communist", *Labor History*, Summer 1989, 101.

great post-war boom in trade union membership and the consequent economic gains of the American labor force would have been in danger.[22]

Many of Rice's regrets were awakened by the McCarthy era and the climate it created.

> My regrets about the whole business, on looking back, cluster around my over intensity and my unremitting enmity, almost a blood feud that went on and on until well after they [Communists] ceased to be a domestic threat, along with my complete acceptance of our country's Cold War stance and rhetoric. I should have been fighting the Arms Race and supporting peace then and been an early anti-war agitator.
>
> Johnson's invasion of the Dominican Republic started me thinking properly, and Vietnam completed the process....[23]

As for specific regrets, Rice says "I talked too freely" on Communism in the UE to Pennsylvania Congressman Francis Walter in connection with an August 1949 House Un-American Activities Committee hearing, on the eve of crucial elections in UE Local 601. "I had his [Walter's] promise that he would not divulge me," Rice noted, "but as soon as there was the slightest fuss he quoted me. That is politics; if you mess with it you may get smeared."[24]

Rice admitted that during the long period of battles between labor's Communists and labor's anti-Communists and their allies, he had contacts with FBI agents, as did other Catholic social actionists. Contacts were a far cry, however, from FBI-directed activities. Rice-FBI contacts ended abruptly in the 1960s, after a Rice remark on Mike Levine's KDKA radio show in Pittsburgh.

> Mike and I were discussing Rev. Martin Luther King, along with whom I had just led an anti-war protest, when a woman called in to say that J. Edgar [Hoover] had branded Doctor King a communist. My rejoinder was that Hoover was "a punch-drunk old man, and totally unreliable."
>
> FBI files reveal that the revered FBI director was informed immediately and reacted angrily. The Most Rev. John J. Wright, Lord Rest Him, was our Bishop and generally approved my tough stances, but this was different. I met him the next day at a confirmation and he said "Cholly, not Hoovah! Not Hoovah!" I then laid off.

---

22 Ibid.
23 Ibid., 102.
24 Rice, "Response" in Symposium on *Fighter with a Heart, Labor History*, January 1999, 67.

> Obviously, before the rest of us knew the ugly truth, John Wright did, namely, that we were dealing with a man as evil as he was powerful.
>
> Later, when I allowed the Black Panthers to use Holy Rosary's cafeteria to serve breakfast for hungry black kids, Hoover again reacted angrily. Handwritten and initialed by him was the injunction to consider using "COINTELPRO"—disruption, sabotage, slander, and wire-taps. I'm glad it was not used.[25]

Some Communistic viewpoints fasten on the regrets and reevaluations of Rice and other Catholic labor activists as if they were exhibits in the Communists' case against the entire Catholic social-action movement. With Rice and the others, however, that case founders on its contentions that Catholic social actionists were all about anti-Communism and that there were no socialistic influences (even of Christian socialism) in the social action movement.

There is much evidence in this volume contrary to that case and to its corollary about the McCarthy era—that all anti-Communists were McCarthyites, and that if you were against Communism you were for capitalism's excesses. Communists, of course, claimed that the only valid socialism was revolutionary socialism, and thus slammed reform socialists, who were (and are) among their bitterest enemies. "I did not make the mistake," Rice was glad to say, "of calling an ordinary Socialist, of whatever variety, a Communist and was reasonably precise in my attacks and accusations. Early I learned to distinguish who was who and what was what among the left, and whacked only the Communists".[26]

At heart, Rice's anti-Communism was simply a byproduct of what he describes as his "extraordinary regard, love would not be too strong a word, for the trade union movement."[27] He traced the origins of that force.

> Along with many other young people of that generation [in the mid-1930s] I held labor to be not just a worthy cause, but virtually a holy one. Unions were not merely something that would make life better for working people but they could lead to the reform of society. They could energize and transform the working class and the rural proletariat and could actually change people, make them less selfish and so on. Even

---

25 Rice, "Cholly, Not Hoovah! Not Hoovah!", *Pittsburgh Catholic*, Sept. 29, 1989, in McCollester, 139.

26 Rice, "Confessions of an Anti-Communist", *op. cit.*, 101.

27 *Ibid.*, 100.

after I abandoned that rather naïve belief I continued to champion unions, still do, and I believe in them today as a necessity for a just society. Stronger unions mean more economic health for most people. Unions should be democratically controlled and have honest leadership, but even less perfect unions are better than none at all.[28]

Throughout Rice's life, his love for labor stayed strong, even when he devoted most of his energies to other aspects of social justice. He spoke out against the increasing conservatism of the labor movement (often backing rank-and-file insurgencies seeking to reform locals and unions), fought racially exclusionary practices in the building-trades unions and elsewhere in labor, and criticized Catholic hospitals and nursing homes resisting unionization.

In 1979, in the midst of the decline in the Pittsburgh-area steel industry and of the plant closings which accompanied that decline, Rice entered another phase of labor activism. Encouraged by Charles McCollester, at that time a machinist in a Union Switch and Signal Plant and a UE chief steward, Rice got involved with the Tri-State Conference on Steel, a group formed to deal with the human and societal impacts of the steel decline and the plant closings.

Rice called upon 40 years of exploring such impacts, going all the way back to his column "The Machine and Society" (summarized earlier), to make significant contributions to this group over the next two decades. The group's members, including Rice and clergy of other faiths, and McCollester and other unionists (officers and rank-and-filers), worked hard to help the victims of decline, to save as much of the steel industry as possible, and to pull in new industries. Rice's call for "ownership and responsibility shared between employees and communities"[29] formed a full circle with those early days when, armed with "the Roman Collar and a little brass," he preached worker justice with the social-action encyclicals as his texts.

Charles McCollester, now a professor of labor and industrial relations at Indiana University of Pennsylvania, compiled a collection of Rice's writings, coupled it with an insightful essay on Rice, and in 1996 published *Fighter with a Heart*. It's a fine book with a fitting title, and editor McCollester captures much of the spirit of the book's subject when he says that Rice "expressed a Catholic social philosophy that

---

28 Ibid.
29 Rice, "Lack of Commitment", *Pittsburgh Catholic*, Apr. 2, 1982, in McCollester, 198.

was politically radical but theologically orthodox"[30]—orthodox in the sense which *America* editor Father John LaFarge conveyed when he said "In preaching the Gospel week after week, one could always avoid the overly-obvious socialistic conclusions of the discourses of our Lord Jesus Christ—or else be suspected of a certain degree of socialism."[31]

Monsignor Charles Owen Rice died in 2005 at 96. He is buried in St. Anne's churchyard not far from the final resting place of his brother in faith and labor Philip Murray. May they rest in peace and inspire us to justice.

---

30   McCollester, *Fighter with a Heart, op. cit.*, xix.
31   LaFarge, John, *The Manner Is Ordinary*, New York: Harcourt, Brace Co., 1954, 246-7.

CHAPTER NINE
PHILIP CAREY (1907–1989)

My father worked as a conductor on the 23rd Street trolley line [in New York City]. See, if you were literate, they made you conductor. Otherwise, they put you on the front end of the car. He was off two days a year. We used to see him Sunday afternoon when he let us ride on the front of the trolley.

There must have been six or eight ferries that came in on 23rd Street. The starter would ring up say a hundred fares. They had a little board on the side of the car, and that's where my father would have to go, because the people were hangin' from the sides. If he didn't collect the fares, they came out of his pocket.

The brutality of the job was incredible. Like on the Fourth of July once, he was an extra man and he was over at the West Farms barn tryin' to get another car. He was over in the back, and there was an open inspection pit. He fell down a whole flight and hit his head against a snowplow. He was pounding at the door for the longest while before they found him. They put him on the front of a trolley car and took him down to the hospital, and he was out about a month. But the guy who was in charge for compensation had skipped off with the funds, so my father didn't get any compensation.

They never got paid for eating time, and he always had to keep his time card because the receiver would cheat him. My father was a man with an enormous sense of justice. God would love him. A normal man would have been bitter at the treatment he was getting. He wasn't that way. He would say "I am thankful to God that I will not have to face my Judgment Day with that on my soul. They will have to do it. I won't."...

There was a trolley strike in 1916. During the strike, he came down to the waterfront to get some work. He worked the barbed wire and cement because no one would handle that. The breathing was awful. The barbed wire just tore all his clothes. There was a wonderful priest at that time at Guardian Angel, Father McGrath, who told my father after two days, "You're not the man for this kind of work. Get back. Don't stay around here."

Soon, we were down to having tea and toast—that's bread and water with a little coloration. Every week the superintendent would come around and beg my father to come to work. Then they brought in all those scabs from the Bowery. They didn't know anything about operating trolley cars. But we knew it was over when they brought in all the fellows from out of state. They were all put up in the yard with Red Cross supplies. When the strike was over my father went back to work, but he always wore his union button inside his hat.[1]

As he describes his dad, John, Father Philip Carey in large measure describes himself—intelligent, intrepid, devout, and dedicated to unionism as the road to self-respect and social justice. His long years of training as a Jesuit priest in the late 1920s and most of the 1930s, a period which coincided with the Great Depression, determined him to make bettering the lot of workers the focus of his priestly career. After being ordained in 1938 and serving a two-year teaching internship in New York City, he had the good fortune to connect with a school which shared his purpose, Xavier Labor School (XLS), a Jesuit institution.

The Jesuit labor-school tradition, like the rest of Catholic social action, grew out of the blending of Catholic worker-justice principles with late-19th-century ideas of democracy and reform socialism. In-

---

1 Carey, Philip, "One Man's Dignity", Dec. 1986. [FU]

deed that blend, as expressed in *Rerum Novarum*, was a primary influence on Father Terence Shealy, SJ, who founded the Xavier School of Social Sciences in 1911. The school lasted for 11 years, with labor as an important part of its curriculum.

Shealy's aim was "to spread among church and workers' associations a sound knowledge of social facts and of the Christian principles in the light of which these facts must be interpreted." The practical had to be coupled with the spiritual, Shealy emphasized, pointing out that every Catholic worker had the potential to be an apostle for Christ by seeking opportunities to translate his faith into action, including in labor school and workplace.[2]

The school Shealy founded fell victim in 1922 to the post-World War I decrease in reform. After the onset of the Great Depression, however, the international head of the Jesuit order (the Society of Jesus, or SJ), Father Wlodimir Ledochowski, challenged North American Jesuits to lead the way in "world-wide systematic warfare" to promote social justice and oppose Communism.[3] He accompanied his 1935 challenge with *An Integrated Program of Social Order*, a document with themes closely resembling those in *QA* and in *The Bishops' Program for Social Reconstruction of 1919*.

A major part of the response to that challenge was the establishment of Jesuit labor schools. XLS was founded in 1936 as Xavier School of Social Sciences, in tribute to its Shealy heritage. In 1938, when the school adopted a totally labor-centered curriculum, it changed its name to Xavier Labor School.

Other early Jesuit labor schools were St. Joseph's College School of Social Service Philadelphia; Crown Heights Labor School, Brooklyn; and schools in Kansas City, Missouri (affiliated with Rockhurst College) and Boston (in conjunction with its Archdiocese). A successor of that latter effort, The Labor Guild in Weymouth, Massachusetts (just outside of Boston), still operates—the last of the Catholic labor schools in the sense of the form they generally followed. (See p. 116.)

Father Joseph McShane, SJ, Fordham University President, is one of the foremost historians of Jesuit social action and of Catholic so-

---

2   McShane, Joseph, SJ, "'To Form an Elite Body of Laymen …': Terence J. Shealy, SJ, and the Laymen's League, 1911-1922", *The Catholic Historical Review*, Oct. 1992, 563.

3   Schmidt, Austin G., SJ, ed., *Selected Writings of Father Ledochowski*, Chicago: Loyola University Press, 1945, 907.

cial action in general. According to McShane, "the Jesuits looked upon union activism as the ultimate and most practical weapon for achieving the goal that their labor schools aimed at: the Christian reform of industrial society."

The leaders of these schools, McShane added, wanted to get away from, and help workers get away from, what Father Shealy described as "that awful superstition that priests alone can do the work of God." These leaders concentrated on imparting to workers a sense of their dignity and the dignity of their work, and on recognizing, developing, and utilizing what McShane called "the ministerial talents of the laity."[4]

The XLS founders, including *America* editor Father John LaFarge, SJ and Dorothy Day, sought a school leader capable both of infusing workers with the Jocist "see-judge-act" principles LaFarge had observed in France and of passing on Catholic social action's teachings to other workers. However, finding someone with the right set of qualifications, especially a thorough grounding in labor experience, proved to be extremely difficult. The school went through three directors in four years—and then Father Philip Carey showed up.

It was May 1940, and the school director at the time, Father Joseph Fitzpatrick, who went on to eminence as a Fordham University sociologist, remembered Carey's arrival as a vision of "a boyish-looking priest with a gray sweater thrown across his shoulders like a wet rag, and with a somewhat strange, halting speech." Carey identified himself as a prospect for the vacancy Fitzpatrick would create by leaving to pursue theological studies.

"Carey sat down and began to talk," Fitzpatrick recalled. "There was a strike on the waterfront at that time and he said 'I spent the afternoon down there and talked with many of the men on the picket line.' Then he began to unfold the issues of the strike and the attitudes of the men. I was amazed. I had never before heard such a clear and sharp analysis of the issues. I had never before come across such penetrating insight into the lives of the men. I told my rector, Father Vincent Hart, 'This is the man you must get for the Labor School.'"[5]

---

[4] McShane, "'The Church is not for the Cells and the Cave': The Working-Class Spirituality of the Jesuit Labor Priests", *U.S. Catholic Historian*, Summer 1990, 300, 303.

[5] Fitzpatrick, Joseph P., SJ, "One-Man Miracle", *Catholic New York*, June 8, 1989, 17.

9 ❧ Philip Carey

Carey also got an excellent recommendation from Father John Delaney, SJ, a member of the XLS faculty since the school's start in 1936. Father Delaney, a key figure in American Jesuits' response to Father Ledochowski's 1935 challenge, saw in Carey great potential for leadership in the Shealy tradition. Carey got the directorship, and Delaney was enormously helpful in the new arrival's adjustment to his position.

Carey and XLS turned out to be a perfect match. His seeming shyness masked immense tenacity, and his halting speech hid an eloquence mingling the directness of worker slang with insights gained from deep study. Carey was cooperative when possible and forceful when necessary. Above all, he combined spirituality with street sense in a way which made his worker-students feel that he was one of them and that he cared about them and their lives. Several years into his tenure he reviewed its start.

> *Of course, the rise of Communist Party intrigues and the danger to the country and the Faith has always been before our minds. In fact, I do think that were it not for the motivation this danger gave, the school here might never have been undertaken.*
>
> *But we are not merely "anti", for I feel that this policy is as self-destructive of any good to be done as it is stupid. Certainly, we have far more on which to base a social program of lasting importance, and we have a motivation in the world supernatural which the Communists cannot reach.*
>
> *We recognize that only through honest, constructive unionism can we come to true democracy in the nation, for only in this way can we control and regulate the greed of corporations and the unreasonable encroachments of the State. Of course, we realize that all unions here are not of that standard; that there are whole branches of it infected with dry rot and racketeering, while whole Internationals are completely Communist-dominated. (I cite the National Maritime Union, the Transport Workers Union, the United Electrical Workers, and the American Communications Association.).... I have heard estimates that Catholics are 30-60% of the industrial and urban workers of the nation, and my own experience seems to confirm these estimates. What then?*
>
> *Unionism can be a means of great sanctification. It can be a practical application of that love of neighbor so constantly insisted upon by our Lord, and it can give great glory to God, if done from the motive of love of Himself. It can demand real sacrifice. In fact, aside from ignorance, the greatest cause of the present industrial chaos has been selfishness. And selfishness can only be conquered by Christ-like selflessness. I think of the Jocist answer to the Communists of France. I think of Charlie Messina of Newark, one of my own men, and of what he told*

me when he had put himself in jeopardy of loss of job for the sake of his fellows. His local was completely company-dominated (though an AFL affiliate), and though he made a perfectly legal and tactful motion on the floor of his union meeting, he was discharged and his family finally had to go on relief. He knew well the consequences of his act. I feared for him, and he said "This school has taught me something I'll never forget, Father. The Communists say they love the other fellow. We know what kind of love that is. As Catholics we are bound not merely to see Christ in the other fellow, but we must also ACT toward him as though he were our brother in Christ. Father, I've got to do it!" And he did, and he turned over a local of 4,000 men, and he is now an officer in the union, feared yet respected by the company he conquered.

I think that the object of the school is not so much information, though that is essential, but primarily a change in attitude. This cannot be done in a day, or in a month, or even in a year. It is a gradual, imperceptible thing. It can't be taught by words, though they help. It is formed as a habit is, by reiteration of act, by continued portrayal of the same attitude toward the problems you touch in the classroom, by the example of your life more than all else....

Within many unions, there is now a cadre of men trained here who think together and act together. Several large unions are now controlled by school graduates, and opinions expressed by the school are listened to with an ever-growing interest. We do not go into organizational lines, for then I should tie the Catholic name and all that it stands for with things political. I'd rather have the men formed here go into their locals and then band together there, as members of that local and not as labeled Xavier or Catholic. It's more successful, while we're still in a minority, and far safer than entrusting your reputation to a man, who may turn out later a disgrace to the cause. The results above all else: that there is some Catholic thinking and some action along Catholic lines going on, and that as the years pass this leaven in the mass may increase and raise the whole.[6]

Noteworthy in this review are its merger of spirituality and practicality and its emphasis on people—reaching out to them as individuals and helping them to help others. Training for leadership was important to Carey, but he valued highly both the leadership of rank-and-filers (often two thirds of the XLS student body) and the leadership of union officers.

The spiritual aspect of XLS came from Father Carey's view that it was in essence a spiritual endeavor. He never forgot, and he lived by,

---

6 Carey, "History of Xavier", Feb. 24, 1943, 2-4. [PR]

the admonition of a priest who helped prepare him for his ordination. Father Frank Keenan, Rector of the seminary where Carey was ordained, Woodstock Seminary in Maryland, told him "a Christian priest has only one reason for his being, the welfare of Christ's brothers and sisters. God will be a very, very severe judge on any of you who uses his priesthood for his own selfish ends."[7]

Carey's favorite activity as XLS director was conducting spiritual retreats for workers or union groups. He felt badly that logistical and scheduling factors meant less of that activity than he expected and desired.

By the time of Carey's review above, early 1943, he and XLS had made considerable progress in nearly three years. Regular attendance averaged about 375 students a year, 125 per term for winter, spring and fall terms, every Wednesday night for nine weeks. Attendees were in every occupation imaginable, blue-collar and white-collar, and in a bewildering variety of unions, CIO, AFL, and independent. They came from all over the New York City metropolitan area, with large numbers from Queens, Manhattan, the Bronx, Brooklyn, and New Jersey.

The school was well on the way towards fulfilling its founders' desires that it be competitive in an area full of labor schools. The Communist Party's New York Workers School was a short walk away. Socialists held forth at the Rand School a block down. The Henry George School was across the street. Several labor unions in the same block conducted their own educational activities, with the International Ladies' Garment Workers Union a leader in that field.

XLS and Father Carey competed with other schools, but not with malice. Carey met the Communists forthrightly, because he was of the opinion that "If we Catholics really put the Pope's plan into effect, we'd make the Communists look like rock-ribbed reactionaries." As for the socialists, he looked "to bring back the spirit of the old-time Socialist.... The old-time Socialist was fighting for the dignity of labor and the brotherhood of man."[8]

For Father Carey, directing XLS was a full-time job, and this kind of commitment enabled him to make the school a magnet for students and graduates, and an appealing choice for prospective students. Carey

---

7   Carey to John Cardinal O'Connor, June 26, 1986. [FU]
8   Carey, editorial in *The Xavier X-Ray*, Feb. 17, 1943. Wershba, Joseph, "Daily Closeup", *The New York Post*, nd [FU].

made sure XLS teachers, mostly laypeople, were skilled, articulate, and personable, and he issued constant reminders that the student body was largely made up of "workers who don't think and pray with the twisting of philosophies, but who come to God with ideas and goals they can squeeze in their hands."[9] Above all, he was always available to his students.

> My guys come to me. They've got a gripe but they don't know how to put it. I tell them 'Look fellas, give it to me in your own patois.' (Of course it isn't the dialect that's spoken in convent boarding schools!) It's pretty wild language. The paint may peel off the walls while they're talking, but they make sense.
>
> I tell them, 'All right, I understand you. Now go back and get ten others that feel that way and come back here.' They come with five men. They talk it out. At long last they finally understand just what is biting them. You have to know the question that ought to be asked. Then, the answer! You don't give them the answer, pat like that! The men have to arrive at it themselves. You prod them with questions. You slant a question: How would Christ do this? What would He think? At the end, they come to group action, team play.
>
> Maybe you'll hear how they made out. Most likely, you won't. But if men can begin to get the habit of thinking and acting like Christians, if they can solve just a few problems in real terms of actual living, they'll begin to form a foundation for their lives. That's the substance of it—teaching men to think for themselves.[10]

The language lacks the gender consciousness Americans arrived at several decades later but its practicality is apparent, and that trait permeated the XLS curriculum. In early years, options for the first period of three were "Public Speaking" and "Parliamentary Procedure." Options for period two were "Labor Ethics" and "A Worker's Life." Options for period three were "Trade Unionism Past and Present" and "Economic Problems."

Carey designed a two-year course sequence to foster the long-term attitudinal changes he sought. A second-year student took "Advanced Public Speaking" in period one, "Social Ethics" in period two, and in period three could choose between "Current Events" and "Making a Contract." Carey insisted on time being allowed for class discussions.

---

9   Fitzpatrick, *op. cit.*
10 Sheehan, Arthur and Elizabeth, "Workingman's Priest", *Today*, Feb. 1957, 17.

He added courses in basic English and math. On Tuesday evenings XLS held labor clinics and courses in labor law. Labor clinics, which were introduced to the school by Walter Maggiolo of the U.S. Conciliation Service (a forerunner of the Federal Mediation and Conciliation Service created in 1947), enabled students to role-play in collective-bargaining situations.

Practicality was emphasized in extracurricular activities as well. Examples included the Center Club, a school-sponsored speakers' bureau; debating teams, first within the curriculum and later representing the school against other labor schools; the Senior Club, which held socials, played a key role in student government, and, early in Carey's tenure, revived and supported the student newsletter *The X-Ray*; and graduation ceremonies which were held as mock union conventions to give students a chance to both apply the skills they were learning and to display them to families and friends.

America's entry into World War II, a year and a-half after Father Phil Carey's arrival at XLS, profoundly changed the American labor scene and Catholic labor schools, a change explored in previous chapters. As the war intensified, many XLS students and faculty members went off to war, including priests who enlisted as chaplains. Father Carey himself served as a chaplain at Fort Totten in New York City, but when he wasn't there saying Mass on Sundays or otherwise helping, he was holding the school together against numerous challenges of staffing, traveling, and scheduling. Attendance stayed fairly steady, a tribute to the success of his efforts.

Entries in XLS newsletters, whether *The X-Ray* or *The Xavier Detail*, a newsletter started by students to keep in touch with members of the XLS community in war service, provide a unique window into the vibrancy of that community and into what happened to American labor in wartime.

> **2/3/43: Pvt. Bill Caul**, *4th Fighter Group, former XLS student and UAW member in Linden, N.J. GM Plant, from "somewhere in England"*: "Hiya, Father, how's the Labor School? Whether you know it or not, we fellows will sure need every advantage that labor can give us when we get home." **9/44: MM2/C Benoit Banville**, *"another old XLS man," in the Navy's 7th Construction Battalion*: "I was in the Guadalcanal campaign. Thanks for your prayers. We're back out to 'somewhere in the Pacific.'" **2/2/44: John Clayton, XLS and Seabee,** *from camp*: "Seabees are about 80% union men, and to hear them talk,

one would wonder whether they ever heard the meaning of unionism and collective bargaining. The great majority signed up in locals and NEVER ATTENDED A UNION MEETING." **John Cifichiello, XLS and a Navy mailman**, from northern Ireland; spoke at St. Vincent de Paul Society and was introduced as John Kelly (an alias Carey had given him), gave his New York accent a real workout and got "a good belly laugh" from his listeners. **11/15/44: Sgt. Edward Chave, XLS economics teacher, with Air Corps, Washington, D.C. writing the Corps' statistical-methods manual:** "I have my doubts that we have any idea of what kind of a peace we want. And where is God in all this? Any state or society even close to succeeding must offer spiritual values as well as material ones.... But we Catholics don't seem to realize the Church's teachings in our lives." **1/45: John "Kelly" Cifichiello, now MM/3C**, on leave, volunteered at Catholic Social Guild, Oxford, England: "I spoke to a Jocist meeting in a slum district. The audiences were 'workers', kids actually working for a living.... It left a heavy impression on me. Europeans look to us for leadership in our new world. It'll be a sad thing if we turn them down. They expect us to help and lead in a material, spiritual, and economic way." **Gerry Frane, XLS Librarian**, reported seeking an overdue book from student John King and finding he was Captain King and had received the D.S.C. in the Italian Campaign. **Faye Goldware, XLS and WAC**, chimed in from Paris that "France may be a little distant from Xavier, but civil affairs, which is the branch I work for, isn't. Remembrances to all the crowd." **Sgt. Chave**, still "statisticating": "Thanks for the Detail. Most of us G.I.'s have a pretty murky idea of labor and its intentions. There's been a pretty well organized, if hidden, attempt to build up an anti-union animus within the services. I guess most of us are wondering when will I get home, and what will be there for me? I think we ought also to be thinking and hoping for a better world, not only for ourselves, but for our neighbors, for those especially of the 'backward' nations." **2/7/45: Carey** addressed postwar challenges: "Do we 'view with alarm', 'toss in the blanket'? God knows we don't, for we have within us, in the Faith and the companionship, one or the other, in the Mystical Body of Christ, enough answer to the tremendous questions that will face all of us in the postwar years. What we do decry is the stupid unwillingness to look embarrassing facts in the face, that cowardly apathy to intellectual effort that so characterizes us, Catholic workers. We may fill the casualty columns (as indeed we do), but to what avail all this blood and sweat and lives if we sit back and let others do the planning, thinking, and organizing of the future? ... We must make heroic efforts." **3/7/45: John Clayton**, now on "one of the little islands of the Pacific": "The war news is going great but the

> stories of these strikes is turning me inside out.... I am doing my best to present the Labor view, but the feeling here is great against me. We don't get all the facts.... Are we going to win the war and come home to find brother fighting brother, and our jobs gone and the country a mess?" **3/14/45: <u>Father Dan Carey, SJ</u>, <u>Phil's brother, an XLS public-speaking teacher, and a chaplain in Germany</u>:** "Today is Ash Wednesday and we had Mass in an old sawmill, with the steel table of a band-saw for an altar.... One of the men asked me to go out with him to a distant outpost to see his sick buddy. I gladly went, and gave the Sacraments to a poor Joe who lay in a wet miserable hole, too feverish to move. The good man who brought me to him is now in Heaven, being rewarded for his Christ-like charity." **Army Pvt. Herb Haas**, Father Phil Carey reported, was a POW in Germany but was well and hoped to be home soon. [Subsequently, the War Department informed Carey that Haas died from pneumonia on Feb. 11; in a Feb. 10 postcard which later caught up with Carey, Haas greeted the Xavier gang, saying "I'm trying to use this time which a most gracious God has so wonderfully spared to me."] **10/30/45: <u>Carey</u>**, after citing several news reports about uncertainty over price controls, hoarding, and record business inventories of $31 billion: "Do you see now why the Church maintains that in an INDUSTRIAL Democracy labor should have a voice in the policies of production, PRICES, MARKETING, and profit? Your job, full employment, and your annual wage depend on those policies."

This is a clear statement of the message at the heart of Catholic social action, and Father Carey's consistent and courageous application of it was a powerful force for good, sound unionism in postwar America. XLS and its labor allies fought hard for such unionism, in the process battling the flare-ups of union Communism in the late forties and union corruption in the early fifties. Significant headway was made despite a lack of enough good, sound unionists to both overcome those obstacles and perform the priority task of countering unrestrained capitalism.

Many of the unionists who did take part in these struggles, however, were good and sound indeed. Consider Ray Westcott and John Brooks, who in 1943 were clerical workers at New York Omnibus Company. Its road and maintenance workers had been organized by the Communist-dominated Transport Workers Union (TWU), but its white-collar workers were unorganized, and though they had decent job security their cost-of-living situations were worsening.

The two men explored forming a union, found widespread support for the idea from their colleagues, and called in TWU organizers. Westcott got 50 signatures on union pledge-cards himself, but grew increasingly uneasy about the union's Communist domination, so he and Brooks went to see Father Carey, who they heard was helpful to workers and unions. This opinion was confirmed by many women in the company comptroller's office, who had already sent a committee to Carey for a lunch-hour conversation about their grievances.

Carey affirmed these white-collar workers' need for a union and, when Westcott asked about their forming an independent local within TWU, Carey said that forming a totally independent union was a better possibility, but that eventually they and their colleagues would probably need TWU's power behind them. Carey invited the workers to attend XLS and offered to set up special classes to help them develop a sensible course of action and one tailored to their objectives. TWU was the union Carey's dad belonged to, so he had lived it and knew it inside-and-out.

Westcott, Brooks, and 10 colleagues took Carey up on his offer—not an easy decision in light of the sacrifices involved. Westcott, for example, had a wife and a sick child at home and his take-home pay was $60 a week, whereas schooling and union activities would cost him in both time lost from the job and in general expenses—books, carfare, suppers out, and so on. Eventually these activities cost him $800, but he never regretted his decision.

XLS itself charged no fees, and the New York Omnibus Company students learned valuable lessons about union formation, contract negotiations, job evaluation, and grievance procedures. They and their colleagues established an independent union, but got off to an inauspicious start.

"The mistake we made," Westcott said, "was to let management split us into three voting groups—stenos, general clerks, and statistical clerks. This meant each unit would vote separately for its bargaining representatives and whether or not they wanted *us*. While we carried the big unit, with enough votes to have carried all the units if their members had voted as parts of a single group, we lost the stenos and the special clerks."[11]

---

11 Weinberg, Jules, "Priests, Workers, and Communists", *Harper's Magazine*, Sept. 1948, 54.

At any rate, a local for the big unit was recognized in 1944 and Westcott was elected president. At the end of the war, however, management told the independent local that the company wasn't going to be pushed around by white-collar workers and that it refused to handle their grievances. The split engineered by management meant that the big-unit local didn't have enough strength to mount a successful strike, especially since it organized in defiance of TWU.

"Here we were," Brooks commented, "trying to stay out of the Commies' hands, and here was management, which was supposed to be so opposed to Communists, forcing us right into their hands. There was nothing we could do but join TWU."[12]

They did join, and within a few months Westcott and Brooks were finagled into registering for an event of the American Labor Party, at that time a vehicle for the U.S. Communist Party's postwar strategy for a third political party. At TWU's next convention, Westcott, Brooks, and their allies supported petitions to the nominating committee for election of well-liked Interborough Rapid Transit organizer Dickie Downs. The committee, Communist-dominated, tried to set aside these petitions in favor of its candidate, Charles Smolikoff. The petitioners took the issue to the convention floor, where Westcott used all his XLS lessons in parliamentary procedure in a successful effort to block Smolikoff and elect Downs.

After the convention the New York Omnibus group joined with union rank-and-filers from the Third Avenue and Fifth Avenue transit systems, in Westcott's words "lads who thought the same as we did, a lot of young guys fresh out of the Army who didn't want to take this domination stuff from anybody, any time."[13] The rank-and-file coalition got a candidate elected to the union's executive board, and before long each of the coalition's members was an XLS graduate.

Events played into the coalition's hands in 1947 when CIO's Communists, under attack by CIO President Murray and his allies, tried to take TWU into a new labor confederation. To gain public support, these Communists opposed an attempt to increase the longstanding five-cent fare for New York City's subways, said to offer "the longest ride in the world for a nickel."

TWU President Mike Quill and others in the controlling cadre opposed the increase until the rank-and-file coalition demonstrated to

12 Ibid.
13 Ibid., 55.

union members that a higher fare would permit a much-needed pay raise. In a referendum, 23,000 members voted for a subway fare increase and 7,000 voted against.

"Mike Quill had one foot on the rowboat and the other on the dock," said Carey, "and the distance widened with each passing day."[14] Finally, in 1948, Quill broke with the Communists and supported his workers. The fare increase went through, the workers got their raise, and the movement to expel CIO's Communist unions picked up steam.

This added momentum heartened rank-and-filers in many other locals and unions, particularly where the objectives of Communist unionists hampered democratic and effective unionism. These rank-and-filers gathered together to form the United Rank and File Educational Committee, seeking, in the words of its director, John Holly, "to restore control of their unions to the members, where it belongs."[15] The unions represented were TWU; UE; American Communications Association; United Office and Professional Workers of America; United Public Workers; American Newspaper Guild; and United Retail, Wholesale and Department Store Employees of America (URWDSEA).

Holly, who had taught the XLS course "Trade-Union Methods" to Westcott, Brooks, and hundreds of other rank-and-filers, learned his subject matter in the trenches. While an elevator operator on Wall Street, he became one of the first union organizers in the building trades and paid for his efforts one night when a bunch of wrench-wielding goons set upon him in his elevator and broke several of his ribs. He was an early head of the Building Service Employees International Union, where he spearheaded an exposé of George Scalise and other union racketeers which led to several convictions. And he spent several years helping break the tyrannical hold Communists had on the URWDSEA locals in Macy's, Bloomingdale's, Hearn's, and Gimbel's; managers of these stores sometimes collaborated with a store union's Communists by punishing their opponents for trumped-up violations of store rules.

The exploits of Westbrook, Brooks, Holly, and many other XLS students and graduates, help explain the school's successes at a time when the national school network was gradually declining. Indeed,

---

14 Carey, "Ray Westcott", nd. [FU]
15 Holly, John, *What If They Are Red?*, New York: United Rank and File Educational Committee, 1948, 22.

XLS experienced a postwar expansion. By the early 1950s, Carey offered extension classes in New Brunswick and Paterson, N.J.; Mamaroneck in Westchester County; Tarrytown up the Hudson River; in the Bronx, at Sacred Heart School and St. Helena's Holy Name Society; and, elsewhere in Manhattan, at Holy Cross in "Hell's Kitchen."

Father Carey's supervisors at the New York Province (regional governing unit) of the Jesuits, while they sometimes had to protect Carey from employers or wealthy benefactors unhappy with his support for labor, were pleased with XLS successes. Shortly after World War II, they assigned a priest to help him.

The new arrival, Father John "Pete" Corridan, SJ, wasted little time proving his usefulness to Carey, especially along the waterfront. As noted earlier, corruption was entrenched there, and Catholic social actionists had met it head-on in fierce yet largely futile battles. Most of the waterfront workers were Catholics, but so were many of their bosses.

Corridan, a big, bluff man with an open, hearty manner, won over the workers in their rough world by approaching them with directness and showing them his sincere interest in their lives and problems.[16] Their worst problem was the "shape-up", or "shape", which John Cort, who got his social-action start on the waterfront, described as "an antiquated slave-market method of hiring."[17]

Twice a day, near 8 a.m. and 1 p.m., workers in Joe Ryan's corrupt International Longshoremen's Association (ILA) lined up in front of a boss stevedore, who picked the cargo loaders and unloaders for the next shift. The union had two or three times as many members as workers, 70 percent of those workers were on the job less than 75 percent of an average work year, 16-hour days were common, and a minority of workers got all the overtime.

This was clearly an arbitrary system. Frank Hogan, New York City District Attorney in the late 1940s, when waterfront corruption reached one of its periodic peaks, said "It [the shape] is responsible for kickbacks, loan-sharking, and a large percentage of the other crimes on the waterfront. The power over employment is so arbitrary that

---

16 See Fisher, James T., *On the Irish Waterfront: The Crusader the Movie, and the Soul of New York*, Ithaca: Cornell University Press, 2009.

17 Cort, John, "The Longshore Strike", *Commonweal*, Dec. 17, 1948, 257.

THESE CONDITIONS NECESSARILY FOLLOW. That has been evident for more than 30 years."[18]

Murderers and thugs of every variety enforced mob rule on the docks, and behind it were the Shipping Association (including its "Mr. Big", William McCormack) and ILA's inner circle, supported by allies among police officers and politicians. The profits of these interests reigned supreme.

Late 1948 marked the beginning of a challenge to these interests through convergence of several factors: one of the bitter strikes through which longshore workers frequently expressed their frustrations; a hard-hitting exposé of waterfront corruption by *New York Sun* reporter Malcolm Johnson; and XLS' increasing involvement in the situation. Corridan, stirred by workers' accounts of their grim experiences and by extensive research, publicized his findings as widely as possible.

Carey and Corridan formed a good one-two punch, with Corridan circulating among the workers and encouraging them while Carey supported those who came to XLS. They "come in like Nicodemuses by night for fear of 'the Ryan,'" Carey recalled. "Most educational work was done among the dock workers during the chore of getting out a mimeographed paper. As the men did the stuffing of envelopes a very lively discussion took place across the table. Attitudes and moral conclusions were arrived at that would have seemed impossible to develop."[19]

XLS assistance focused on helping the workers attain practical, short-term goals—a closed shop and hiring-hall-system, decent welfare and pension plans for an occupation which was among the nation's most dangerous, better pay, and shorter hours. Most of these goals were met over the next half-dozen years, and considerable progress was made on longer-term goals to change the climate of corruption through political and legal reforms. The New York State Crime Commission held hearings, Ryan and others were indicted, a Bi-State Waterfront Commission was created, and the ILA was ejected from the AFL in 1953. Never again would longshore workers be as exploited as they had been in the previous 40 years.

---

18 "An Open Letter to *The New York Sun*", *The Xavier Detail*, Dec. 13, 1948.
19 Carey to Dennis Comey, SJ, Sept. 22, 1947. Carey, "Industrial Relations Report", nd. [PR]

The "fear of 'the Ryan'" prevailed in the end, however. When the workers had a choice in a 1955 election between the old ILA and the newly-created International Brotherhood of Longshoremen-AFL, they voted for the former, 9,407 to 9,144. Father Corridan asked for a transfer and ended up at St. Peter's Institute labor school in Jersey City, in the same line of work but in almost total disillusionment. "Over the whole mess," Carey summed up, "is 'FEAR', a blinding, paralyzing fear inculcated by men who claim to be very prominent Catholic laymen."[20]

The dockworkers' vote for the past was but one irony in a seven-year struggle full of them. Another was that although these workers were better off at the end of that period, New York City's waterfront economy was not, as it experienced declines in the face of increasing automation and competition. Yet another was that although XLS heroism in the long struggle was nationally celebrated in the 1954 hit movie *On the Waterfront*, with Karl Malden as Father Corridan, the end of the real-life drama showed just how fleeting fame and attention can be.

There had been and would be many other XLS struggles with corruption, and just as in the struggles with Communism, some were won and some were lost. As mentioned earlier, however, Father Phil Carey kept his focus on what he considered to still be the Catholic social-action movement's major foe, unrestrained capitalism. Indeed, Carey's extraordinary realism in this respect stands above most other leaders in Catholic social action. This, and the strong spiritual sense underlying and permeating his entire ministry of social justice, account for XLS lasting until 1988, long past the time when nearly all other labor schools had folded their tents.

"We've done far more work protecting men against the thugs and racketeers in the union movement than helping them against injustice on the part of management," Carey wrote to fellow Jesuit Father Thomas O'Brien in 1949, "but our deep drive is to prevent the drift of workers away from the Church, as happened in Europe.... I've been criticized for not being sufficiently conscious of management's problems, but in a city such as this and in a time of prices such as this, I haven't the luxury of complete impartiality."[21]

XLS was somewhat of an anomaly among Jesuit labor schools, but it played a key role in their development. In December 1940, XLS teacher Father John Delaney was instrumental in founding the Jesuits'

20 Carey to Thomas Murray, Feb. 15, 1952. [FU]
21 Carey to Thomas O'Brien, Oct. 31, 1949. [PR]

Institute for Social Order (ISO) and headed its New York regional office. ISO's mission was coordinating the Society's labor schools and other social-action efforts, and in October 1941 it published Delaney's *How to Run a Labor School*, a practical outline informed by the XLS experience.

Delaney came to ISO with an ambitious goal—to found a labor school in every Jesuit parish and to link a labor school to every Jesuit high school and college. World War II intervened and realization of the goal was not to be, but one Jesuit labor school started in fall 1941, in affiliation with Marquette University, in Milwaukee. Starting between 1943 and 1945 were eight more university-affiliated labor schools: Holy Cross Institute of Industrial Relations (IIR), Worcester, Massachusetts; John Carroll University Labor School, Cleveland; Xavier University Institute of Social Order, Cincinnati; Creighton University IIR, Omaha; St. Louis University Labor College; Gonzaga Labor School, Spokane; Syracuse School of Industrial Relations (at LeMoyne College), and Scranton University School of Industrial Relations.[22]

Delaney was out of the Jesuit labor-school picture by war's end, having been reassigned to the Philippines, and most Jesuit labor schools had diverged from the Shealy tradition Delaney and XLS represented, and were moving in a direction emphasizing social order and an intellectual, academic approach to labor education. In part this was to keep up with the competition and attract returning veterans eligible for G.I. Bill assistance, and in part to focus on harmony between labor and management and to treat them neutrally or even-handedly.

As their names imply, these newer Jesuit labor schools were generally founded as part of an institute of industrial relations, with a labor school existing side by side with a management school. In postwar many of these schools became (or led to) four-year degree programs, as did one of the earliest Jesuit labor schools (founded around the same time as XLS), St. Joseph's College School of Social Service in Philadelphia—later St. Joseph's College IIR. It exists today as the Dennis Comey IIR of St. Joseph's University, having been renamed for the Jesuit priest who headed it from 1943-81 and died in 1987. (See p. 142.)

---

22 Among postwar Jesuit initiatives were the University of Portland Institute of Industrial Relations and San Francisco University Labor-Relations School.

Under Comey, the Institute was one of several labor schools welcoming considerable numbers of both labor and management representatives into its courses and training them together. The idea behind this technique was that if cooperation between workers and managers happened at the Institute, they would be inspired to promote such cooperation in their workplaces, and in many instances this happened.

Carey used a different method, based upon his conviction that while labor-management harmony was a desirable goal, there would always be variances between the viewpoints of workers and the viewpoints of owners and managers, that these variances could only be worked out where there was true partnership and respect, and that most owners and managers were far from providing those requisites. Regarding the simultaneous-training method, he said "I can't see how I could ever combine management and labor in the same rooms on the same night in view of our peculiar situation here. It seems to me that if you dilute justice to the vague and vapid rantings of a pulpiteer, you end up by pleasing neither labor nor management and certainly you're not doing much to better things."[23]

Clearly, among Jesuit social-action programs—as among Catholic social-action efforts generally—there were contrasting styles and methods. However, there was also dedication to the same cause, social justice. The Catholic social-action umbrella was an extremely roomy one; indeed, it is remarkable that so many personalities, perspectives, and ways of doing things were able to fit under it in relative comfort.

Jesuit labor schools banded together through ISO headquarters in St. Louis, Missouri, and also coordinated with other Catholic labor schools through the national Social Action Department, where Father George Higgins (see Chapter Ten) replaced Father John Hayes as schools coordinator in 1944. The Jesuit schools' group served as a clearing-house and held conferences of school representatives. Jesuit schools in particular regions took part in cooperative activities, among them interscholastic debating; in the Northeast it involved XLS (later Xavier IIR), St. Joseph's College IIR, Crown Heights Labor School, and Holy Cross College IIR.

XLS considered debating to be an excellent way for worker-students to apply their lessons and to be more effective in union meetings. Topics were selected for their timeliness, and questions addressed in debates involving XLS teams included: Should unions be required to

---
23 Carey to Walter Hogan, SJ, Oct. 10, 1950. [PR]

provide a financial accounting to their states? Which is better, the affiliated union or the independent union? Should World War II's no-strike pledge be retained? Is Reuther's 30-percent pay-raise proposal in the 1945-46 GM strike justified? Should veterans receive super-seniority? Should the federal government require arbitration of labor disputes in all basic American industries? Should there be a dues check-off?

The debates and the preparation for them were exciting and informative—even humorous. When XLS debater Jim Murphy visited the Brooklyn Library and asked for material on the check-off, he drew a blank, so he asked the librarian to look under "anti-checkoff". "Oh," she exclaimed, "I have just what you want," and she brought back an armful of books on Russian author Anton Chekhov. Murphy and his team won anyway!

Every Catholic social actionist—Jesuit, diocesan, ACTU, Catholic Worker, or any combination of these—was a product of the totality of that person's life experiences. Phil Carey had a powerful sense of where he came from, a deep commitment to social justice, and a strong belief that he was being faithful to the teachings of the Church he loved.

Monsignor George Higgins, praising Carey after his death, saw Carey's perspective in terms of Pope Paul VI's 1971 description of economic conditions at and since the time of *Rerum Novarum* 80 years earlier: "Although the two [capital and labor] cooperated in the joint task of production, he [Paul VI] noted, a division of minds and interest brought about a systematic struggle between the parties. Thus, he said, was created a society destined to inevitable collaboration as well as inevitable conflict."[24] Surface or illusory harmony, Carey felt, was no substitute for constructive conflict resolution.

Father Carey was certainly not anti-business. He was highly regarded as a labor-management negotiator and arbitrator. He was an active public member of the War Labor Board in World War II and of state and national mediation boards over several decades thereafter, contributing to the resolution of scores of disputed cases and in 1965-66 helping New York City draft its Code of Labor Relations. "He was neither belligerent nor contentious by nature," said Monsignor Hig-

---

24 Higgins, George, "The Undivided Road: Father Philip Carey", *The Yardstick*, June 15, 1989.

gins, "yet he never ran away from a good fight when it was forced on him."²⁵ Why this is so in clear from Carey's own words:

> I can't ask men to die for collective bargaining, and you really can't ask men to suffer for democracy, and it's pretty meaningless to ask a fellow to love another man for the man's sake, especially when you don't like him. So much of this is watered-down charity. So much of it is the pious mouthings of post-Christian pagans. We've got to make men realize that they really are brothers, that their brotherhood and solidarity with one another can only have meaning in their brotherhood in Christ, that the concept of solidarity of all workers is nothing but a weak version of the Communion of Saints and the participation of all of us in the Mystical Body of Christ. If these things aren't known in the world, maybe it's because we Catholics haven't talked about them or lived them.²⁶

This message is at the heart of everything Father Philip Carey did for labor. He was extraordinarily realistic because he was extraordinarily spiritual. "There is a social problem," he said, "but it isn't primarily an economic one or legal or even sociological. It is a religious one."

Carey considered what he called "laissez-faire capitalism" or "industrial paternalism" to be a bitter foe because "it can destroy the souls of employees by making them so selfish they have no apostolic spirit, no great width of character and of love to all the other workers in the country, and no sense that they, too, have to take their share with the rest of the workers in bettering the condition of all workers."²⁷ The stands he took on specific labor issues were largely determined by this moral sense.

Consider what he said about the Taft-Hartley Act soon after its enactment:

> In an industrial society, unions are necessary organizations for the protection and the ADVANCEMENT of the workers' just rights. Unions are no different than any other man-made society. Every such society needs an elected authority to guide them under laws of the membership's choosing. No authority can work without the effective power of imposing proportionate punishments for acts against the laws and welfare of the group. Without that power, authority cannot function and the group tends to disintegrate. BUT the T-H law—AS A LAW in full opera-

---

25 Ibid.
26 Carey to Maurice Hennessy, Feb. 16, 1949, 2.
27 "Carey Speaks to Interracial Council", *Catholic News*, Sept. 12, 1953. Carey to William McIntosh, SJ, Aug. 1, 1950.

tion—takes away the power of imposing effective sanctions from union leadership. Therefore, the T-H Law, in destroying the effectiveness of union leadership, good or bad, is destructive of unions.[28]

As for the "right to work" provisions in Taft-Hartley, Carey quoted with approval, in the November 10, 1948 issue of *The Xavier Detail*, Santa Fe Archbishop Edwin Byrne's response to a proposed "right to work" amendment to the New Mexico Constitution. "As one desirous of industrial peace and desirous to aid in the prosperity of my State and of my Country, as a friend of the worker," Byrne stated, "I cannot approve this proposed amendment, which, if it does not outlaw unionism, deals it a death blow. Rather it seems to me that it should be opposed by men of good will and peace, who reverence the individual dignity of man and the spirit of the Constitution of the United States."

Father Carey also saw moral implications in the relationship between workers and technological change, as had Father Charles Owen Rice (see p. 198). In the decade after Rice's remarks, the complexity of this key issue grew tremendously.

In a 1948 speech to Allied Printing Trades members, Father Carey bemoaned what had just happened in an International Telephone and Telegraph Cable strike, when, in Carey's words, "a tremendous technological change was made without the advice or control of the workers' organizations." Catholic social thinking, Carey added, "always insists that efficiency is not a final goal in itself. The state and economic systems and industrial processes exist for workers, as means to help them live happily under God. It is therefore of the first importance that the installation and control of these new processes which will affect the lives of so many be done by the organizations of both parties involved."[29]

At the mid-point of the 20th century, XLS and director Carey were active and productive, sharing the creative ferment of American labor generally as it fought to repeal Taft-Hartley and regain momentum. While outbreaks of anti-Communism, conservatism, and conformity would soon eclipse those pursuits, it was a good time for Catholic social actionists to take stock of their progress and their prospects. In 1950, Carey wrote to his Jesuit superior Father T. E. Henneberry that "the Province has come a long way from the smugness of the cloistered

---

28 Carey, "Taft-Hartley", *Xavier Detail*, Feb. 3, 1948.
29 Carey, speech to Allied Printing Trades, Apr. 11, 1948.

life.... No Communist or labor leader can now challenge the Church with lack of interest in organizations of working people, as has been done in the past. Now, they might even say we were too interested."[30]

Catholic social action's progress also had a positive impact nationally, including favorable mentions in *Time*, *Look*, and *Harper's*. In late 1948, in the wake of CIO's expulsion of its Communist-dominated Greater New York Council, the widely-respected *Louisville Courier-Journal* singled out for praise the United Rank and File Educational Committee. The newspaper remarked of the Catholic social-action movement in general that "it has had a healthy effect upon union organization, and has taught what the unions themselves signally failed to teach—the importance of an informed and participating membership which can keep the union in possession of the workers instead of allowing it to become without a struggle the tool either of racketeers or of dangerous political movements."[31]

This had to come as music to Phil Carey's ears, because he taught that lesson from day one at XLS and proclaimed it again in *Look* in March 1949 when he said "the greatest enemy to democratic unionism is the immense apathy and ignorance of the rank-and-file.... We'd like to have every worker attend his local meetings, voice his opinions coherently, and act constructively for the good of his brothers and the common good of all."[32]

For nearly 40 more years Father Carey would go on proclaiming that message, living it, and seeing it lived by the thousands of worker-students from every walk of life who went though Xavier Labor School and then applied its lessons in their unions. Carey felt that he belonged with these worker-students, that it was his spiritual calling to share in their lives and livelihoods.

Carey enjoyed ministering to workers from every occupation represented at XLS, but his favorites were the sandhogs, the workers who built the tunnels tying New York City together or linking it to other places. Their work was dangerous, dirty, and brutally hard, but the sandhogs were proud of being tough and of doing something vital. They loved Carey, and he loved them. He said May Day Mass for the

---

30 Carey to T. E. Henneberry, Feb. 14, 1950.
31 "A Significant Episode in Labor's Development", *Louisville Courier-Journal*, Nov. 24, 1948.
32 Riesel, Victor and Aaron Levenstein, "Labor Priests", *Look*, March 1949, 39.

deceased of their local at St. Cecilia's Church, and he said Mass in the third tube of the Lincoln Tunnel to give thanks that there were no serious injuries on the project, a safety record testifying eloquently to these workers' skills.

Sandhog or statistician, laborer or lathe operator, Carey loved all the workers he taught and guided. There was no anti-intellectualism in him—he was an associate professor in labor and industrial economics at Fordham University for 16 years—but he was trying to impart above all the dignity of work and the brotherhood and sisterhood of workers. A major concern of his was workers "slipping into secularism and materialism", and he did everything he could to help workers stem that slippage in their lives and to blend spirituality and social justice.[33]

He did this not only in labor work on weekdays, but in Church work on weekends. For 22 years before he died in 1989, he was a regular visiting priest at Our Lady of Grace Church in West Babylon, Long Island. Many parishioners affectionately called him "the parking-lot priest" because he often stood among the cars behind the church to greet people or say good-bye. He also said Masses, baptized babies, officiated at weddings and funerals, helped people find jobs, and generally just helped parishioners in any way possible.

Tom Lilly, Senior, a New York City labor lawyer from Garden City, Long Island, knew Father Carey in both his weekday and weekend roles. Lilly taught labor law at XLS for 30 years. Frequently, he picked Carey up at the train station and the Lilly family welcomed him for visits before Tom returned him to the station for the trip back to the city. Lilly recalled that what most impressed him about Carey was "his saintliness, his selflessness, his interest in anyone other than himself, and his willingness to drain himself—whether to give up clothing, money, time, or whatever."[34] Carey, he said, knew all the conductors on the Long Island Rail Road and all the homeless people in Penn Station.

In the final analysis, Father Philip Carey was all about values, in a way which speaks across the years to every member of American society. At XLS' 25th anniversary, then-U.S. Secretary of Labor James Mitchell said that Carey and XLS stood firmly for "a rigorous shaking out of the superficial values from our lives. The corporation official

---

33 Carey to McIntosh, *op. cit.*
34 Crowe, Kenneth C.,"Honoring His Priestly Labors",*Newsday*, June 9, 1986,25.

who measures his profits by what the traffic will bear, the union member who tolerates a corrupt leadership as long as he gets his share, the share owner who ignores the employment policies of his company so long as the dividends remain high, history will sweep them all under the rug."[35]

Father Carey understood the worker and he understood work. By "worker" he didn't mean the narrow definition of the word which capitalism's "rugged individualists" have created over the decades, whether by restricting the term to manufacturing; by reclassifying supervisors of all varieties as "capital" rather than "labor"; by crippling the union-shop arrangement through the Taft-Hartley Act and other measures of economic tyranny; or by every sort of old-fashioned and modern-day union busting. He meant all those employed by the owners and managers of property, whom social justice requires to be good stewards of what is owned and to be just employers of the workers entrusted to their care.

> Work is not just a means of making a living. Work is living, or should be. And yet how many people really live at work? How many people rest secure in the knowledge that they have a job for as long as they want to work; that favoritism plays no part; that race, color, or creed doesn't enter in; that they work in a decent place, earn good money, have vacations with pay, and have welfare and pension funds to protect them and their families; and that they are treated like human beings, children of God, and brothers and sisters of Christ? How many work hard for the success of the firm they work for because they have full confidence that they will share justly in any extra contributions they make? How many are not afraid of working themselves out of a job, and are not afraid of the sickening effects of a depression that they have seen in their wives, children, themselves, and others? How many take an active interest and pride in helping their unions shape their policies for the good of their fellow members; of management and owners, their co-partners; and of the country and the world? Such work would be prayer and living, for most of us come closest to God when we do a real unselfish job for our fellowmen out of the love of God.[36]

---

35 "Mitchell Speaks at XLS 25th Anniversary", *Catholic News*, Feb. 13, 1960.

36 Carey, editorial in *Xavier Detail*, Jan. 13, 1948.

Social Action Vignette
NEW ORLEANS: "A STORMY PETREL"

There's a fine line between being intrepid and being impetuous. Restraining the latter without reducing the former challenged the trainers of Catholic social-action priests. Father Reynold Hillenbrand met the challenge admirably in the case of Father Jerome Drolet, a Louisiana priest whose passion sometimes outran his prudence.

Hillenbrand took Drolet under his wing when the latter attended the 1938 priests' summer school in Chicago. Drolet returned home to an onslaught of criticism for sending a telegram to state and local officials complaining of a "police reign of terror" against National Maritime Union-CIO organizers. Hillenbrand responded to Drolet's request for advice about the onslaught with a letter counseling caution and patience, and Drolet replied to the letter with thanks and the assurance that "I have taken to heart all its contents."

This lesson enriched Drolet's labor activism, especially in terms of his relationship with New Orleans Archbishop Joseph Rummel. Rummel was so incensed at the telegram incident that he closed down a Catholic Worker reading room and house of hospitality and forbade Drolet from "social work," but as Drolet and other priests forged ahead with the hard work of developing labor schools and fighting for sound unions, Rummel became a staunch labor advocate. He led the fights against a state "right-to-work" law and for the drive by the National Agricultural Workers' Union to organize the workers in Louisiana's sugar-cane fields.

Drolet never stopped being "a stormy petrel," as Father Phil Carey called him (after the seabird which shows up at the first sign of trouble), but he allowed himself to be tempered by experience. This increased his effectiveness as archdiocesan priests, in tandem with Father Lou Twomey, SJ and his associates at Loyola University of the South, New Orleans, stood side-by-side with workers throughout the city and the state of Louisiana, and became stormy petrels in their own right.

CHAPTER TEN
GEORGE HIGGINS (1916–2002)

*F*or a postal clerk with an eighth grade education, Charles Vincent Higgins took his children far and wide. Not literally, of course. My father never traveled (he didn't have the money to travel) and never owned a car. Before visiting me years later in Washington, his longest journey came when he and my mother [Anna] left their home in south-central Illinois [Springfield], logging a grand total of 175 miles.

In Springfield my father and his brothers worked as machinists, firemen and engineers on the railroad.... Each of my uncles took his place in the active ranks of organized labor. My father, too, became a strong union man, but his interests ran wide....

My father had a virtual obsession with getting his children interested in serious things, and in an urban center like Chicago, the possibilities were numberless. In the days before television and before most people owned a radio, lectures were big business, much bigger than today. They were the only way to see or hear the great writers and thinkers of the time, and my father rarely missed a major lecture in Chicago. If the circuit brought around a G.K. Chesterton, a Hilaire Belloc or a John A. Ryan (big names then, particularly in the American Catholic subculture), he would go hear them and take me with him.

Charles Higgins may not have been a public person, but he did enjoy a small measure of celebrity, in his way. Some of the more attentive readers in Chicago and elsewhere were familiar with the name of C. V. Higgins—the signature he affixed to hundreds of "letters to the editor." He held forth on many and various subjects, from the New Deal and League of Nations to liturgical arts and literary criticism. The media of his message were usually daily newspapers in Chicago, America and Commonweal, and New World (the newspaper of the Chicago Archdiocese)....

When I got old enough, he would have me read aloud, for relief when he was too tired as well as to further my own education. He worked the nightshift in the post office and was always home for lunch, so I would rush home at noontime from the parish school and take my place at the kitchen table to read from the small-print columns of America and Commonweal. To underline the educational point of this, he would have me look up all the words I didn't know (an exercise that I have appreciated more in retrospect than I did at the time).

My father had a way of measuring the value of education outside the classroom. "The investment I've made in your education," he often said, "will be worthwhile—if you're impatient whenever America or Commonweal is late in the mail."[1]

In later life George Higgins was thus impatient, a natural result of following his father's sage advice to keep up with current events. George also shared his father's reading habit, a colleague of George estimating he spent about 40 hours a week reading—that is, in addition to the extensive reading he did for his job at the Social Action Department of the National Catholic Welfare Conference (renamed the U.S. Catholic Conference, or USCC, in 1967). Higgins was SAD assistant director from 1944 to 1954, when he took over as director from Father Ray McGowan; director from 1954-1967; and, from 1967-1980, director or top staffer of several USCC departments or units.

Higgins started his reading habit early, as a consequence of not only his dad's influence, but also the influence of Father John Henry Nawn, pastor of the Higgins family's church, St. Francis Xavier. It was in La-

---

1   Higgins, George with William Bole, *Organized Labor and the Church: Reflections of a "Labor Priest"*, New York and Mahwah, N.J., Paulist Press, 1993, 10-13.

Grange, a town just to Chicago's west. Father Nawn had amassed a good parish library and encouraged George Higgins to borrow from it whenever he wanted, and George did.

Nawn was ecumenical for his day, creating quite a stir in LaGrange when he took tea with the vicar of an Episcopal church in town. Nawn's church, however, was the only Catholic church in LaGrange, amid 12 Protestant churches—so there wasn't a great deal of opportunity for ecumenicalism to flourish.

Nevertheless, C. V. Higgins wanted his kids to learn religious and cultural diversity, so on Sundays he took George and his brother and two sisters into the Near West Side Jewish neighborhood of Chicago, which George remembered as a settlement "bustling with the trade of small things, a pound of smoked salmon here, a pair of socks there, and maybe a radio or two," a settlement with "the charged atmosphere of a bazaar."[2]

C. V. had gotten to know Jewish co-workers at the post office and was impressed with the great value they placed on books and studies. Warm friendships developed, inspiring C. V. to nurture in his children the ecumenical sense which they developed and which George later displayed in Catholic social action. One of George's best friends was Arthur Goldberg, who grew up in Near West Side and whom we mentioned earlier as a teacher in Chicago's Catholic labor schools. Goldberg and Higgins didn't meet until 1949, but they quickly discovered their Chicago connections and they worked together for many social-justice causes.

By the time George Higgins finished grade school, he was convinced by the example of Father Nawn to become a priest.

> Wanting to be a priest meant that I would pass up high school in LaGrange. It meant that every day, for five years, I would take a train and two streetcars to downtown Chicago, near the North Side. Notwithstanding our family day-trips to the urban jungle, I really did not know the city. My commutes to Quigley Preparatory Seminary of the Archdiocese of Chicago were an unfiltered exposure to the big city, in the middle of the Great Depression, as well as to the children of the Depression....
>
> Yet, while exposed to the sights and sounds of urban life during the Depression, I heard little of this behind the high walls of the seminary. We did what all high school students preparing for the priesthood did—Latin, Greek, algebra and the like. We had only a vague aware-

---

2 Ibid., 9.

ness of social ferment of the time, the battles of organized labor and experiments of the New Deal. We knew even less that our own cardinal [Mundelein], a princely and somewhat mysterious figure, was figuring in some of the more intriguing of these events.... To us the cardinal was a distant figure, yet he was close to his seminarians, in his way. He knew all of our names (quite a number to keep in mind) and monitored the progress of each one of us. He even knew about our families, once asking me, in a surprise encounter, how my father was doing at the post office. This quiet yet engaged style of leadership carried over into his public life. Although speeches and high-profile appearances did not appeal to him, Mundelein was a strong F.D.R. supporter, a social-minded prelate who supported the New Deal agenda....

Among those encouraged by Mundelein was a young, quiet priest named Reynold Hillenbrand. An English teacher in the minor (mainly high school level) seminary, Hillenbrand took students seriously. He would enter the classroom with a briefcase full of books and empty it out onto the desk. Those interested could take the books and bring them back whenever they wanted. At the time I assumed that Hillenbrand's main interests were in literature and related subjects, not knowing of his social outlook. Less than two years into my major seminary studies, Cardinal Mundelein took the rising professor out of Quigley Preparatory and (after an appointment to the Archdiocese's "mission band") made him rector of the seminary in Mundelein, Illinois. That move would have a far-reaching effect on priests of my generation.

A reflective, soft-spoken, and deeply spiritual man, Hillenbrand had a quiet sort of German determination about him. He had a tremendous influence on people, and, in short order, ushered in an ecclesiastical New Deal at Mundelein.... He called attention to social problems and the labor problem in particular. With a crowded seminary curriculum, he started evening courses in Catholic social teaching and related subjects. And though his experiment would be short-lived, Hillenbrand had a lasting effect on us seminarians. He helped us realize that social action was not an extra-curricular activity, not a hobby that we may or may not want to pursue outside of our "real" priestly work. It went to the heart of our mission.[3]

Higgins was ordained in 1940, and in August of that year, on Father Hillenbrand's recommendation, he and several other newly-ordained priests were sent by Chicago Archbishop Samuel Stritch (a replacement for Mundelein, who died the previous year) to The Catholic University of America, Washington, D.C. They were sent for gradu-

---

3   Ibid., 15-6, 19-20.

ate study in areas which would strengthen the faculty of St. Mary of the Lake Seminary. Father Higgins pursued a doctorate in economics, which he received in spring 1944 after writing the dissertation *Voluntarism in Organized Labor in the United States 1930-40*.

Shortly before Father Higgins received his degree, Father John Hayes, whose role as SAD's labor-school coordinator we explored in Chapter One, had to leave that position because of his TB. Higgins and Hayes had come to Washington within a month of each other in 1940. Before they went east, Higgins assisted Hayes' social-action efforts in Chicago.

In Washington, Higgins visited frequently with Hayes and his SAD mentors Fathers McGowan and John Ryan. Hayes called upon Higgins to help locate good labor-school materials. So Higgins was a natural choice to fill the SAD vacancy, and Stritch approved him doing so on a temporary basis.

In 1945, when Ryan died and McGowan replaced him as SAD director, Higgins became an assistant to McGowan and somehow "temporary" became longer-term, although Higgins still belonged to the Chicago Archdiocese.

> *The only time Stritch ever referred to it was after I'd been in D.C. for a long time. He was here for a bishops' meeting, and we went up to his room—he was a cardinal by that time—for a drink before dinner. He had a dinner appointment, and was almost out of the door, and said "Higgins, what diocese do you belong to?" This was after a very nice conversation, and I said "Well, I've been working on the assumption it was Chicago, and I was kind of hoping that you had the same assumption." He said, "Well, I'd think we'd see more of you; we never see you." I answered, "Well, I work here." After that I went to Monsignor Howard Carroll, who was NCWC's general secretary then, wondering what this was all about, and we decided that perhaps I ought to take a trip out to Chicago. So a few days later I flew out there and went to the Cardinal's office, and I said "Your Eminence, I was just passing through and I thought I'd say hello," and he said, "Yes, Father, come in any time, we're always glad to see you." I walked out and that was the last time I ever was in the chancery office. I never even sat down, and I'd spent a hundred bucks to get out there.*[4]

---

4   Costello, Gerald, *Without Fear or Favor: George Higgins on the Record*, Mystic, Conn.:Twenty-Third Publications, 1984, 23.

Washington turned out to be an ideal place for Father Higgins to work. Congress and the headquarters of labor federations and international unions were nearby, and Higgins' recent labor studies and SAD position helped him get the information he needed to perform his duties. In addition to labor-school coordination, these included representing Church positions on social and economic issues and advising Catholic social actionists around the nation. "He served," said labor leader Tom Donahue, "as the premier translator of the Catholic Church to the American trade-union movement and of that movement to the Church."[5]

An important vehicle for this translation was *Social Action Notes for Priests*, the monthly newsletter Father Hayes started four years earlier; Higgins issued it until 1968. Even more important was *The Yardstick*, a series of weekly columns enabling SAD directors, first McGowan and Higgins, to reach the social-action community. Columns in the series, started years earlier by McGowan under the title *Father McGowan Says*, were distributed to diocesan newspapers which subscribed to the series through the National Catholic News Service.

Father McGowan, who took over as SAD director after Ryan died in 1945, asked George Higgins to write *The Yardstick* for a couple of weeks in that year, and by the end of it the task was one of Higgins' regular assignments. He wrote *The Yardstick* for the next 56 years, and his 3,000 columns constitute a unique window into the history of Catholic social action.

Other outreach vehicles for Higgins were speeches around the country, the SAD statements issued every Labor Day, and invocations at labor conventions. Father Higgins, whom friends described as having a deep prayer life privately, also valued these invocations, feeling that "through prayer for God's blessing, the church makes visible its presence in the labor movement."[6]

Higgins set the tone for his extensive and extended contributions to America's labor apostolate in his *Yardstick* column for February 11, 1946.

> *The social encyclicals are admittedly impartial in the sense that they stand for even-handed justice, but they are not by any means neutral or impartial ... in their presentation and appraisal of the facts of modern*

---

5 Ibid., 59.
6 Higgins, *op. cit.*, 5.

economic life. They recognize and flatly affirm ... that labor does not yet enjoy equality of status and power with organized capital. The encyclicals unashamedly take the side of organized labor in its quest ... for an expanding participation in ownership, profits, and management.[7]

Inequality of status and power between labor and management was the dominant motif of the United States in 1946 (as it had been since the Civil War except for industrial unionizing's mid-1930s heyday), and the Taft-Hartley Act of 1947 made that inequality the law of the land. Higgins wrote the statement SAD issued regarding this infamous legislation.

The Taft-Hartley Bill does little or nothing to encourage labor-management cooperation. On the contrary, it approaches the complicated problem of industrial relations from a narrow and excessively legalistic point of view. It runs the risk of disorganizing and disrupting industrial relations by hastily and completely recasting the whole range of federal labor legislation just at the time when collective bargaining shows definite signs of moving towards collective cooperation for the common good. Instead of encouraging labor and management to work together in harmony for the general economic welfare, the bill puts a number of legal restrictions on collective bargaining and particularly on the activities of trade unions—restrictions which will almost inevitably lead to industrial strife and unrest. The bill is an open invitation to management to have recourse to the courts and to the Labor Board at almost every turn and thus to sidetrack or evade the normal processes of constructive collective bargaining....

More specifically, we oppose the Taft-Hartley Bill because of the following unfair and unworkable provisions: 1) By outlawing the closed shop [similar to union shop], the bill disregards completely the history of industrial relations in the United States during the past fifty years or more. Hundreds of thousands of American workers are now covered by closed shop contracts, which, in the vast majority of cases, have operated and are now operating to the mutual benefit of labor and management alike.... 2) The bill denies to foremen and to certain other supervisory employees the legal protection of their natural right to organize into trade unions of their own free choosing.... 3) The bill, in effect, would tend to encourage the separate States to enact anti-labor legislation. It would do so by going out of its way in a most unprecedented manner to

---

7   Yardstick columns and Higgins' other papers, and Social Action Department records, are in the Archives, Catholic University of America, Washington, D.C.

provide that in spite of the federal law the States are free to outlaw the union shop in any of its various and long-established forms....

We urge the Congress to reconsider its vote and to ... concentrate seriously on discovering ways and means of going beyond the limits of traditional collective bargaining into an organized system of labor-management cooperation on the whole range of industrial and economic problems. Anything less than this will tend to encourage class conflict by setting off organized management and organized labor as contestants in a continuing struggle for power.[8]

For George Higgins, the Industry Council concept of the social encyclicals was the kind of "organized system" needed; and "[I]f a misguided industrialist—Catholic or non-Catholic—tells you that the plan is socialistic," Higgins advised, "tell him politely that you are proud to be in the company of such distinguished 'socialists' as Pope Pius XI." The plan, however, while it proved useful in promoting labor-management equality, was too vague, long-term, and macro-level to be truly effective. (See discussion of the plan in Chapter Seven.) Higgins eventually conceded the point, admitting the need for more "flexibility" and for "hard-headed pragmatism" by local unions in negotiating for greater profit-sharing and co-management.[9]

American capitalism's "rugged individualists" did not take kindly to Higgins' talk of labor and management coming together to work out major economic decisions regarding wages, prices, profits, production schedules, and related matters. The National Association of Manufacturers and its allies in the media and the Church hierarchy attacked Higgins' statements and called on his superiors to rein him in, but Bishop Karl Alter of Toledo, who in 1945 succeeded Cardinal Mooney as NCWC's episcopal chairman, backed Higgins strongly.

Higgins and the rest of the Catholic social-action movement continued to see application of the social encyclicals as a communitarian (community-oriented, or for "the common good") middle way between the individualism of unrestrained free enterprise and the collectivism of Communism. They saw the successes of capitalists' concerted drive to decimate or destroy unionism, they knew the successes came mainly because not enough unionists fought to determine their own destinies, and they tried valiantly to inspire unionists to do so.

---

8 Higgins, "Statement on Taft-Hartley Bill", SAD, 1947.
9 "Industry Council Plan", *The Wage Earner*, Oct. 1949, 2. Costello, *op. cit.*, 173-4.

Many sound, honest unionists did fight, as we have seen, and fought hard, but their energies were dissipated by their battles on other fronts. These unionists ejected most of labor's Communists, who on balance were a detriment to the labor movement, but this internal warfare weakened the movement and diverted attention from labor's capitalist foes. The sound, honest unionists also confronted the corruption in many locals and unions, with partial success in the case of the International Longshoremen's Association, as we've seen, and less success in the case of Jimmy Hoffa, Dave Beck, and other officers of the Teamsters, a focus of ballyhooed Congressional investigations throughout the 1950s.

These were tough times for fighters for worker justice, in both the labor and Catholic social-action movements. No one battled against union corruption more fiercely than these fighters did, so it was especially tough for them to see unrestrained capitalists railing against union corruption even as they opposed unions' existence or turned labor-management relations into hostile encounters. In the 1960s and 1970s, however, as various groups in American society—including African-Americans, women, and farmworkers—also fought to determine their own destinies in the face of establishment intransigence, Higgins and other worker-justice advocates found common cause with these empowerment efforts.

In his invocation to the UAW convention in Atlantic City, New Jersey in 1947, Father George Higgins made clear his belief that the union's African-American members and other members were equal brothers and sisters in Christ. Higgins' commitment to racial justice in employment practices and in every other aspect of the labor movement was obvious and influential.

Father Higgins and SAD supported the Civil Rights Act of 1964. He praised Philip Randolph, Bayard Rustin, and Martin Luther King for stressing the vital link between economic justice and civil rights, and he joined their call for a labor-civil rights coalition. He took part in the civil rights march following King's assassination in Memphis in April 1968, and noted that King came to Memphis in support of a strike by the city's sanitation workers.

> *He did so, at the cost of his life, because he was convinced that the time had come for the civil rights movement to turn its attention to the economic root causes of racial justice. Memphis was to have been the first step in his so-called Poor People's Campaign, a preliminary local skir-*

mish, if you will, before he moved on to Washington to launch his highly-publicized campaign at the national level. It wasn't too surprising, of course, that Dr. King should have agreed to throw the full weight of his enormous influence and prestige behind the striking sanitation workers of Memphis. These were his people, desperately poor Negroes fighting against almost impossible odds for elementary economic justice. They needed him and, characteristically, he heeded their anguished plea for help, even though he must have known that, in coming back to Memphis for a second demonstration, he was putting his own life in jeopardy. His courage and sense of dedication will be forever held in highest honor.[10]

In the April 13, 1953 *Yardstick*, George Higgins argued for equal pay and equal opportunity for women, in wages, hiring, promotion, training opportunities, and seniority. As the number of working mothers increased, so did his acceptance of that trend. He initially opposed the Equal Rights Amendment, but later switched to open support, and championed inclusion in the amendment of provisions to protect the special interests of working women.

Higgins focused on gender bias for working women around the world, in industrial as well as developing countries. In *The Yardstick* for April 5, 1993, he called the persistence of such bias "depressing and unacceptable." He called for equality of access to economic resources, for freedom from sexual harassment, and for jobs with greater prospects for economic gain and self-esteem.

The involvement of Father Higgins with farmworkers, the labor connection for which he is best known, started in the 1950s, when he wrote *Yardstick* columns denouncing low wages, long hours, and poor housing and health care for migratory farm laborers. These workers were largely unorganized.

The drafters of the Wagner Act of 1935, bowing to large growers and their lobbyists, omitted these workers from the Act's protections. In addition, the U.S.-administered bracero program enabled growers to contract for Mexican farmworkers and guaranteed these workers decent housing, free transportation, and a 50-cent minimum hourly wage, thus denying U.S. farmworkers economic leverage.

Thanks to George Higgins and other farmworker advocates, the bracero program ended in 1964, but organizing continued to be the main priority. At this time, Higgins met California farmworker, World War II veteran, and organizer Cesar Chavez at a Boston Catholic so-

---

10 Ibid., 158-9.

cial action meeting (social action priests assisted Chavez' earliest organizing efforts), and praised him in *The Yardstick* for "charismatic leadership" of the National Farm Workers Association (NFWA), the union Chavez founded in 1962.

In 1965 NFWA went on strike to organize California's table-grape industry, an effort boosted two years later when the union and AFL-CIO's Agricultural Workers Organizing Committee joined to form the United Farm Workers Organizing Committee (UFWOC). Chavez, quoting *Rerum Novarum,* led the strikers in an eleven-year drive which captivated the nation through grape boycotts, Senate hearings, a 300-mile march growing from 100 people to 4,000, and Chavez going on a long fast.

Higgins supported the strike publicly, citing Monsignor John Ryan's teaching that a boycott is justified "when the injustice inflicted by the employer is grave, and when no milder method will be effective."[11] Higgins could not get the nation's bishops to support the boycott officially, but they did form the Bishops Ad Hoc Committee on Farm Labor in November 1969, with Higgins as a consultant. Under the chairmanship of Bishop Joseph Donnelly of Connecticut, whose contributions to social action this volume has already recognized, the committee brought Chavez and the growers together in 1970.

It took six years before the growers finally recognized Chavez' union, a period filled with numerous cross-country trips by Higgins and Donnelly and with courageous efforts by Chavez and UFWOC members to beat off an attempt by the Teamsters union to muscle in on the organizing drive. Higgins' role was instrumental in bringing about final recognition of the United Farm Workers (UFW) union because he had the confidence of both the growers and Chavez, who said "He knows how to move in the whole field of labor relations. The growers knew that he liked us, but he never lost his credibility with them for a minute."[12]

The Bishops' Committee dissolved in 1976 but not before helping Governor Jerry Brown secure passage of the California Agricultural Labor Relations Act, which gave farmworkers many of the protections unavailable to them under federal legislation. Sadly, within a year the growers waged a successful campaign to severely weaken the new state law. UFW accomplished much, however, and Catholic social action-

11 *Ibid.,* 102.
12 *Ibid.,* 105-6.

ists have continued to support labor's efforts to improve the lot of the nation's farmworkers.[13]

This episode displayed George Higgins' stature as both an articulate and influential labor advocate and a front-line soldier in worker-justice struggles. That stature, recognized by the Church's naming him a Domestic Prelate in 1959 (although he much preferred "Father" to "Monsignor"), was also exemplified during this period by his strong support for UAW and for the Amalgamated Clothing and Textile Workers Union (ACTWU).

Allied with bishops in the U.S. Southeast and with ACTWU members throughout that region, Monsignor Higgins backed the 1980 boycott of J. P. Stevens Company products. This boycott helped bring about eventual recognition of the union in a region where economic individualism has long dominated worker interests.

In 1957, at the height of union bashing, UAW established a seven-member Public Review Board and Walter Reuther appointed George Higgins as one of its members. The board was an ethics guardian, providing an avenue of final appeal to any UAW member who alleged that the union violated its constitution and by-laws. Higgins, a valued member of the Board for 44 years, called it "one of the most innovative vehicles for the enhancement of union democracy."[14]

Monsignor George Higgins officially retired in 1980—two years after his friends in Church and labor successfully prevented a USCC attempt to eliminate his position.[15] Over the next 22 years, however, he performed his greatest service—one which not only bridges the gap between the worker-justice struggles (Catholic or otherwise) of yesterday and the struggles of today, but which offers American society a much-needed organizing principle for the present and the future. This service was to proclaim loudly and persistently that organized labor in the United States—and the organizing of labor in the United States—are alive, vibrant, and wide-open to workers of every kind

---

13   A helpful resource is *Cesar Chavez, the Catholic Bishops, and the Farm-workers' Struggle for Social Justice*, Marco G. Prouty, Tucson: University of Arizona Press, 2006.

14   Higgins, *Organized Labor, op. cit.*, 180.

15   USCC presented the attempt as a means of budget cutting, but a bit of "muscle-flexing" by some well-placed Church conservatives cannot be discounted.

as means of realizing their demands for justice and of democratizing their nation.

This message of George Higgins resonates powerfully and universally for Americans because it says that contrary to the prognoses of the labor movement's terminal illness avidly promoted by today's "rugged individualists," the movement is in transition to an era where its realities and potentials for social justice can be reclaimed and fulfilled. Higgins acknowledges labor's declines and difficulties, but, as he put it, "the main danger is not that the labor movement may go out of business ... but that it would be rendered so weak as to be ineffectual."[16]

> The labor problem is not a matter of ancient history. It is an ongoing problem that calls for active involvement on the part of those who believe in social justice. While organized labor is undoubtedly far from perfect—I have even gotten intimations at times that my own church is far from perfect—no other movement in sight would enable American workers to protect their legitimate economic interests. No other movement would enable American workers to play an effective and responsible role in helping to promote the general economic welfare both at home and abroad.
>
> At the height of the Great Depression, in one of his many books on industrial ethics, John A. Ryan wrote two sentences that sum up his views on labor. This is my credo, as well as his: "Effective labor unions are still by far the most powerful force in society for the protection of the laborer's rights and the improvement of his or her condition. No amount of employer benevolence, no diffusion of a sympathetic attitude among the public, no increase of beneficial legislation, can adequately supply for the lack of organization among the workers themselves."[17]

Here is "Go to the worker" in modern form. "Go organize!", George Higgins' life and work says to labor, Catholic social action, and all of American society. Experiences like the grape-industry and J. P. Stevens boycotts resonate, Higgins stressed, because they involved labor, Catholic social action, and the public answering American workers' sharp and continuing cry that their interests be fairly represented. In this sense, Higgins acted pastorally in a wide parish as his message cut across lines of class, gender, ethnicity, section, religion, race, or whatever other category.

---

16 Ibid., 72.
17 Ibid., 78.

In *George G. Higgins and the Quest for Worker Justice*, published in 2005, Father John O'Brien explored the meanings of Higgins' 1944-2001 *Yardstick* columns and of the NCWC/USCC Labor Day statements from 1945-2001. Higgins wrote the statements through 1980 and the others, in O'Brien's words, "continued to reflect Higgins' agenda and mentality."

Before Higgins died, he reviewed O'Brien's cataloguing of *Yardstick* columns and declared it to be "an invaluable service." O'Brien's distillation of the Higgins/USCC output in the 1980s and 1990s traces the social and economic issues of those decades and illumines the deep need for worker justice in today's America.

> Several issues touched the lives of workers in new ways in the 1980s and 1990s. First, the gap between the rich and the poor kept getting bigger. In fact, the gap in the United States was larger than anywhere else in the world. Upper-income families experienced substantial income growth in the 1980s, and the bottom 40 percent experienced stagnation or a decline in wages. The disproportion between the earnings of CEOs and the salaries of ordinary workers was increasing. Younger people, especially those with a minimum amount of education, were more likely to be poor. Many of the new jobs in the 1990s were part-time, provided meager wages, and offered few benefits. People increasingly felt uneasy. Even with low unemployment, many workers felt insecure about their future.
>
> Another major issue was that the country was becoming a single nation with three economies.
>
> The first economy was prospering and moving ahead. People in this economy had the skills that enabled them to flourish in a global economy and in an information age. This economic class had power and prestige.... The ability of transnational corporations to transcend national borders suited many in this economy.
>
> The second economy was just getting by, but it was being squeezed by the decline in real incomes. People in this economy feared the loss of their jobs, their health care benefits, and their retirement pensions when companies downsized or relocated. They worried that they would be unable to educate their children. This economic class had limited power and prestige. Many in the middle were at a breaking point. Temporary illness or disability could plunge them into poverty.
>
> The third economy was losing ground. People in this economy were on the margins and not getting by. They worried about not having enough to pay the rent, buy food, and afford decent health care. Sometimes they had to settle for one over the other. This economic class had no power

and prestige. Many, even those working full-time at the minimum wage, were unable to afford safe, quality child care, decent housing, and transportation to and from work.[18]

Obviously, recent economic events in the United States have underscored the truth of these observations, and have deepened the crises which demand the ministrations of social justice.

Social justice is based upon constructive anger. It is stoked by such signs of the times as those George Higgins just cited and by those all around us. It is stoked by the comparison of the percentage of American workers organized in the mid-1960s, about a third, to the percentage today, 12, one of the lowest figures among industrialized nations. It is stoked by 2005 U.S. Bureau of the Census figures showing that the number of Americans living in severe poverty grew by 26 percent from 2000 to 2005, while "the share of national income going to corporate profits has dwarfed the amount going to wages and salaries." And it is stoked, above all, by the fact that, as George Higgins noted, "employer opposition is a major cause of labor's decline since the 1960s."[19]

No wonder many of the economic ideas infusing the work of John A. Ryan and other early Catholic social actionists—and of the Midwestern progressives, German social democrats, and English economists who influenced these pioneers—were based upon distributive justice: fair distribution of the proceeds of production. The gross unfairness of distribution in the United States today defies the bedrock beliefs of the nation, especially when its dominant economic interests are bent on destroying or decimating the worker organizations through which some fairness of distribution has been accomplished—and through which much more worker justice could be accomplished.

"The bulk of U.S. employers have never accepted the permanent, institutional role of unions, especially in their own companies," said Industrial Relations Association President Everett Kassalow in 1985.[20] Among disturbing indicators of this lack of acceptance, Higgins noted declines in union victory returns in elections supervised by the National Labor Relations Board, increases in union decertification (abo-

---

18 O'Brien, John J., *George G. Higgins and the Quest for Worker Justice: The Evolution of Catholic Social Thought in America*, Lanham, Md.: Rowman & Littlefield Publishers, Inc., 2005, 171.
19 Pugh, Tony, "Poverty Numbers at Record High, Study Says", *Atlantic City Press*, Feb. 25, 2007, A8. Higgins, *Organized Labor*, op. cit., 152.
20 Ibid., 151.

lition) and in industry bargaining for concessions of job security, and a whole new spin on union-busting where briefcases have replaced bludgeons and consultants are hired to keep unions out. These "professionals" receive personal information from supervisors and use it to influence employees' votes in representation elections, and they "divide-and-conquer" by pitting black against white, old against young, educated against uneducated, and so on.

Higgins constantly reminded readers that the Wagner Act of 1935 (still on the books despite its emasculation by the Taft-Hartley Act of 1947) declared it to be U.S. policy "to encourage the practice and procedure of collective bargaining ... by protecting the exercise of workers of full freedom of association, self-organization, and designation of representatives of their own choosing...." One right guaranteed by "the neglected NLRA," Higgins added, was the right to strike without fear of reprisal.

In 1981, President Ronald Reagan fired 12,000 striking members of the Professional Air Traffic Controllers' Organization (PATCO), signaling a new and alarming era in American labor-management relations. PATCO members were in the public sector and thus not covered by the National Labor Relations Board, but private employers, heartened by a U.S. President depriving striking workers of their jobs and getting away with it, started doing the same thing under the provisions of a 1938 Supreme Court decision which few employers had dared to use prior to the PATCO fiasco.

That decision, *NLRB v. Mackay Radio and Telegraph Company*, held that strikers have the right to return to their jobs after a strike settlement. Then, in the same decision, the court negated this finding by ruling that employers have the right to keep their business going during a strike even if it means hiring permanent replacements for the strikers.

After President Reagan's punitive PATCO action, more employers hired permanent replacements. One year after a strike, NLRB allows the affected employer to petition for an election to decertify the striking union. Consequently, hiding behind *Mackay* has great appeal for anti-union employers because the strikers can't vote, yet the strikebreakers who replaced them can.

The appalling injustices of the resulting outbreak of assaults on the rights to organize and to bargain collectively moved the American bishops, in their 1986 pastoral letter on Catholic social teaching and the American economy, to state that they "firmly oppose organized efforts, such as those regrettably now seen in our country, to break existing unions and prevent workers from organizing."²¹ This forthright statement directly results from the efforts of the Catholic social-action movement and of its allies of whatever faith or persuasion.

The great majority of labor-schools within the Catholic social-action movement faded away through the 1950s and into the 1960s, but their legacy remains, and Catholic social action lives on in new ways. A key question now and in the future, in the words of Monsignor Higgins in his 1993 book *Organized Labor and the Church*—a must-read for any friend of worker justice—is "Will the Catholic Church, my church, reclaim its heritage of support for the organization of working people? I am afraid I cannot say for sure. In fact, the church stands in danger of losing forever its tradition of cooperation with organized labor. It is for that reason, above all, that I wrote this book."²²

Recent developments show just how real this danger is. Part of it is simply that too many Catholic workers, like too many workers generally, have moved up the economic ladder so rapidly that they have become indifferent to the needs of workers on the ladder's lower rungs. Such climbers seem to think, according to Higgins, "that in a society as affluent as our own, workers can readily fend for themselves in the so-called free market; workers have no need to organize."²³

The bulk of the danger, however, comes under the "physician, heal thyself" heading which, as already mentioned, has fit many instances of how Catholic institutions, as employers, relate to their employees. According to Higgins, "the right to organize and bargain collectively in Catholic institutions—or the propriety of doing so—has yet to be universally acknowledged. A troubling case in point, is those Catholic health care facilities that have waged open warfare with their employees over this issue. Some of the hospitals have gone so far as to hire notorious anti-union consulting firms to prevent their workers from organizing."²⁴

---

21   National Conference of Catholic Bishops, *Economic Justice for All: Pastoral Letter on Catholic Social Teaching and the U.S. Economy*, Washington, D.C.: USCC, 1986.
22   Higgins, *Organized Labor, op. cit.*, 5-6.
23   *Ibid.*, 66.
24   *IIbid.*, 113.

Higgins called Catholics back to their heritage. He frequently reminded them that in the latter part of the 19th century, "it was the American labor movement that held out hope of advancing the American experiment." He reminded them also that the Knights of Labor, an inclusive national organization with many Catholic members, played a vital role in that contribution.[25]

In 1886, the Vatican was preparing to forbid American Catholics to join this group when James Cardinal Gibbons of Baltimore, representing the U.S. bishops, successfully petitioned the Vatican to desist. "Since the great questions of the future," Gibbons declared, "are the social questions, the questions which concern the improvement of the condition of the great masses of the people, and especially of the working people, it is evidently of supreme importance that the church should always be found on the side of humanity, of justice toward the multitudes who compose the body of the human family."[26]

In the aftermath of the Second Vatican Council, the four-year-long process in the 1960s through which the Catholic Church re-explored social questions and the Church's teachings in response to them, constructive institutional innovations were adopted and supported at every Church level. Higgins welcomed this development, but he welcomed even more Catholic laypeople empowering themselves during and since that renewal process.

This empowerment emphasizes what Higgins called the "layperson's independent and autonomous role as a citizen and a member of secular organizations, in solving social problems." Foremost among those organizations for Higgins, of course, were labor unions, and he applauded Pope John Paul II's characterization of them as "indispensable."[27]

Higgins also welcomed the fact that following the recent concerted assault upon unions, the labor movement and the worker-justice movement are re-energizing themselves. Unions have mounted a multitude of new drives to organize the unorganized, among them service workers, computer operators, white-collar workers, and immigrants.

Higgins especially welcomed the fact that the health-care field, which included many Catholic hospitals, had become a priority in organizing efforts. He wrote of taking part in these efforts in the early 1980s with labor leaders such as Gerry Shea, now the AFL-CIO Pres-

25 Ibid., 47.
26 Ibid., 48-9.
27 Ibid., 39, 72.

ident's Assistant for Governmental Affairs but at that time the head of the hospital unit of the Service Employees International Union.[28]

Community activists and groups, with Catholics significantly represented, have increasingly supported organizing drives and labor's renewed efforts to strengthen and expand collective bargaining. Higgins cited as an example of this support the victory in the United Mine Workers 1989-90 strike against the Pittston Coal Company in southwestern Virginia, where an inter-denominational network of religious organizations was instrumental in the successful outcome.

Religion, labor, and other segments of America's communities are rediscovering the value of coalition-forming around worker justice as a means of focusing new energies. The media abound with accounts of profit-making elevated to the supreme value, skyrocketing executive compensation, lagging competitiveness, multiple plant closings and relocations, questionable investment policies, and chaotic corporate reorganizations. All this happens while "regular American families have received a shrinking portion of the American pie," as Higgins put it.[29] More and more Americans are becoming aware that unions are sorely needed—just as much if not more than in the ferment of the mid-1930s.

> Several years ago I stayed in a hotel in Disneyland for a two-week conference. Anyone who knows anything about Disneyland hotels knows that the rooms are almost always booked, and so the owners make lots of money. I got to know some of the hotel workers, including the woman who cleaned my room. I asked her how long she had worked there. "Twenty years," she said. I asked if she would mind telling me how much she earned. "Minimum wage," was her reply.
>
> I am often asked, "Why are unions needed in this day and age? People should not ask me. They should ask the maid at Disneyland and other low-wage workers. If her situation was like that of other minimum-wage workers, she probably had no health insurance, in addition to no living wage. Health insurance, which originated at the bargaining table, represents one of organized labor's great contributions to the American worker. Without this coverage, people can run up bills for health care that would otherwise land them in the poorhouse. And yet, millions of non-union workers have no health insurance; as a result, more than 30

---

28   Ibid., 125-6, 129.
29   Ibid., 169.

million American workers are not covered and several times as many are under-insured.[30]

Two years before those words were written, in 1991, Pope John Paul II celebrated the 100th anniversary of *Quadragesimo Anno*. Higgins recalled a related incident which occurred in that memorable year.

> George P. Shultz spoke the truth when he told the National Planning Association in 1991 that "free societies and free trade unions go together." Those words—in a speech that lamented the decline of organized labor—came from a man who has held the top cabinet posts in several Republican administrations, including Ronald Reagan's State Department. Ray Marshall, like Shultz a former secretary of labor, has elaborated on this message: "We should be particularly concerned about the weakening of labor organizations since the 1960s, because we are not likely to have a free and democratic society without a free and democratic labor movement. Trying to have economic democracy without unions is like trying to have political democracy without political parties."[31]

Thank God for all of George Higgins' ministries towards the spiritual fulfillment and economic democracy of America's workers and unions. Higgins and the other American labor apostles profiled in this volume have done everything they can to "Go to the worker." May each of us do the same.

---

30   Ibid., 181-2.
31   Ibid., 190.

SUGGESTED BOOKS FOR FURTHER READING

GENERAL

Seven Great Encyclicals. Glen Rock, N.J.: Paulist Press, 1963.

American Catholicism and Social Action: A Search for Social Justice, 1865-1950, Aaron I. Abell. Westport, Conn.: Greenwood Press, 1960.

"Sufficiently Radical": Catholicism, Progressivism, and the Bishops' Program of 1919, Joseph M. McShane, SJ. Washington: The Catholic University of America Press, 1986.

Right Reverend New Dealer John A. Ryan, Francis L. Broderick. New York: The Macmillan Company, 1963.

The Mystical Body and Social Justice, Virgil Michel. Collegeville, Minn.: St. John's Abbey, 1938.

Selected Writings: By Little and By Little, Dorothy Day. New York: Orbis Books, 1992.

Voices from the Catholic Worker, Rosalie Riegle Troester, ed. Philadelphia: Temple University Press, 1993.

Breaking Bread: The Catholic Worker and the Origin of Catholic Radicalism in America, Mel Piehl. Philadelphia: Temple University Press, 1982.

Franklin D. Roosevelt and the New Deal 1932-1940, William E. Leuchtenberg. New York: Harper & Row, Publishers, 1963.

American Catholics and Social Reform: The New Deal Years, David J. O'Brien. New York: Oxford University Press, 1968.

The End of Reform: New Deal Liberalism in Recession and War, Alan Brinkley. New York: Vintage Books, 1995.

The Dynamics of Industrial Democracy, Clinton Golden. New York: Harper & Brothers Publishers, 1942.

The UAW and Walter Reuther, Irving Howe and B. J. Widick. New York: Random House, 1949.

The State and Labor in Modern America, Melvyn Dubofsky. Chapel Hill: University of North Carolina Press, 1994.

Christian Socialism, John Cort. Maryknoll, N.Y.: Orbis Books, 1988.

A New Deal: How Regional Activism Will Reshape the American Labor Movement, Amy B. Dean and David B. Reynolds, Ithaca: Cornell University Press, 2009.

The Big Squeeze: Tough Times for the American Worker, Steven Greenhouse, New York: Alfred A. Knopf, 2008.

CHAPTER SUBJECTS

Dreadful Conversions: The Making of a Catholic Socialist, John Cort. New York: Fordham University Press, 2003.

This Confident Church: Catholic Leadership and Life in Chicago, 1940-1965, Steven M. Avella. Notre Dame: University of Notre Dame Press, 1992.

Seasons of Grace: A History of the Catholic Archdiocese of Detroit, Leslie Woodcock Tentler. Detroit: Wayne State University Press, 1990.

The Word Made Flesh: The Chicago Catholic Worker and the Emergence of Lay Activism in the Church, Francis Sicius. Lanham, Md.: University Press of America, 1990.

Fighter with a Heart, Charles J. McCollester, ed. Pittsburgh: University of Pittsburgh Press, 1996.

A Canterbury Tale: Experiences and Reflections 1916-1976, John Cogley. New York: The Seabury Press, 1976.

Organized Labor and the Church: Reflections of a "Labor Priest," George Higgins with William Bole. New York: Paulist Press, 1993.

George G. Higgins and the Quest for Worker Justice: The Evolution of Catholic Social Thought in America, John J. O'Brien. Lanham, Md.: Rowman & Littlefield Publishers, Inc., 2005.

INDEX

A

Abood v. Detroit Board of Education 109
Abraham, Steven 109
Acropolis, John 149
Adamczyk, Chester 179
Adams, John Q. 167–168
Addes, George 97
AFL-CIO 113, 189, 256
Agricultural Workers Organizing Committee, AFL-CIO 249
Alamo Register 50
Alden Hosiery Mills 43
Alinsky, Saul 46
A Living Wage 46
Allied Printing Trades 234
Alter, Karl 246
Amalgamated Clothing and Textile Workers Union 250
Amalgamated Meat Cutters and Butcher Workmen of North America, Local 590 197
America 103–104, 123, 212, 216, 240
American Communications Association 217, 226
American Federation of Labor 39, 57, 59, 65, 69–70, 72, 86, 101, 126, 131, 146, 149, 189, 193–194, 196–197, 202, 218–219, 228
American Freedom and Catholic Power 138
American Labor Party 225
American Maid Shoe Company 36
American Newspaper Guild 40, 63, 126, 140, 157, 226
Americans for Democratic Action 186
American Sociological Society 103
Anderson, Joseph 45
An Integrated Program of Social Order 215
Anti-Communism 70, 95, 137, 153–159, 162, 164, 166, 176, 186, 199, 204, 206, 208–210, 217, 234
Anti-Semitism 84
Archdiocesan Labor Institute 82, 85, 171, 176
Armstrong, John H. 166
Army-McCarthy hearings 207
Association of Catholic Trade Unionists 60–66, 68, 77, 81–82, 84, 86, 90, 92, 95, 106–108, 125–128, 138, 143, 152–153, 160–162, 167, 173–178, 186–188, 192, 197, 204, 232
Atlantic Mills 64
Auto-Lite Company 67
Avery, Sewell 133–134

B

Back of the Yards Council 46
Bajork, Leonard 124
Ballam, Deborah 110
Baltimore Archdiocese 156–157
Banville, Benoit 221
Barwick, Helene 179
Beck, David 247
Beckmann, Joseph 40
Belloc, Hilaire 240
Bell, Thomas 160, 162
Benedictine order 123

Bennett, Harry 85–86
Biddle, Francis 133
Bishops Ad Hoc Committee on Farm Labor 249
Bishops' Program for Social Reconstruction, The 46–47, 215
Bi-State Waterfront Commission 228
Black Panthers 210
Blanshard, Paul 138
Block, Harry 162
Bloy, Leon 56
Bohn Local 208-UAW 90
Boland, John 107, 143
Booker T. Washington Workers School 153
Bosch, Marie 145, 148
Boston Archdiocese 215
Boston Newspaper Guild 77
Boulton, William 160, 162
Bowe, James 149
Boyd, William 40, 45
Boyle, Hugh 206
Boys' Catholic High School 197
Brennan, Brother Justin 66
Brennan, William 63
Bresette, Linna 42, 47
Bricklayers Union 149
Bridges, Harry 201
Bronx Home News 148
Brooklyn Diocese 102, 105, 107
Brooklyn Prep High School 103
Brooklyn Priests' Social Action Committee 102–106, 111, 114
Brooklyn Social Action Department 106, 167
Brooks, John 223–226
Broun, Heywood 40
Browder, Earl 89, 134
Brown, Ben 33
Brown, Jerry 249
Brown, Leo 162
Buckley, Joseph 101–115
Buffalo Labor College 44
Buhl Local 772-UAW 179
Buick Local 599-UAW 87
Building Service Employees International Union 112, 226
Burke, John 155
Burns, Bernard 126
Business Week 132
Byrne, Edwin 234
Byrne, John 151

C

California Agricultural Labor Relations Act 249
Calvary Cemetery 110
Candy Workers Union 114
Canning and Pickle Workers-AFL 194
Cantwell, Daniel 45–46, 48, 50, 99, 129–130, 138
Capitalism, unrestrained (rugged individualism) 34, 58, 68, 70, 77, 83, 89, 96, 104, 108, 113, 115, 122, 137–138, 155, 158, 165, 182, 189, 192, 195, 210, 217, 223, 229, 231, 233, 237, 245–247, 250–254, 257
Carey, Daniel 223
Carey, James 162–163
Carey, John 213, 224
Carey, Philip 44, 104, 106, 148, 213, 233, 236
Carnegie Public Library 197
Carnegie Steel Corporation 67
Carrabine, Martin 118
Carroll, Howard 243

Index

Carstens, Arthur 124
Carter, Jimmy 109
Casey, George 40
Cathedral College 168
Catholic Action 46, 130
Catholic Business Education Association 167
Catholic Conference on Industrial Problems 47
Catholic conservatives and labor 35, 41, 45, 47–48, 78, 114, 137, 139, 159, 193, 196, 229, 234, 246, 250, 255
Catholic Council on Working Life 139
Catholic employers and labor 40, 97, 107, 110, 120, 137, 146, 166, 187, 211, 227, 255
Catholic, Jewish and Protestant Declaration on Economic Justice 135
Catholic Labor Alliance 124–127, 129–131, 133–135, 139
Catholic Labor Defense League 61
Catholic Labor Guild (later Labor Guild) of Boston 77, 215
Catholic labor schools 38–39, 41–44, 50–51, 61–62, 66, 77, 82, 85, 102–105, 107, 111, 113, 125, 130, 137, 157–159, 172–173, 175–178, 181, 188, 197, 199, 206, 214–216, 221, 226, 229–231, 241, 243–244, 255
Catholic liturgy 31, 49, 123, 125
Catholic News 108
Catholic Radical Alliance 192, 194–195, 197
Catholic Social Action 174
Catholic Social Guild 222
Catholic Transcript, The 139

Catholic Union of the Unemployed 124
Catholic University of America, The 46, 48, 130, 158, 242
Catholic Worker movement 31–32, 38, 46, 55, 58–59, 66, 118, 123–125, 140, 192–193, 196, 199, 232
Catholic Worker, The 32, 55, 59–60, 66, 117–119, 192, 194
Caul, Bill 221
Chave, Edward 222
Chavez, Cesar 248–249
Chesterton, G.K. 240
Chicago ACTU 126
Chicago American, The 39
Chicago Archdiocese 40, 45–46, 125, 240–241, 243
Chicago Catholic Worker, The 32, 50–51, 119–121, 124, 128, 164
Chicago Daily News, The 133–134
Chicago Herald-American, The 39
Chicago Herald-Examiner, The 39
Chicago Inter-Student Catholic Action 118
Chicago Newspaper Guild 39
Chicago Sun-Times, The 140
Childs Restaurant 197
Chisholm, Al 179
Christian Brothers, The 66
Christianity and American Capitalism 139
Christian Socialism 77
Chrysler Corporation 81, 84–85
Chrysler Local 7-UAW 81, 88–91, 97, 179
Chrysler Local 490-UAW 179
Cicognani, Amleto 155
Cifichiello, John 222

CIO-PAC 75, 91
City College of New York 81
Civil Service Employees Union 113
Clancy, Raymond 85, 135, 171–173, 177, 181, 187
Clayton, John 221–222
Clericalism 83, 157
Click, James 162
Clinton, William 109
Coen, Harry 93
Cogley, John 119–120, 123–124, 164
Cold War 209
Collective bargaining 37, 39, 48, 61, 67, 70–72, 74, 88, 92–93, 96, 108–111, 121, 127, 131–132, 185, 221–222, 224, 233, 245–246, 251, 254, 256–257
College of New Rochelle 66, 77, 143, 145, 166
Collins, Joseph 113
Comey, Dennis 231
Commission on Human Relations (Chi.) 140
Committee for Maritime Unity 202
Committee for Rank-and-File Democracy, District 4-UE 161–162
Committee for the Study of Social Thought, University of Chicago 124
Commons, John 46
Commonweal 66, 68, 73, 75, 77, 136, 139–140, 164, 173–176, 240
Communications Workers of America 112, 179
Communism in the United States 155
Communist Party 32, 38, 43, 49–50, 57–60, 64–66, 68–70, 77–78, 81–84, 86, 89–90, 94–95, 97, 104–105, 112, 119–120, 122, 126, 128–129, 131–134, 137, 146–147, 151–165, 177, 182, 186, 189, 192–194, 196, 198–206, 208–210, 215, 217, 219, 223–226, 229, 235, 246–247
Confidential Report on Communist Activities 157
Congress of Industrial Organizations 32, 36–37, 39–40, 57–58, 63–65, 67–73, 75, 78, 81, 84, 87, 89, 91, 93, 101, 125–126, 131–132, 135, 137, 147, 153, 162–163, 170, 179, 181, 184, 189, 191–194, 196–206, 208, 219, 225–226, 235
Conlon, Joseph and Angela 114
Conroy, James 161
Consumers' roles 122
Cooney, Rita Clare 125, 131
Corridan, John 227–229
Cort, Helen (Haye) 68, 77–78, 145
Cort, John 53–78, 94, 135, 139, 227
Coughlin, Charles 48, 84–85
Cox, James 194
Creighton University Institute of Industrial Relations 230
Crisano, Louis 107
Cronin, John 154, 156–159, 174
Crown Heights Labor School 103, 106, 215, 231
Crusaders of Christ the Worker 103
Cunningham, Paul 166
Curley, Michael 49, 156
Curran, Joseph 202

D

Daily Worker, The 64, 193, 199, 206
Dairy Employees Union-AFL 39, 124

Index

Daley, Richard J. 140
Dalrymple, Sherman 67
Darby, Thomas 143, 175
Day, Dorothy 31–32, 38, 40, 55–60, 65, 124, 192, 214, 216
Dearden, John 206–207
Decline of the Catholic social-action movement 137, 139–140, 165
Delaney, Frank 39, 230
Delaney, John 217, 229
Dennis Comey Institute of Industrial Relations, St. Joseph University 230
Detroit ACTU 81–82, 84, 95, 165, 171, 173–177, 179–181, 185–189
Detroit Archdiocese 83–84, 172–173, 177
Detroit Federation of Teachers 177, 179, 187
Detroit Newspaper Guild 82, 95, 179, 189
Detroit Times, The 180, 188–189
Dewey, Thomas 91
Dignity of work 34, 121–122, 195, 216, 219, 234, 236
Diocesan Labor Institute (Hartford) 50, 165, 186
Distributism 253
District 2-UE 162
District 4-UE 153, 160–161
District 6-UE 162
District 8-UE 162
District 50-UMW 202
Divini Redemptoris 32, 57, 155
Dodge Local 3-UAW 179
Doherty, Thomas 179
Dominican Commercial High School 105, 107
Donahue, George 65–66

Donahue, Thomas 113, 244
Donlin Bert 79–99
Donnelly, Joseph 50, 135, 162, 165, 186, 249
Dorfman, Isaiah 39
Dorney, William 43
Downs, Dickie 225
Dreadful Conversions 77
Drohan, William 162
Drolet, Jerome 43, 135
Dubofsky, Melvyn 71, 74
Duffy, John 162
Duquesne University 192

E

Edison Electrical Workers Union 60
Eisenhower, Dwight 137, 207–208
Ely, Richard 46
Emspak, Julius 163
Engel, Frances 44
Enright, Bart 162
Epiphany Church (Chi.) 51
Equal Rights Amendment 248

F

Faidel, Michael 197
Fair Employment Practices Committee 48
Farm Equipment Workers 37, 203
Farmworkers 247–249, 251
Federal Bureau of Investigation 156, 158–159, 189, 209
Feldhaus, Margaret 145, 148
Fenton, Frank 146, 149
Fenton, John 149
Ferrer, Sister Vincent 125
Fighter with a Heart 211

First National Catholic Social Action Conference (Milwaukee) 33, 48
Fitzgerald, Albert 163
Fitzgerald, Gareth 149
Fitzpatrick, Joseph 216
Flynn, Joseph 64
Foery, Walter 96
Food, Tobacco, Agricultural and Allied Workers-CIO 112
Forbes, Robert 173
Fordham University 62, 66, 106, 114, 168, 215–216, 236
Ford, Henry 85
Ford Local 600-UAW 97, 179
Ford Motor Company 85, 96
Foremen's Association of America 110
Fort Totten 221
Frane, Gerry 222
Frankensteen, Richard 67, 85
Frick, Henry 67

G

Gahagan, Marguerite 179, 188–189
Gallagher, Michael 84
Garvey, Jack 162
Gem Razor strike 63
General Motors Corporation 59, 72–73, 75, 81, 85, 87, 92–94, 96–97, 185, 221, 232
George G. Higgins and the Quest for Worker Justice 252
Gibbons, James Cardinal 256
Gillespie, Frank 39, 124
Goldberg, Arthur 39, 241
Goldware, Faye 222
Gompers, Samuel 202
Gonzaga Labor School 230

Goodyear Tire and Rubber Company 67
Gosser, Richard 97
Grant's 5&10 63
Great Depression 30–31, 47, 55, 58, 65, 79–81, 84, 87, 117, 161, 192, 198, 214–215, 241, 251
Greater New York Council-CIO 235
Gregory, Wilton 29–30
Grimm, George Jr. 149
Guardian Angel Church (NYC) 214
Guardian Angels Church (Det.) 173

H

Haas, Francis 48–49, 64, 70–71, 82, 108–109, 123, 156
Haas, Herbert 223
Haener, Dorothy 179
Hamilton, Pat 179
Hammond, Joseph 105, 107, 113, 151, 167
Hannan, Jerome 82
Harold, John 111
Harper's 235
Harris, Herbert 98, 136
Hart, Vincent 216
Hathaway, Clarence 199
Hayek, Friedrich 158
Hayes, A. J. 131
Hayes, John 29–52, 60, 66, 94, 117, 135, 231, 243–244
Hearst Guild Strike Committee 39
Heidelberger, Ronald 180–181
Helgans, Edward 166
Henneberry, T. E. 234
Henry George School 219
Hensler, Carl 192–193, 195, 197

Index

Herberg, Will 136–138
Higgins, Anna 239
Higgins, Charles 239–241
Higgins, George 48, 135, 159, 174–175, 184, 231–233, 239–258
Hillenbrand, Reynold 30, 32, 35, 38, 40–41, 45–46, 130, 135, 158, 242
Hillman, Sidney 72
Hitler, Adolf 69, 84, 86, 198
H. J. Heinz Company 193–195
Hoffa, James 247
Hogan, Frank 227
Holleman, Henry 43
Holly, John 226
Holy Cross Church (NYC) 227
Holy Cross College Institute of Industrial Relations 230–231
Holy Name Cathedral 38, 126
Holy Name Society 150, 157, 227
Holy Rosary Church (Pitt.) 84, 207, 210
Holy Trinity Church 168
Holy Trinity Church (Det.) 172
Homestead strike 67, 206
Hoover, Herbert 80
Hoover, J. Edgar 209
Hotel, Bar, and Restaurant Workers-AFL, Local 705 179, 181
Hotel Service Employees Union 77
House Un-American Activities Committee 157, 209
Howe, Irving 89
How to De-Control Your Union of Communists 200
How to Run a Labor School 230
Hubbard Company 197
Hubble, Karl 76, 169–190
Hudson, Roy 158

Hutton, Barbara 63

I

Illinois Department of Labor 39
Illinois Manufacturers Association 45
Immaculate Conception Church (Washington, Pa.) 207
Incarnate Word College 50
Indiana University of Pennsylvania 211
Industrial Relations Association 253
Industry Council plans and ideas 71–73, 87, 137, 167, 181, 183–185, 246
Institute for Social Order 230–231
Institute of Catholic Social Studies 158
Interborough Rapid Transit 225
International Association of Machinists 131
International Brotherhood of Electrical Workers-AFL 149
International Brotherhood of Longshoremen-AFL 229
International Brotherhood of Teamsters 144, 247, 249
International Confederation of Free Trade Unions 51
International Harvester Corporation 36–37
International Ladies' Garment Workers Union 138, 219
International Longshoremen's Association 58, 65, 227–229, 247
International Longshoremen's & Warehousemen's Union 201
International Seamen's Union 55, 58

International Telephone and Telegraph 234
International Typographical Union 148
International Union of Electrical, Radio and Machine Workers 163, 206

J

Jackson, Robert 48
James Mullenbach Industrial Institute 135
Jesuits (Society of Jesus) 103, 107, 123, 187, 214–217, 227, 229–232, 234
Jeunesse Ouvrière Chrétienne (JOC or Jocists) 31, 38, 123, 130, 216–217, 222
John Carroll University Labor School 230
Johnson, Lyndon 209
Johnson, Malcolm 228
J. P. Stevens Company boycott 250–251

K

Kaiser, Anthony 169–171, 173, 181
Kassalow, Everett 253
KDKA Radio 209
Keeley, Clarence 166
Keenan, Frank 219
Keller, Edward 139
Kelly, George 62, 107–108, 110–111, 174–176
Kern, Clement 43, 172–173, 181, 187
King, John 222
King, Martin Luther 209, 247–248
Knights of Columbus 102, 105, 157
Knights of Labor 256
Knudsen, William 72, 87

Kuhle, Albert 39

L

Labor Day Mass (Chi.) 126, 131
Labor Leader, The 61, 64, 66, 77
Labor-management partnership (industrial democracy) 33, 36, 47–49, 52, 55, 57, 59, 61, 71–77, 87, 92–94, 96–99, 121–123, 137, 164–165, 168, 184–185, 189–190, 196, 223, 229–233, 237, 245–246, 251, 258
Labor violence 61, 64, 67
Lacey, Michael 179
LaChapelle, Lloyd 179
LaFarge, John 123, 136, 212, 216
LaFollette Committee, U.S. Senate 68
Laity social-action roles 36, 41, 102, 118, 121, 124–125, 130, 140, 194, 215–216, 256
Landrum-Griffin Act 109
Lannon, Albert 158
Lappan, Thomas 193
Larkin, Roger 161
Lavelle, Richard 102, 105
Lawrence, Robert 166
League of Nations 240
Ledochowski, Wlodimir 215, 217
Leibfred, Albert 166
Leonard, Richard 97
Levine, Michael 209
Lewis, John L. 64, 68–69, 72, 74, 184, 202
Lilly, Tom 236
'Little Steel' 74, 195–196, 207
Livingston, John 97
Local 29-UAW 179
Local 101-UE 162
Local 104-UAW 173

Index

Local 155-UCW 170
Local 293-UCW 112
Local 404-UE 160
Local 419-UE 160–161
Local 428-UE 162
Local 453-UE 150, 152–154, 159–160
Local 456-UE 149
Local 475-UE 161
Local 1102-UE 162
Local 1202-UE 160
Local 1237-UE 160–161
Long Island Daily Press 63
Look 220, 235
Loose-Wiles Company 193
Louisville Courier-Journal 235
Loyola University of Chicago 118, 124
Lucey, Robert 64
Ludlow Massacre 67
Lyon, James 147–148

M

Maggioli, Albert 44
Maggiolo, Walter 106, 221
Malden, Karl 229
Manhattan College 65–66
Manhattan Refrigerating Company 168
Marble Helpers Union 44
Marciniak, Ed 117–141
Marquette University 230
Marshall Field's store 39–40, 45
Marshall Plan 127, 164, 200
Marshall, Ray 258
Marshall, William 90
Martin, Homer 83
Marx, Karl 95, 104, 154, 167, 184
Materialism 98, 124, 236

Matles, James 94, 163
Maurin, Peter 59–60
Mazey, Emil 85, 97
McCabe, Frank 197
McCarthy, Frank 33
McCarthyism 163, 186, 189, 206–208
McCarthy, Joseph 137, 157, 163–164, 206–210
McCollester, Charles 211
McCormack, William 228
McCulloch, Frank 135
McCusker, Henry 179
McGill, John 87
McGill, William 148
McGowan, Raymond 47, 49–50, 83, 135, 159, 197, 240, 243–244
McKenna, Norman 173
McShane, Joseph 215–216
Meany, George 131, 189
Meegan, Joseph 46
Memorial Day Massacre 59, 195
Memphis sanitation workers' strike 247
Merrill, Lewis 202
Messina, Charles 217
Michel, Virgil 31, 49, 123
Michigan CIO News 173
Michigan Labor Leader (later *WE*) 95
Mies, John 84
Military-industrial complex 207
Miller, Raymond 82
Millor, William 188
Mine, Mill and Smelter Workers 202
Mitchell, James 236
Molloy, Thomas 102
Monaghan, John 62, 107–108, 135

Montgomery Ward Company 133–134
Moody, Joseph 144, 148
Mooney, Edward 64, 82–85, 96, 156, 172–173, 176–177, 179, 181, 187–188, 246
Mother of God Church (Waukegan, Ill.) 38
Moving Picture Operators Union 149
Mulvey, James 166
Mundelein, George Cardinal 35–36, 41, 130, 242
Murdock, Curtis 73
Murphy, James 232
Murray, Philip 71–73, 87, 93, 131, 163, 181, 185, 198, 200–203, 205, 207–208, 212, 225
Mussolini, Benito 84, 184
Mystical Body of Christ 31, 119–120, 218, 222, 233, 237

N

National Association for the Advancement of Colored People 99
National Association of Manufacturers 44, 76, 98, 246
National Catholic News Service 244
National Catholic Welfare Conference 33, 41, 47, 60, 81, 83, 154–156, 159, 194, 197, 240, 243, 246, 252
National Center for the Laity 140
National Conference of Catholic Bishops 255
National Farm Workers Association 249
National Federation of Telephone Workers 112

National Industrial Recovery Act 48
National Labor Relations Act (Wagner Act) 48, 57, 67, 76, 108, 248, 254
National Labor Relations Board 37, 39–40, 58, 85, 125, 131–132, 136, 195, 204, 245, 254
National Maritime Union 58, 202, 217
National Planning Association 258
National Recovery Act 48–49, 72
National Religion and Labor Foundation 135
Nawn, John 240–241
Nazi-Soviet pact 69, 86, 89, 128–129, 198
Near West Side (Chi.) 241
Nell-Breuning, Oswald von 47
Nelson, Donald 73
New City 139
New Deal 47–48, 70, 72, 137, 240, 242
New Masses 202
New Rochelle Labor School 143
New World 40, 240
New York ACTU 63, 111–112, 125, 174, 176
New York Archdiocese 110–112, 168
New York City Code of Labor Relations 232
New York City waterfront 216, 227–228
New York Omnibus Company 223–225
New York Shipping Association 228
New York State Crime Commission 228

Index

New York State Department of Labor 145
New York State Federation of Labor 146
New York State Labor Relations Board 107, 143
New York Sun 228
New York Times, The 98
New York Workers School 219
Niederauer, W. J. 166
Nixon, Richard 157, 159
NLRB v. Mackay Radio and Telegraph Company 254
Novak, Michael 179
Novak, Ralph 173
Novena Notes 39–40
Nugent, Michael 149

O

O'Brien, John 252
O'Brien, Thomas 229
O'Connor, Kate 39
O'Donoghue, Kevin 114
O'Gara, James 119, 124, 164
Ohio State University Business Law Program 110
Oleksinski, Anthony 179
On the Waterfront 229
Organized Labor and the Church 255
O'Toole, George Barry 192–193, 195
Our Lady of Grace Church (West Babylon, L.I.) 236
Our Sunday Visitor 200
Owen, Blaine 67

P

Pacifism 124
Packing-house Workers Organizing Committee 33

Page, John 150, 153
Papalardo, Michael 148
Pastuszka, Ann 179
Paulist Press 150
Paul, Marty 123
Pegler, Westbrook 180
Personal reform and social reform 55, 118, 121, 139
Peterson, Kenneth 161
Petro, Joseph 45
Pittsburgh ACTU 197
Pittsburgh Catholic, The 192, 197–198, 200, 207
Pittsburgh Diocese 207
Pittston Coal Company 257
Playboy Club 172
Poor People's Campaign 247
Pope John Paul II 256, 258
Pope Leo XIII 31, 34, 114, 134, 159, 166, 170, 181
Pope Paul VI 232
Pope Pius XI 31–32, 34, 38, 41–42, 44, 51, 57, 59–62, 66, 84, 101, 115, 121, 135, 137, 145, 155, 170, 181, 246
Pope Pius XII 41, 114, 137, 167
Popular Front era 68, 120
Postwar period 73, 75, 92–93, 96, 98–99, 108, 135, 137, 148–149, 154, 158–159, 164, 169–170, 175, 181, 189, 200, 223, 225, 227, 230
Premier See, The 157
Priests' social-action roles 42, 57, 62, 102, 121, 193, 216, 219, 242
Primer on Roman Catholicism for Protestants 136
Primer on the Taft-Hartley Law 108
Problem of American Communism, The 154, 156, 1945

Professional Air Traffic Controllers'
    Organization 254
Progressive Party 200
Protestant, Catholic, Jew 137
Ptaszynski, Joseph 179

Q

Quadragesimo Anno 31, 38, 46,
    48–49, 51, 53–54, 57, 59, 61,
    71, 101–102, 114, 125, 166, 168,
    170, 184, 192, 215, 258
Quigley Preparatory Seminary 31,
    40, 117–118, 241–242
Quill, Michael 202, 225–226

R

Racial justice 30, 39, 98–99,
    118–119, 123–124, 133, 135,
    191, 207, 211, 237, 247, 254
Randolph, Philip 247
Rand School 219
Read, Harry 45
Reagan, Ronald 254, 258
Red-baiting 129, 134–135, 163
Region 1-UAW 179
Region 6-UCW 179
Reintjes, William 43
Religious openness 46, 62, 123–
    126, 133, 135–136, 138, 140,
    147, 149, 151, 160, 162, 165, 167,
    175, 241, 257
Remington-Rand Corporation 204
Republic Steel Company 59, 195
Rerum Novarum 31, 57, 102, 159,
    166, 168, 170, 215, 232, 249
Reser, Albert 123
Retail Food Stores Employees Local
    424 197
Reuther, Walter 81, 85, 87–89,
    91–94, 96–99, 123, 131, 165,
    171, 185–186, 189–190, 232, 250

Rice, Charles Owen 162, 191–212,
    234
Rieff, Louis 149
Right-to-work states 108–109,
    139–140, 234, 246
Riordan, Mary Ellen 179
Road to Serfdom, The 158
Roche, Edward 39
Rockhurst College 215
Romig, Walter 169
Roosevelt, Franklin 47, 70–76, 91,
    99, 101, 117, 133, 242
Roosevelt University, Labor
    Education Division 136
Rosary College 125
R. P. Scherer Corporation 170
Rummel, Joseph 139
Rustin, Bayard 247
Rutgers University Labor Program
    109
Ryan Forum 131
Ryan, John 46–49, 60, 78, 82–83,
    94, 134, 159, 243–244, 249, 251,
    253
Ryan, Joseph 58–59, 65, 227–229
Ryan, William 173

S

Sacher, Harry 151
Sacred Heart School 227
Sacred Heart Seminary 173,
    188–189
Sarah Lawrence College 153
Scalise, George 226
Schools of Social Action, SAD 33,
    35
Schrembs, Joseph 193
Schuyler, Joseph 106
Scranton University School of
    Industrial Relations 230

… *Index* 273

Searchlight, The 161–162
Second Vatican Council 256
Sectarianism 106, 127, 146, 173–175, 177
Secularism 138–139, 170, 186, 195, 218, 236
Senser, Robert 131
Service Employees International Union 257
Shea, Gerry 256
Shealy, Terence 215–217, 230
Sheehan, John 111
Sheil, Bernard 125, 164
Sheil School 125, 131
Shrine of the Little Flower (St. Theresa) 84
Shultz, George 258
Siedenburg, Frederic 81
Sleeper, Ernest 104
Smith-Connally Act 75
Smith, William 103–104, 106
Smolikoff, Charles 225
Social Action Bulletin 187
Social Action Department (NCWC) 41–42, 46–48, 50, 60, 81, 83, 156, 159, 174, 184, 231, 240, 243–245, 247
Social Action Notes for Priests 42, 44, 244
Social Gospel movement 46
Socialism 41, 47, 77–78, 81, 83, 90, 92, 94–96, 114, 134, 138, 152, 164–165, 171, 182, 184–186, 189, 210, 212, 214, 219, 246
Spalding, Thomas 157
Spellman, Francis 110–112, 168
St. Agnes Church (Pitt.) 192
Stalin, Josef 69, 86, 200
St. Angela Church (Chi.) 31

St. Anne Church (Castle Shannon) 207, 212
St. Ann Church (Chicago Heights) 45
St. Boniface Church (Brooklyn) 105
St. Brigid Church (Brooklyn) 105
St. Carthage Church (Chi.) 29, 51
St. Catherine Church (Det.) 179
St. Cecilia Church (Brooklyn) 105–106, 111, 114, 236
St. Edward Church (Det.) 172
Steel Workers Organizing Committee 59, 195–196
St. Francis Xavier Church (Ecorse) 179
St. Francis Xavier Church (LaGrange) 240
St. Gregory Church (Det.) 179
St. Helena Church (Brooklyn) 227
St. Joseph Church (Natrona) 207
St. Joseph Church (Port Huron) 179–181
St. Joseph College Institute of Industrial Relations 230–231
St. Joseph College School of Social Service 215, 230
St. Joseph High School 66, 107
St. Leo Church (Det.) 172, 181
St. Louis University Labor College 230
St. Mark the Evangelist Church 66
St. Mary of the Lake Seminary 30–32, 36, 45, 242–243
St. Mary Seminary 154, 158
St. Michael Church (Queens) 105
Stockell, Victor 166
Stockyards Transit Company 33
St. Paul Seminary (Minn.) 46
St. Peter Church (Chi.) 126

St. Peter Institute of Industrial Relations 106, 229
Stritch, Samuel 41, 45, 126, 130, 242–243
St. Sebastian Church (Queens) 105–106
Sts. Peter and Paul Church (S. Chi.) 38
St. Sylvester Church (Brooklyn) 102
St. Theresa of the Infant Jesus Church (Chi.) 38
St. Therese Church (Brooklyn) 105
St. Thomas Aquinas Church (Nahant, Mass.) 78
St. Thomas Church (Ann Arbor) 179
St. Thomas More Service Club 51
Stuber, Stanley 136
Sturmer, Henry 149–150
St. Vincent Church (Pontiac) 179
St. Vincent de Paul Society 157, 193, 222
St. Vincent Seminary 192
St. William Church (Pitt.) 199
Sullivan, Joseph 173, 180
Summer School of Social Action, Chicago 35
SUNY-Oswego Business School 109
Swanstrom, Edward 65, 102
Sweeney, John 113
Syracuse School of Industrial Relations 230

T

Taft-Hartley Act 76, 98, 108–110, 130–132, 136, 140–141, 167, 175, 181, 204, 233–234, 237, 245, 254
Technology's impact 198, 211, 234
Temporary National Economic Committee 113
Tennessee Coal and Iron Company 67
Textile Workers Union of America-CIO 64
Thomasine, Sister (O.P.) 132
Thomas Jefferson Workers School 153, 202
Thomas, R. J. 83, 86, 91, 97
Time 195, 235
Timmes, Edward 160–161
Tobin, Maurice 131
Tom Paine Workers School 146, 153
Toward Social Justice 197
Townsend, Willard 131
Tracey, John 179
Transport Workers Union 202, 217, 223–226
Tri-State Conference on Steel 211
Troy, Philip 44
Truman, Harry 76, 92–93, 108–109

U

UAW and Walter Reuther, The 89
UE Members for Democratic Action 162–163, 165
Union corruption 65, 102, 147, 217, 223, 226–229, 235, 237, 247
United Association of Journeymen Plumbers 148
United Auto Workers 67, 73, 75, 81, 83–94, 96–97, 99, 151, 164–165, 171, 173–174, 177, 185–186, 189, 202, 221, 247, 250
United Cemetery Workers 112
United Chemical Workers 170, 179

Index

United Electrical, Radio and Machine Workers of America 94, 149, 160, 162–163, 201, 203–206, 209, 211, 217, 226
United Farm Workers 249
United Farm Workers Organizing Committee 249
United Financial Employees 112
United Mine Workers of America 64, 68, 72, 74, 257
United Office and Professional Workers of America 202, 226
United Packing-house Workers of America-CIO 33
United Public Workers 202, 226
United Rank and File Educational Committee 226, 235
United Retail, Wholesale and Department Store Employees of America 40, 226
United Rubber Workers of America-CIO 67
United Shoe Workers 36
United States Steel 38, 67, 195
United Steel Workers of America 72, 74, 93, 202
United Transport Service Employees-CIO 39, 124, 131
University of Detroit 81, 187–189
University of Wisconsin 46
Ursuline nuns 143
U.S. Bureau of the Census 253
U.S. Catholic Conference 240, 250, 252
U.S. Chamber of Commerce 158, 182
U.S. Conciliation Service 106–107, 149, 221
U.S. Conference of Catholic Bishops 30
U.S. Department of Labor 39, 131
U.S. Office of Price Administration 124
U.S. Office of Production Management 72
U.S. Social Security Board 39
U.S. Supreme Court 39, 48, 85, 109, 254

V

Vanderpoel, Robert 140
Vicinanza, Joseph 162
Vietnam war 207, 209
Visking Corporation 124
Vogel, Cyril 197
Vogt, George 43
Volunteerism in Organized Labor in the United States 1930-40 243
Voos, Paula 109

W

Wage Earner, The 95–97, 173, 177, 179–181, 185, 187–188
Wallace, Henry 200
Walsh, Francis 143
Walsh, T. A. 166
Walter, Francis 209
Wangerin, Otto 134–135
War Labor Board 74, 148, 232
War Manpower Commission 88
War Production Board 73
Waterfront Labor Problem, The 65, 102
Weber, Gerald 29–30
Weber, Paul 82–83, 90, 94–96, 135, 157, 165, 171, 173, 179–180, 185, 188
Wersing, Marty 60
Westbrook, Raymond 226

Westchester County Federation of Labor 149
Westchester Management Forum 167
Westcott, Raymond 223–226
Westinghouse Local 601-UE 199–201, 203, 209
Whelan's drug store 197
White-collar workers 112, 144, 150, 190, 219, 223–225, 256
White, Walter 99
Widick, B.J. 89
Williams, Charlie 86
Williams, G. Mennen 171, 180
Willkie, Wendell 72
Willock, Edward 140
Wilson, Charles E. 73, 185
WJAS Radio 192
Women's rights and roles 47, 62, 125, 132, 135, 144–145, 197, 206, 224, 247–248
Woodstock Seminary 219
Woolworth stores 63
Work 50, 124–125, 131–135, 139, 141, 205
World War II impact 41, 50, 69–71, 73–76, 81, 87, 89, 91–92, 94, 97, 103–106, 119, 124, 128–130, 132, 136–137, 148, 156–158, 166, 170, 175, 181, 197–199, 221, 230, 232
Wright, John 207, 209–210
WWSW Radio 192

X

Xavier Detail, The 221–222, 234
Xavier Labor School 44, 103–104, 106, 113, 213
Xavier School of Social Sciences 215
Xavier University Institute of Social Order 230
X-Ray, The 221

Y

Yalta Conference 164
Yancey, John 39, 124, 133–134
Yardstick, The 244, 248–249, 252
Young Christian Workers 31